Women in the Films of John Ford

Women in the Films of John Ford

DAVID MEUEL

McFarland & Company, Inc., Publishers
Jefferson, North Carolina

LIBRARY OF CONGRESS CATALOGUING-IN-PUBLICATION DATA

Meuel, David, 1950–
  Women in the films of John Ford / David Meuel.
     p.   cm.
  Includes bibliographical references and index.

  ISBN 978-0-7864-7789-0 (softcover : acid free paper) ∞
  ISBN 978-1-4766-1456-4 (ebook)

  1. Ford, John, 1894–1973—Criticism and interpretation.
  2. Women in motion pictures.   I. Title.
  PN1998.3.F65M48   2014
  791.4302'33092—dc23   2014001666

BRITISH LIBRARY CATALOGUING DATA ARE AVAILABLE

© 2014 David Meuel. All rights reserved

No part of this book may be reproduced or transmitted in any form or by any means, electronic or mechanical, including photocopying or recording, or by any information storage and retrieval system, without permission in writing from the publisher.

On the cover: Grace Kelly and Ava Gardner in *Mogambo*, 1953 (MGM/Photofest)

Manufactured in the United States of America

McFarland & Company, Inc., Publishers
  Box 611, Jefferson, North Carolina 28640
  www.mcfarlandpub.com

To the memory of my parents,
Charlie and Harriett Meuel,
who shared their love of John Ford's films with me

Contents

Preface 1
Introduction: Spotlighting Women in John Ford's Films 5

1. The Dark Side of Mother Love: Henrietta Crosman's
   Hannah Jessop in *Pilgrimage* 15
2. Fearless Free Spirit: Jean Arthur's Wilhelmina Clark
   in *The Whole Town's Talking* 25
3. "Swamp Gal": Anne Shirley's Fleety Belle in
   Steamboat Round the Bend 34
4. The Innocent Turned Imperialist: Shirley Temple's Priscilla
   in *Wee Willie Winkie* and Philadelphia in *Fort Apache* 43
5. All About Attitude: Claire Trevor's Dallas in *Stagecoach*
   and Joanne Dru's Denver in *Wagon Master* 52
6. Colonial Spunk: Claudette Colbert's Lana and Edna May
   Oliver's Mrs. McKlennar in *Drums Along the Mohawk* 62
7. Family First: Jane Darwell's Ma Joad in *The Grapes of Wrath*
   and Sara Allgood's Beth Morgan in *How Green Was My Valley* 72
8. More Than the Sum of Her Parts: Mildred Natwick's
   Four Small Gems for John Ford 83
9. "On the very edge of eternity": Donna Reed's Sandy Davyss
   in *They Were Expendable* 90
10. Ford's Wild Irish Rose: Maureen O'Hara's Kathleen in
    Rio Grande and Mary Kate in *The Quiet Man* 99
11. Female Supremacy: Ava Gardner's Honey Bear and
    Grace Kelly's Linda in *Mogambo* 109

12. "Way out on a limb": The Women Who Trigger Ethan's Quest in *The Searchers* and the Women Who Must Face Its Consequences 120

13. Reconnection and Regret: Vera Miles' Hallie in *The Man Who Shot Liberty Valance* 135

14. No Other Way Out: Anne Bancroft's Dr. Cartwright in *7 Women* 142

15. Snapshots: Other Fine Female Roles and Performances in Ford Films 152

16. Dare We Call Ford a Feminist? The Director's Achievement in Context 172

Conclusion: Electric Moments 180
Recommended Resources for Further Reference 183
Chapter Notes 187
Selected Bibliography 191
Index 193

Preface

"With all the brilliance, the intelligence and sophistication that goes into filmmaking today, with all the multiplicity of elaborate and costly techniques, there is still this lack of feeling, of emotional exposure and commitment. Which is one reason why, again and again, we return in our dissatisfaction (not just with nostalgia) to the great films of the past in which we can still feel 'the freshness of the early world' and from which we can still receive refreshment. So it is with the films of Ford."—Lindsay Anderson, *About John Ford*

I grew up with John Ford.

I'm not being literal, of course. Really growing up with John Ford would make me about 120 years old. More precisely, when I grew up, I often watched his films on television. Usually, I did this with my parents, who had been watching Ford films since long before I arrived on the scene. My father, who loved westerns, marveled at how he could watch some of Ford's westerns over and over and never be bored. My mother, whose own parents were born in Wales, often remarked that *How Green Was My Valley* was her favorite film. She also had a special fondness for one of Ford's other Celtic masterpieces, *The Quiet Man*.

When I became an adult, I continued their tradition in my own way: watching Ford films, being entranced by their emotional intensity as well as their artistry and, in an amazing number of cases, never finding repeated viewings boring. Along with millions of others (including many of the world's most celebrated film directors), I consider him America's greatest and most influential director and his films an endless source of inspiration. Without Ford, it is often said, films as we know them would simply not exist. I heartily agree.

As time has passed, however, I have found myself increasingly at odds with how many people (including some film historians and critics) view his work today. For them, Ford is mainly the specialist in westerns, the visual poet, and the man's director. For me, that viewpoint barely scratches the surface.

Everyone agrees that Ford excelled at westerns. But, during the last 45 years of his career, westerns accounted for only about 20 percent of his feature film output, and, in one 20-year period between 1926 and 1945 — when Ford made 41 feature films — only one of them, *Stagecoach*, was a western. It's interesting too that, of Ford's record four best directing Oscars, none was for a western. This has something to do with Hollywood's condescending attitudes toward the western genre, of course, but it also suggests another truth: that during Ford's time, people understood his great versatility — his ability to excel in many genres — better than they do now.

Ford's visual compositions are often breathtaking. Yet, he also excelled at every aspect of directing, from selecting stories to developing scripts, giving characters greater depth and complexity, selecting actors, getting great performances from those actors, staging big action sequences, staging intimate scenes, choosing the right music and precisely when to use it, influencing the editing process, and putting all the elements together. He did it all as well as anyone, and he did it for half a century.

While Ford's films focus on male characters and their concerns more often than not, women figure prominently in nearly all of his films and are the central characters in many more than most people assume. What is noteworthy, too, is the variety and complexity of so many of these female characters and the great sensitivity and mastery with which they are portrayed (occasionally by unproven actresses) over several decades. If we look closely at Ford's work (which includes the more obscure as well as the more popular films) the range of female characters and perspectives is very impressive — especially for a so-called man's director and especially for one working at a time when women were routinely represented as projections of male fears or fantasies and their viewpoints often trivialized or dismissed.

To appreciate Ford more fully, it's critical to better understand *all* these facets of his work, and among them I believe the one that most urgently needs to be told is his interest in women's stories and his ability to tell them so well. This, in essence, is why I wrote this book.

To convey these stories also meant collaborating with hundreds of actresses over the decades, women whose lives were often as fascinating and varied as the females they portrayed for Ford. This is why I've also chosen to feature brief biographical sketches of actresses along with analyses of the roles they played in Ford films. Some of these actresses such as Shirley Temple, Maureen O'Hara, Ava Gardner, Grace Kelly, and Anne Bancroft remain household names. Many others will be major surprises, even for ardent classic film fans, but relative obscurity today has no bearing on the acting talent of these women. *All* of them should be much better known than they are.

* * *

Preface

This project began as a perfect storm of Ford-oriented forces. The first was a series of film studies classes I began taking in 2010 at Stanford University's Continuing Studies program taught by Elliot Lavine, one of the most knowledgeable (and enthusiastic) film authorities I've ever met. In the last few years, he has helped me to see classic films (including Ford's) in a very different and much richer way, and for that I am deeply grateful. In addition, Elliot introduced me online to writer Moira Finnie, who posted an early version of my profile of Shirley Temple in Ford films on her classic films blog, *The Skeins*. The second was a first reading of Joseph McBride's seminal 2001 biography, *Searching for John Ford*, and follow-up correspondence with the author. This led me to read numerous other books about Ford and his work and fueled my Ford obsession all the more. The third was initial contact and an ongoing correspondence with April Lane, the creator of *directedbyjohnford.com*, the only site on the web dedicated solely to Ford and his work. April, a lifetime "Fordie," as she describes herself, has been extremely supportive of my interest in Ford and happy to post some of my initial writing on her site. The chapters in this book on Ford's films *Pilgrimage* and *Mogambo*, for example, first received public exposure in earlier versions on April's site.

Photographs are always a vital part of any book on film, and I would like to thank the staff at the New York–based stock photo archive Photofest, who found photographs for every actress featured in this book and from the films I wanted to discuss. The staff's knowledge and professionalism were very impressive.

I also want to acknowledge the support and insights of friends and family—my kitchen cabinet of film advisors, if you will—who have been so encouraging throughout this process. They have urged me forward with the project, put forth ideas, offered frank criticism when they deemed it appropriate, and generally told me to "just do it." These include Kathryn Diamond, James Meuel and Annette Hulbert, James Daniels, Paul Bendix, Bob and Melanie Ferrando, Peter Nelson and Natalie Varney, Gerald Nachman, and Scotty Martinson.

In addition to Joseph McBride, I want to pay an appreciative thanks to several of the authors (both living and deceased) whose books on Ford have been huge inspirations and valuable resources for me as I have gone through this process. These include Lindsay Anderson, Peter Bogdanovich, Scott Eyman, Tag Gallagher, James Kitses, and Andrew Sarris. To paraphrase Isaac Newton: they are the giants on whose shoulders I have stood.

* * *

As this book went through its various stages of development, I made many exhilarating discoveries about John Ford, his films, many of the female characters that populate them, and the talented actresses who brought these characters to life on the screen. And I hope that everyone who reads this book experiences some of the same: seeing how these characters pulsate with life today as much as they did decades ago when filmgoers paid in hard-earned nickels and dimes to see their stories told at the neighborhood picture shows; seeing why *their* work will outlive us all.

Introduction
Spotlighting Women in John Ford's Films

To separate her son from the woman he loves, a selfish, spiteful Arkansas farmwoman has him drafted into the Army during World War I, a decision that leads to his death and, eventually, her transformation.

On the Mississippi River in the 1890s, a teenage "swamp gal" pilots a broken down riverboat in a race to Baton Rouge to save her young husband from an unjust fate at the gallows.

In nineteenth-century India, a nine-year-old girl fresh from America joins her grandfather at a British colonial outpost, befriends a hostile native leader, and helps avert a local war.

In the African jungle, an American party girl takes up with a big game trapper and safari leader, loses him to another woman, and then finds a new path in life for herself—and for him.

In China in 1935, a tough-talking atheist doctor strikes an unholy bargain with a Mongolian marauder so she can help free a group of hapless Christian missionaries from his brutal occupation.

As amazing as it seems, these are all snippets of plots from films made by John Ford (1894–1973), the legendary American director whom many regard as a specialist in westerns, the one who made major stars out of John Wayne and Henry Fonda, the ultimate man's director. Yet, none of these films is a western, and none of them stars either Wayne or Fonda. The actresses playing these roles range from household names to brilliant but virtually forgotten performers. And they represent only a small fraction of the great actresses who brought to life scores of complex and compelling female characters in more than 100 Ford feature films during the director's more than half-century career.

* * *

The passing of time has a way of simplifying our understanding of what exceptional people did in the past, of reducing what's usually a very complex reality down to a few sketchy (and sometimes misleading) bullet points. In the four decades that have past since John Ford's death, his achievements have been subject to this kind of historical typecasting. Today, most people who know about Ford may know him only for a handful of westerns; his two great social dramas, *The Grapes of Wrath* and *How Green Was My Valley*; and perhaps his cantankerous personality. If their interest is more than passing, they may also know that he started his career in silent films and — as well as westerns — directed comedies, historical dramas, adventure stories, films starring the great humorist Will Rogers, films set in Ireland, documentaries, and a few television shows. They may even know that he is the only director to receive, among numerous honors, four Academy Awards for his feature films and two more for his documentaries, six in all, a record not likely to be broken any time soon.

Even with this knowledge, however, we see only the tip of an enormous iceberg.

John Ford was, and remains, one of the world's greatest cinematic storytellers, a poet who blended intense feeling for his characters; crisp, incisive dialogue; stunning visual compositions; highly evocative music; and brilliant, often startling editing to create films of enormous intellectual energy and emotional power. And he is also one of the most influential. Just a partial list of the filmmakers who have acknowledged their debt to Ford includes Ingmar Bergman, Frank Capra, Francis Ford Coppola, Clint Eastwood, Jean-Luc Godard, Howard Hawks, Akira Kurosawa, David Lean, George Lukas, Jean Renoir, Martin Scorsese, Steven Spielberg, Oliver Stone, and Orson Welles. And, whether they know it or not, the billions of people who have seen films either by Ford or by any of his numerous disciples have also felt his influence. Perhaps more than any other filmmaker in history, Ford has directly or indirectly shaped both the character of modern cinema and our own perceptions of who we are, where we've come from, and maybe even where we are headed. To better know Ford, we may conclude, is to better know ourselves.

Yet, while Ford's work is widely respected and imitated, it is also widely debated. Even today, decades after his death, the arguments continue.

One of these great debates focuses on his attitudes toward women and female points of view in his films. Was Ford, as many people assert, basically a man's director who was dismissive of, or at best not particularly attuned to, his female characters? Or were women much more integral to his stories and, by extension, to his attitudes toward a wide range of human issues?

It is easy to see why Ford is usually viewed as a man's director. Most of his films have male leads, predominantly male casts, and themes associated with male concerns such as honor or duty. A few — 1934's *The Lost Patrol* comes to mind — have no female characters at all. And another early talkie, 1930's *Men Without Women*, says it all in the title. With the exception of Maureen O'Hara, he is not readily associated with any major actresses the way George Cukor, for example, is associated with Katharine Hepburn, Josef von Sternberg with Marlene Dietrich, or Clarence Brown with Garbo. In fact, he is far better known as the person who made stars out of several *male* actors, most notably Wayne and Fonda.

But, to say that Ford is simply, or almost exclusively, a man's director is far from true. Women play leads in many more of his films than we assume. Just some of the major female stars who made Ford films — in addition to Maureen O'Hara — include Jean Arthur, Anne Bancroft, Madeline Carroll, Claudette Colbert, Ava Garner, Helen Hayes, Katharine Hepburn, Janet Gaynor, Shirley Jones, Grace Kelly, Myrna Loy, Donna Reed, Barbara Stanwyck, Shirley Temple, Gene Tierney, Constance Towers, Natalie Wood, and Loretta Young. Then there is the fine work Ford received from such accomplished character actresses as Sara Allgood, Mary Astor, Billie Burke, Linda Cristal, Jane Darwell, Joanne Dru, Mildred Dunnock, Lucille La Verne, Anna Lee, Margaret Leighton, Hattie McDaniel, Vera Miles, Karen Morley, Mildred Natwick, Marian Nixon, Edna May Oliver, Flora Robson, Anne Shirley, Claire Trevor, Arleen Whelan, and many, many others. Then, there is the riveting performance Ford drew out of the now forgotten stage actress Henrietta Crosman in his 1933 drama, *Pilgrimage*. Then there are, of course, many more examples. Well-defined, complex, and excellently portrayed female characters are prominent in dozens of Ford works.

When he sat for this studio portrait in the mid–1930s, John Ford, who had begun his career in silent films two decades earlier, had firmly established himself has one of Hollywood's elite directors.

* * *

These characters didn't appear immediately in Ford's work. It would take him a good two decades of making silent films and early talkies before the women in his films began to take on real complexity and distinctiveness.

When he ended his three-year apprenticeship with his older brother Francis and began directing his own films in 1917, both Ford and his chosen arts medium were still quite young. He was just 23, and the practice of projecting filmed stories to audiences (which began in 1895) was even younger. In all, Ford made more than 60 silent films, both shorts and features. Today, most are assumed lost, but of the ones that remain we can see glimpses of the artist who would express himself so forcefully in the decades to come. Two of his earliest surviving films, 1917's *Straight Shooting* and *Bucking Broadway*, for example, show his humor, inventiveness, and great gift for outdoor visual compositions. In *Straight Shooting*, his displays of galloping men on horseback, swirling dust, and impressive rock formations remind us of memorable moments from great films such as *Fort Apache* and *She Wore a Yellow Ribbon* made more than 30 years later. As he kept making silent films in the 1920s, other Ford trademarks emerge. His 1924 western *The Iron Horse*, for example, is a true epic, portraying a group of people (and an amazingly multicultural one that that) caught up in a major historical event, the building of America's transcontinental railroad in the late 1860s.

Almost from the beginning, Ford also showed an interest in presenting nuance and complexity in key male characters. A big part of the credit here very likely goes to Harry Carey, Sr., a veteran western actor who made more than 20 early films with Ford, developed stories with him, and clearly exerted a major influence over the young director. Carey's characters are often "good bad men," individuals with a shady past who have a change of heart and do the right thing, even if that means making a sacrifice. We see these characters become more clearly defined in Ford's later (post–Carey) silent films such as *3 Bad Men* and *Hangman's House*. In the years to come, these kinds of characters would take on far more depth and complexity in several of the great John Wayne roles, most notably Ethan Edwards in *The Searchers* and Tom Doniphon in *The Man Who Shot Liberty Valance*.

Chomping on a cigar and sporting both a baseball cap and a patch over his left eye, Ford (shown here in 1962) strikes a familiar pose of his later years.

During these years, however, the intriguing women's roles were virtually non-existent in Ford. His principal female characters were usually one- and two-dimensional ingénues: pretty, wholesome, spirited young women who usually had eyes for the hero and, as critic Andrew Sarris has noted, "fairly marginal creatures in Ford's masculine cosmos."[1] In fairness, Ford sometimes focused on other kinds of female characters as well. One example is 1928's *Four Sons*, a late silent film that tells the story of a Bavarian widow, Mother Bernle (Margaret Mann), and her sons before, during, and after World War I. One of the sons, Joseph, goes to the U.S. and runs a delicatessen, and, when the war breaks out, her three other sons join the German army and Joseph joins the U.S. army. All three of the sons fighting for Germany are killed (one ironically in Joseph's arms on the battlefield), and eventually Mother Bernle relocates to the U.S. to live with Joseph.

Four Sons is significant in the development of Ford's portrayals of women for several reasons. First and most obvious, it shows a desire to move beyond the stock-character ingénues that were usually the main female characters in Ford's early films. Second, it is a very early example of Ford drawing his subject matter from a story by a female writer whose principal focus is a female character. In this case, the story is taken from the a story that first appeared in the *Saturday Evening Post* by I.A.R. Wiley (the initials are for Ida Alexa Ross) called *Grandmother Bernle Learns Her Letters*. (Five years later, Ford would return to Wiley's work for inspiration, this time to a story called *Gold Star Mothers*, which would serve as the basis for his film *Pilgrimage*.) Finally, Mother Bernle is also an early example of the "Fordian mother," a selfless and sometimes long-suffering champion of home and family solidarity perhaps best personified by Jane Darwell's Ma Joad in Ford's 1940 *The Grapes of Wrath*. Over the years, some film historians have often been less than charitable in their assessments of these characters, criticizing them for being too sentimental and more idealizations of characters rather and flesh-and-blood people. In reality, many of these characters, notably Darwell's Ma Joad and Sara Allgood's Beth Morgan in 1941's *How Green Was My Valley*, are much more complex, distinctive, and nuanced than these critics have given them credit for. But, unfortunately for *Four Sons*, Mother Bernle isn't one of these complex females. As developed by Ford and portrayed by Mann, the character is designed almost solely to pull at the heartstrings and draw easy tears.

A huge commercial success when it was first released, *Four Sons* is rarely seen today. Yet, while it hasn't proven to be enduring art, it is clear evidence that Ford had a genuine interest in women's stories, especially when it involved either a literal family or close-knit community that effectively served as a family.

Almost immediately after newly developed sound technology brought the silent era to a screeching halt, the 1930s arrived, and it is during this decade that Ford made the transition from respected studio director to major artist. At the beginning of the 1930s, his work largely consisted of lackluster studio assignments, often action or adventure films such as *The Black Watch* or *The Seas Beneath*. By the end of the decade — to be specific, during an 11-month period from February 1939 to January 1940 — Ford made *Stagecoach*, *Young Mr. Lincoln*, *Drums Along the Mohawk*, and *The Grapes of Wrath*: three widely acknowledged masterpieces and one very artfully made adventure/love story (*Drums*). Ford and film had grown up together; now they had reached a new level of maturity together.

Numerous factors contributed to Ford's growth spurt during this decade. One was the work of F.W. Murnau, the master of German expressionism who worked for a while at Ford's home studio, Fox, in the late 1920s and whose influence on the younger director was immediate, strong, and lasting. Another was the addition of sound, which allowed Ford to, among other things, use music to great emotional effect. Still another was his ongoing partnerships with talented scriptwriters such as Dudley Nichols and Lamar Trotti, who helped Ford shape stories that were more sophisticated in their structures and more satisfying both intellectually and emotionally. Yet another was 20th Century-Fox's brilliant and supremely opinionated studio chief, Darryl Zanuck, who wrangled with Ford from time to time but who also challenged him as an artist in ways no one else ever had. Of all the factors, however, probably the most significant was Ford's own growth both as an artist and as a person. During this decade, his work deepened considerably. More and more, his stories reflected real and complicated human concerns, the characters in those stories became more fully fleshed out, and the actors playing those characters brought more to their portrayals. Many of these actors, of course, were simply better than most of the people Ford had worked with during the silent era. (Most of us, for example, would take a Henry Fonda over a Hoot Gibson any time.) Nevertheless, we also get a sense that Ford was now pushing these actors harder to get as much as he could from them.

As Ford's male characters deepened, so did his understanding of the women also portrayed in his films. In the early 1930s, some very interesting female characters begin to emerge. These are not simply the ingénues we see in *Straight Shooting* or *The Iron Horse* or the idealized mothers we see in films such as *Four Sons*. They are much more distinctive, complex, and memorable. They begin to appear in little known but fascinating films such as 1932's *Flesh* and 1933's *Pilgrimage*, and they continue for more than three decades, up through Ford's later features such as 1962's *The Man Who Shot Liberty Valance* and 1966's *7 Women*.

For a director of his day, when nearly every director was a male, Ford (and those who worked with him, of course) also created a remarkably varied gallery of female characters during this 34-year run. Many of Ford's contemporaries, even the most gifted among them, often fixated on certain kinds of women and featured them repeatedly in their films. Alfred Hitchcock, for example, had his icy blondes, and Howard Hawks had his cool, wisecracking babes. Often these characters seem interchangeable too — so alike that we can easily substitute a Hitchcock character played by Grace Kelly for one played by Eva Marie Saint or a Hawks character played by Lauren Bacall for one played by Angie Dickinson. In contrast, women in Ford's films have very different personalities, confront a wide range of issues, and offer numerous perspectives. They are young and old, rich and poor, assertive and passive, kind and cruel, strong and weak, honest and conniving, good mothers and bad ones. In fact, they are nearly as varied as the hundreds of male characters they share the screen with in those more than 100 feature films.

Ford not only distinguished himself by developing distinctive and varied female characters with great consistency during this period, but he did this while also bucking the pervasive gender trends of the time in films. This is especially true from the mid–1940s to the mid–1960s, when directors and screenwriters (the vast majority of whom were also men) routinely depicted women in very disturbing and condescending ways. The late 1940s and early 1950s, for example, was the era of both the "weepie" woman's film, in which heroines were often shown as self-pitying and enormously dependent on men, and film noir, in which women were frequently rotten-to-the-core *femme fatales*. Then, in the 1950s and 1960s, the objectification of women reached new levels in a wide assortment of films ranging from Marilyn Monroe and Jayne Mansfield vehicles, which prominently featured their large breasts, to the James Bond series with its assortment of "Bond girls," the most memorable of whom was named Pussy Galore. During this time, however, Ford continued to tell stories with well-defined, complex, respectfully treated female leads in such films as *They Were Expendable, Wagon Master, Rio Grande, The Quiet Man, Mogambo, Sergeant Rutledge, The Man Who Shot Liberty Valance,* and *7 Women* and to include memorable female supporting roles in these and numerous other films.

Ford is sometimes criticized for being old-fashioned in part because so many of his films are set in the past. Yet in most of his films, regardless of the setting, many of his women are strong, assertive, independent, and quite modern while still being vulnerable, often flawed, and always very human. In contrast to many of the women in other films made during Ford's time, they have real depth and dimension. Certainly in contrast to the *femme fatales* and female caricatures of the era, Ford treats women — as he treats nearly all his characters — with respect and empathy. They are never the inferiors of men.

Taking all this into account, Ford's achievement with female characters becomes all the more remarkable — for someone known mainly as a man's director, he helped create varied and vivid female characters and treated those characters with a maturity that today seems well head of his time.

In addition to developing strong, striking female characters, Ford was a master of follow through. Just as he did with actors, he often saw potential in actresses that others missed and made brilliant casting decisions. For example, he chose a young and relatively untried Grace Kelly for *Mogambo* over numerous objections, and the role led to Kelly's first Academy Award nomination and instant stardom. Ford also had the ability to get great performances out of actresses, sometimes the best performances of their careers. Just compare Ava Gardner's performance in *Mogambo* with literally any performance she did before that. Or put Jane Darwell's Ma Joad in *The Grapes of Wrath* up against any role she had either before that film *or* afterward. While Academy Award nominations are often dubious indicators of quality, Ford's record with actresses here helps to make an important point. Of the 11 Academy Award acting nominations performers received for their work in Ford films, five — or almost half— were for females.[2] And these don't include the actresses scholars have singled out over the decades for their fine work in Ford films: performers from Henrietta Crosman in 1933's *Pilgrimage* to Anne Bancroft in 1966's *7 Women*.[3]

Ford jokes with Ava Gardner during the filming of 1953's *Mogambo* in Africa. As "Honey Bear" Kelly, a "playgirl" who re-evaluates her life after a soured romance with safari guide and wild animal trapper Vic Marswell (Clark Gable), Gardner received her only Academy Award nomination for her work in this film.

* * *

It is natural to wonder why Ford's work with actresses and the care he usually took developing female roles isn't more widely known, and several factors may contribute.

First, some Ford films with major female stars in lead roles, while well-intentioned, are simply not very good. The director's one film with Katharine Hepburn, 1936's *Mary of Scotland*, and his one film with Barbara Stanwyck, 1937's *The Plow and the Stars*, are both, sadly, painful examples. In fact, Thomas Mitchell, the terrific character actor who worked for Ford on several films, used to respond to Ford's harsh criticisms of actors by gently reminding him that the man responsible for *Mary of Scotland* wasn't in a position to criticize anyone.

Second, there are sometimes special circumstances associated with the history of a film. *Pilgrimage*, for example, was thought lost for more than 30 years and, when it was finally rediscovered in the 1960s, its star, Henrietta Crosman, had long been forgotten. As a result, its studio, Fox, did nothing to market the film until it was finally released on the backside of a double-bill DVD in 2007. Today, few people even know about it. Likewise, *7 Women*, another very interesting film, was initially panned by critics and did almost non-existent box office. Even though several Ford scholars now consider it a masterpiece, it has never been available on either VHS or DVD formats.

Third, there's Ford himself, who consciously cultivated a tough-guy, man's-man image in order — according to many accounts — to mask his extraordinarily sensitive nature. Always insecure about not appearing strong and in total control among his peers, he may have been tentative about touting his ongoing interest in women's characters and issues that were important to them. For a man of his time, it may have seemed a bit unmanly. This is a shame because, if he had felt differently, he might have done more to promote the achievements of the actresses who worked with him, and he might have even made a few more films that prominently featured women.

Lastly, there's that historical typecasting. As time passes, the complicated reality associated with a person's life and achievements tends to become more simplified in people's minds. In Ford's case, of course, the tendency is to remember the later westerns and little else when there is so much more to his work that's worth learning about.

* * *

Despite the relative obscurity of many Ford films in which women prominently figure, however, a significant body of outstanding work exists, and this work attempts to bring readers closer to several of these films and to the complex female characters featured in them. Fourteen of the chapters focus on specific actresses and the characters they played in specific films. The fifteenth is a series of brief portraits of still more actresses whose work in certain Ford films is admirable and noteworthy. The sixteenth attempts to put some historical context around Ford's overall achievement in developing and portraying female characters.

This book is not, by any stretch of the imagination, meant to be a definitive examination of this subject. All the selections of actresses and roles as well as the book's appraisal of Ford's achievement in this area are unabashedly subjective, and undoubtedly readers familiar with Ford will have their own thoughts on this subject.

Ford (right) chats with Vera Miles, dressed as the older Hallie, on the set of 1962's *The Man Who Shot Liberty Valance* while James Stewart (left) and John Wayne look on. Ford biographer Joseph McBride has called Miles' acting in this film "one of the richest female performances" in the director's work. Miles, who had worked with Ford six years earlier on *The Searchers*, is also well known for her roles with Alfred Hitchcock in 1956's *The Wrong Man* and 1960's *Psycho*.

With luck, this book also will help to correct the commonly held, and grossly incorrect, assumption that Ford wasn't especially interested in the issues, concerns, and perspectives of half the human race. And, with luck, it will help to give us a more complete understanding of Ford's films — films that are sometimes dismissed as simple and quaint but that are actually filled with complexity, ambiguity, and fascinating contradictions; films that stir us today with their great visual poetry, intellectual vigor, and emotional power as much as they ever have; films that offer vivid, lively portrayals of many kinds of women as well as men.

"John Ford knows what the earth is made of," Orson Welles famously said.[4] For anyone who has looked closely at Ford's work — and especially at Ford's efforts to convey the broad spectrum of female as well as male experience on this earth — it's impossible to disagree.

1

The Dark Side of Mother Love

Henrietta Crosman's Hannah Jessop in *Pilgrimage*

"A stunning comment," was how Ford biographer Joseph McBride once put it.

McBride was referring to a remark film preservationist David Shepard made in a conversation the two had in the late 1960s. Of all of Ford's films, Shepard declared, he considered a 1933 "woman's film" called *Pilgrimage* to be the director's best. McBride, then an avid student of Ford's work, was floored. He had never heard of the film. When he checked around, he discovered that very few other people knew anything about it either.[1]

When McBride eventually saw *Pilgrimage*, he better understood what had so impressed Shepard. While he is hesitant to single out *Pilgrimage* as Ford's best effort ever, he has said that it "belongs without question on a short list of the director's greatest films."[2]

McBride and Shepard are by no means alone in their enthusiasm. Among others, Ford specialists Tag Gallagher and Peter Bogdanovich have also sung the film's praises.

Yet, despite such accolades, *Pilgrimage* remains almost as obscure as it was when McBride first heard about it. One explanation is the film's troubled history. For decades, it was thought to be lost. Then, after being "discovered" in the mid–1960s, 20th Century–Fox was reluctant to market it. Never available in VHS format, it only became available on DVD as part of the 2007 *Ford at Fox* release. So, until 2007, there was very little opportunity for film viewers even to see it. Fox's reluctance to market the film suggests another explanation: for many people, *Pilgrimage* can be a hard sell. First, it's the largely tragic story of a harsh, oppressive mother — not the stuff that attracts huge audiences. Second, it has no name stars. By the time the film came to light in the 1960s, its lead actress had been dead for more than 20 years and was long forgotten. Third,

As Hannah Jessop in Ford's riveting 1933 drama *Pilgrimage*, Henrietta Crosman attempts to repair a photograph of her dead son, a photograph she had apparently torn up in anger before he was killed in World War I. Crosman, born during the U.S. Civil War and one of the leading American stage actresses from the 1880s to the 1920s, made several films in the late 1920s and 1930s before her retirement at age 76 in 1937. She shines in *Pilgrimage*.

the film is quite daring in its design, beginning with tragedy and then moving to a curious mix of comedy and drama. While intriguing for some, this can be disconcerting to viewers who prefer a more conventional story line. Finally, it seems atypical of Ford, who is much better known both for his positive portraits of mothers and for his work in male-dominated genres such as westerns.

Despite the film's persistent obscurity, however, Shepard, McBride, Gallagher, Bogdanovich, and a small but growing list of other admirers have good reason to be enthusiastic. *Pilgrimage*, while in some ways uncharacteristic of Ford, is also a superb Ford film. In fact, it's filled with much that is Ford at his best: the visual poetry, vivid characters, sharp dialogue (most of it courtesy of frequent Ford collaborator Dudley Nichols), a sharp critique of society, striking ironies, and great emotional power.

At the center of the story is Hannah Jessop. Played by the veteran American stage actress Henrietta Crosman, Hannah is — among women in Ford films —

in a class by herself: cold, hard, selfish, cruel, and deeply repressed, but also strong, determined, highly competent, and courageous enough to own up to terrible truths about herself and make a major personal transformation. Among all of Ford's characters, she is as complex, fully realized, and convincingly portrayed as any, including John Wayne's Ethan Edwards in *The Searchers*. When we scratch the surface, the connection between Hannah and Ethan runs even deeper: many of the traits they share are so striking and so central to the essence of each character that they sometimes appear to be cut out of the same cloth.

* * *

Virtually unknown today, Henrietta Crosman was — between the 1880s and 1920s — one of the most popular and highly regarded actresses in the American theater. She was born in 1861, during the first year of America's Civil War. Her father, George Crosman, was a career military man and her mother, Mary Wick, was the niece of songwriter Stephen Foster, best known for such American standards as "My Old Kentucky Home," "Oh! Susannah," and "Jeannie with the Light Brown Hair." After a youth largely spent moving from one military post to another, she began acting in 1883 and, for more than 40 years, performed throughout the U.S. in stage plays ranging from Shakespeare to contemporary pieces. She was especially adept in both the adventure-romances and drawing-room farces that were popular during those years. It's also possible (but only speculation) that Ford, who, as a teenager, ushered at a theater in Portland, Maine, may have seen her on stage. During this time, she also married twice and had two sons, one by each of her husbands.

In 1914, like many stage actors of the period, Crosman began to dabble in silent films. She made a film version of the play *The Unwelcome Mrs. Hatch* for legendary Hollywood mogul Adolph Zukor. But, after this, she focused mainly on the stage and her silent appearances were rare. With the coming of sound, however, all of that changed. Experienced theater actors were much in demand, and Crosman began to work more frequently in Hollywood. Her first screen hit was the 1929 film *The Royal Family of Broadway*, a comedy loosely based on the Barrymores and co-directed by George Cukor. She starred in *Pilgrimage* four years later.

From Three Cedars to the Argonne and Back

Pilgrimage opens on Hannah's farm near Three Cedars, Arkansas, where she and her adult son, Jim (Norman Foster), live and work. It is 1918. World War I is very much on Jim's mind, and so is Mary Saunders (Marian Nixon), who lives on the adjacent farm with her alcoholic father (Charlie Grapewin).

Jim and Mary want to get married. But Hannah, afraid of losing Jim, frustrates him at every turn. No, he can't enlist and go off to war, even though he feels a responsibility to do so. No, he can't draw a salary. No, he can't be with Mary, whom Hannah considers "trash." At night, Hannah even reads a few lines from the *Bible* aloud to Jim, imploring him, "Keep thee from the evil woman."

Jim and Mary are adamant, however, and the three confront each other.

"I'd rather see him dead than married to you," Hannah tells Mary.

"If you love her, you can't love me," she then says to Jim.

When she sees she's not getting anywhere, Hannah tells Mary: "I'll take him away from ya. For his own sake, I'll save him from ya."

Hannah immediately goes to the local Army enlistment officer and signs the waiver that paves the way for Jim to be drafted. "I want the Army to take him away," she says.

So, Jim is drafted and trained, and — on his way to the front in Europe — his train passes through Three Cedars and stops at the station for just a few minutes. Although Jim has wired her, Hannah apparently has not come. But Mary is there, and she has news: she is pregnant. Jim wants to stay at least long enough to marry her, but he can't. He is forced back on the train, which quickly steams away.

Jim's war experience is horrifyingly brief. We see him at night in the trenches. A battle begins. The unseen enemy advances. Then Jim and all those with him are buried in a mountain of sandbags and dirt.

The film cuts back to Hannah's farm. A storm rages at night. She wakes up from a nightmare calling out Jim's name, as if she's had a premonition of his death. Then Mary's father comes down the road in the storm. Mary's baby is about to be born, and he needs Hannah's help. Grudgingly, Hannah obliges, but this child, Hannah swears, "will never bear the name of Jessop."

Now, it is winter. A sleigh carrying the mayor of Three Cedars (Francis Ford) arrives at Hannah's farm. Inside, Hannah, betraying her immense internal conflict, is knitting an item of clothing for the newborn baby but tells a friend that she doesn't want Mary to know that the gift is from her. The mayor enters, and everyone learns that Jim has died. Hannah, overwhelmed with grief, says a few words and exits.

Then, in a wrenching piece of elliptical storytelling, we see Hannah sitting at a desk trying to piece together a photograph of Jim, which she had previously (we assume) ripped up in anger. With her fingers, she lightly caresses Jim's face in the photograph. As we watch, we also hear a very soft rendition of a song that plays occasionally during the film, "Dear Little Boy of Mine" by Ernest Ball. After this, we hear just a few notes of the George M. Cohan song and World War I theme "Over There," referring not merely to Europe where Jim died but now also to the place — wherever that may be — where death has taken him.

This is a heartbreaking, marvelously rendered moment, one Peter Bogdanovich has called "as beautiful as any" in Ford's work.[3] The gentle mix of imagery and music says it all—a good young man's life, like his photograph, is destroyed out of anger and can never be properly put back together again.

After a fade to black, the story picks up ten years later. Hannah, her hair much whiter now, is still hard as nails. Mary continues to live on the neighboring farm, but now it is with her and Jim's son, Jimmy (Jay Ward). The boy is terrified of Hannah, who has never acknowledged that he is her grandson or even given him a kind word.

The mayor, along with a general's daughter from Washington D.C., pay Hannah a visit. Jim, we've already learned, was the only soldier from their county killed in the war, and they want Hannah to represent the county in a "pilgrimage" the government is sponsoring consisting of "Gold Star Mothers," the mothers of American soldiers killed in the war. The mothers will go to France for various ceremonies and then to visit the graves of their sons. At first, Hannah is against the idea of participating, but the mayor manipulates her, cleverly appealing to her pride, and she agrees to go.

At this point, as Hannah's own geographic and emotional pilgrimage begins, the whole look and tone of the film change. First, the isolated, stifling, suffocating world of her farm and Three Cedars is left behind. Hannah is now just one of many people in a wide, bustling world. She seems less certain and more curious, less formidable and more ordinary. She meets other Gold Star mothers, hears their stories of loss and sorrow, and, as best she can, bonds with them. Amid the sadness, humor begins to appear. We see very unflattering passport photographs, provincial mothers fascinated by a very "modern" French fashion show, and a hillbilly mother named Hatfield, who spies chic French women smoking cigarettes after dinner and gives herself permission to smoke her corn cob pipe along with them. Hannah even laughs and has some fun.

Yet, as Hannah softens and begins to connect with the other mothers, the guilt she has long repressed becomes more apparent. She feels embarrassed and unworthy to be with mothers who had such good, loving relationships with their sons. She even confesses to the group that she was a bad mother.

After saying she can't visit Jim's grave, she has a chance meeting with a young man who is in roughly the same situation Jim once was: he's in love with a woman his mother won't accept. Hannah befriends him and the young woman and learns she is pregnant, just as Mary was when Jim went to war.

The scene when Hannah hears this news is a curious one. We see her face in close-up and then we see her mind flash back to the fateful scenes at the train station in Three Cedars ten years before when Mary tells Jim she's pregnant, Jim fights not to be put back on the train, and Mary looks at Jim for the last time. Something doesn't quite fit here, however. As we recall, Hannah *didn't* go the train station that night. That's what Jim and Mary assumed. That's what we assume too, because staying away would be entirely in character for this proud woman. But could she have actually come and, for whatever reason, chosen *not* to reveal herself? That would be in character too. The flashback that at first seems to be a lapse in continuity could actually be another fine piece of elliptical storytelling. Let's assume Hannah was at the train station. If she were, she not only would have seen Jim and Mary together but she would also have seen the great love they shared, have known that Jim knew that Mary was carrying his child, and — as a result — have been burdened with a deeper guilt for her own selfish and cruel actions.

Eventually, Hannah confronts this young man's mother with the harsh truths about herself, saying: "I guess it's our love that makes us cruel." The mother better understands her own shortcoming and accepts the young woman.

This intervention gives Hannah the strength she needs to visit Jim's grave. It's a painful scene. We see Hannah walking erectly among many graves until she finds Jim's. She places flowers various people have given her on the grave. She says: "Jim, forgive me." And then she collapses on the grave in tears.

Back again in Three Cedars, it's now Hannah's turn to ask forgiveness from the living too. She does, but even here the force of her fierce personality is jarring for Mary and downright scary for little Jimmy. It's clear that it will be a while, if ever, before these relationships are comfortable ones. As someone in Three Cedars might say, "Hannah still has a heap of fence-mending to do."

* * *

Hannah's wrenching personal journey is of course the heart and soul of *Pilgrimage*, but the film is also noteworthy in many other ways.

Throughout the story, for example, are pointed comments about the kind of society Hannah lives in and which, we assume, has shaped her values. In many respects, this is a very narrow, repressed, Puritanical world in which work and sacrifice are everything and joy and fun are frowned upon. In one very telling (and humorous) scene, Hannah curtly yells at her hens, "Earn your keep! Lay some eggs!" And, when she reads from the *Bible* to Jim, she is doing it as much because she believes it is the right thing to do as she does to control his desire to be with Mary. This is also a society in which a government and politicians routinely manipulate ordinary people and even exploit their grief by trying to "ennoble" their own selfish interests. As portrayed in the film, the Gold Star Mothers program has a very patronizing and self-serving air about it. When the general's daughter tells Hannah, "Think of how wonderful and reconciling it will be to really stand beside the grave of one of those heroic dead," we feel hollowness in her voice, as if she's just reciting government propaganda. And, when the mayor tells Hannah, "Your boy's gonna put our town on the map," he sees her decision to participate mainly in terms of how it benefits him.

Of special note too is the film's remarkable visual scheme. Heavily influenced by F.W. Murnau, the German expressionist director, the entire look of the first part of *Pilgrimage* captures the stifling, suffocating world of Hannah's farm. At times, fog seems to be seeping in from everywhere to confine and isolate. The farmhouse also seems dark, foreboding, and painfully alone. Needless to say, we never see sunlight. But, when the story shifts to New York and then to France, everything lightens and loosens up. There are more people. There are things to do other than work. When Hannah appears to be at her happiest and most carefree, she is in the French countryside, which is bathed in warm, energizing sunlight. Then, near the end of the film, when Hannah must confront her dark deed at Jim's grave, the setting is again dark, fog-bound, and oppressive: the same stifling, suffocating environment that was present at the outset of this tragedy. In its way, this scene strikingly reaffirms a major point the film wants to make: that just as Jim died as a result of Hannah's pride and selfishness, all the young men buried here have died in an unnecessary war, not to defend freedom, but to further the selfish, proud, and often petty interests of their respective nations. *Pilgrimage* is not only the story of one family's tragedy but of an entire world's tragedy.

Not Your Typical Ford Mother

One criticism often levied against Ford is that he idealizes mothers in his films, portraying them again and again as the good, true, steadfast, and usually one-dimensional champions of home and hearth. Yet, while this is sometimes true (as with Margaret Mann's Mother Bernle in 1928's *Four Sons*), Ford's mothers are actually much more varied. When maternal roles are important ones, for example, the characters can also be quite layered and flawed. Maureen O'Hara's Kathleen York in *Rio Grande*, who is determined that her son lead the life that she has mapped out for him, is a good case in point. Sometimes, too, mothers are not even up to the job. Maureen O'Hara's troubled Min Wead in *The Wings of Eagles* succumbs to alcoholism and neglects her children, and Betty Fields' emotionally stunted Florrie Pether in *7 Women* seems little more than a child herself, and an obnoxious one at that.

But, even in relation to other flawed and even profoundly troubled mothers in Ford films, Hannah stands apart for her selfishness and cruelty. While her fear of losing Jim is understandable, her treatment of him is deplorable. And, while she disapproves of Mary and is embarrassed by little Jimmy's illegitimacy, her treatment of them is just as bad.

This kind of behavior also points to another key difference between Hannah and most other Ford mothers. In *The Grapes of Wrath*, *How Green Was My Valley*, and other films, mothers do their utmost to protect the family from threatening forces from the outside. In *Pilgrimage*, the threat comes from inside the family: from the mother herself, with her ultimate act of destruction paving the way for Jim to go to war and his death.

With all this baggage, it's remarkable that Hannah is capable of making the enormous changes she does as she goes on her "pilgrimage." It's also remarkable that these changes appear so credible. Part of the credit goes to Crosman, who portrays Hannah with such insight, authority, conviction, and genuine empathy. Part also belongs to Hannah herself. People need great courage and determination to face and eventually address horrible truths about themselves. Although Hannah is deeply flawed in so many other ways, courage and determination are two qualities she has in abundance.

Kindred Souls: Mother Hannah and Uncle Ethan

While Hannah clearly stands apart from other mothers in Ford films, she earns the right to stand beside another dark and complex Ford character: Ethan Edwards in *The Searchers*.

At first glance, the two cannot seem more different. Hannah is a stout, older woman who steadfastly works her Arkansas farm during and after World War I. In contrast, Ethan is a towering middle age Civil War veteran who harbors forbidden feelings for his brother's wife and is by nature a wanderer.

Yet, once we glimpse more closely into the cold, stern eyes of each character — once we consider their essential natures — the similarities quickly become apparent. Both Hannah and Ethan are highly capable, headstrong, emotionally repressed, lonely, embittered, intolerant, and extremely intimidating people. While both have families, they are clearly outsiders in those family units, people unable to connect in conventional and emotionally healthy ways. Hannah, for example, does everything she can to keep her son Jim from following his natural instincts and finding happiness with Mary. And, when *The Searchers* begins, Ethan has been a complete mystery to his family for at least three years. No one knows exactly where he has been or what he has been doing.

As well as being very much alike, the two — as the titles of both films tell us — embark on physical (and emotional) journeys to reconnect with a departed family member: Hannah's dead son and Ethan's niece, who, while still alive, is, from his racist perspective, as good as dead. And through their journeys, Ethan's obsessive searching and Hannah's "pilgrimage," both are at least somewhat redeemed. Hannah finally accepts Mary and little Jimmy, and Ethan does something similar, taking his terrified niece into his arms and famously saying: "Let's go home, Debbie." Even after both these transformations, however, Ford slyly avoids conventional happy endings. Hannah's request for forgiveness as *Pilgrimage* ends is so strong it seems to come in the form of a demand, and the grandson she has treated so cruelly until this point still appears to be terrified of her. And, although Ethan brings Debbie to her new home, he can't bring himself to walk through the door—and into an emerging, more civilized society—as everyone else does. Both characters have done the right thing, but, because of who they are, neither can fully integrate with their communities going forward. Both, to a greater or lesser extent, will always be loners.

Of the similarities the two characters share, perhaps the most striking and disturbing is the willingness of both to consider the killing of a loved one in order to maintain a perverted sense of family purity. As Hannah emphatically states before she gives the Army the permission it needs to draft her son,' she would rather see him dead than married to a woman she deems unworthy. Likewise, as two other characters in *The Searchers* (Martin and Laurie) both admit, the fanatically racist Ethan would rather kill his niece than allow her to remain alive because, as the sexual partner of a Comanche "buck," she is forever tainted and now less than a human being. In these instances, we see the horrifyingly repressed natures, intolerance, and resulting capacity for evil that binds Hannah and Ethan together. At the core of their beings, they share the same dark soul.

Considering who they are, it's striking that both Hannah and Ethan also have the capacity to rise above their most disturbing qualities and make peace with others and themselves. Yet this, paradoxically, is also because of who they are: people courageous enough to face and, at least to an extent, manage the demons within themselves.

On a number of levels, Hannah and Ethan share the worst—and the best—of each other. They are true kindred spirits, and, in trying to size Hannah up against the hundreds of characters that populate Ford films, maybe the place to look is not at the other Fordian mothers but through the open doorway of the Edwards' homestead at the big man who rides up on the brown horse.

Still Something Now

Just as *Pilgrimage* may very well be John Ford's first great film, Hannah Jessop may very well be the director's first great character: someone worthy of standing beside Ethan Edwards, Tom Joad, Tom Doniphon, Mary Kate Danaher, Dr. Cartwright, and a handful of other people in the director's work. As loathsome as she is at times, she is always captivating, vulnerable, and utterly believable. Her personal pilgrimage from denial to revelation and ultimately to some level of redemption is a truly moving journey to observe. And we are with her every step of the way.

Along with many other discoveries a viewer makes watching this film for the first time is the actress who brings Hannah so vividly to life, Henrietta Crosman.

While Crosman is virtually unknown today, the quality of her work was certainly recognized at the time. When *Pilgrimage* opened at the Gaiety Theater in New York in July 1933, reviewer Andre Sennwald from *The New York Times* was on hand. Writing for the following morning's edition, he noted: "Miss Crosman, by some strange magic of her own, makes the old, commonplace virtues of motherhood not only dramatic, but fresh and clean and very touching. 'My hair is growing white,' she said in a short stage appearance last night. 'If you like Hannah Jessop, you make me the happiest woman in New York.' This morning she has had her wish.... It is a triumph for Miss Crosman and for Mr. Ford that *Pilgrimage* achieves delicacy and tact where those commendable qualities seem beyond reach."[4] (It's also curious to note that — in this last bit of praise — Crosman's name is cited ahead of Ford's.)

Unfortunately for Crosman, however, youth and time were no longer on her side. She stayed in films for several years, appearing in 15 more films but often in supporting roles in forgettable efforts. One highlight during this period is her role in 1936's *Charlie Chan's Secret*, one of the better efforts in the Charlie Chan mystery series. Crosman died at age 83 in 1944, near the end of another great conflict, World War II.

On one hand, it's sad that so little of Crosman's work survives today. On the other hand, it's almost miraculous that her work in this film — considered lost for decades — is now readily available. Watching her as Hannah, we have to wonder about what we missed during those 40 years when she was one of the leading actresses of the American stage. As they say, she must have been something then. Seeing her on film, however, we realize that she's still something now.

2

Fearless Free Spirit
Jean Arthur's Wilhelmina Clark in *The Whole Town's Talking*

When Ford was making the comedy *The Whole Town's Talking* in the fall of 1934, the American film world was undergoing one of the most dramatic changes (and, by most accounts, darker chapters) in its history. The Motion Picture Production Code, a set of moral censorship guidelines for films, which had been established in 1930 by the Motion Pictures Producers and Distributors of America (MPPDA) but largely ignored, was — as of July 1, 1934 — now being enforced with a vengeance. The "anything goes" spirit of what we now call the "Pre-Code" period of the early 1930s, in which films were routinely irreverent toward traditional notions of morality and propriety, edgy in tone, frank about sex and sexuality, and (for the time) graphic in their depictions of violence, was purged from nearly all mainstream releases. Plainly put — if film studios, directors, scriptwriters, and actors, were to remain viable — they had to conform to the new, more sanitized order of things.[1]

As one might imagine, most of the creative people in Hollywood hated working under these conditions. For the most part, however, they also took a deep breath and soldiered on. If they wanted to be part of the mainstream movie business, they needed to be working for a Hollywood studio. In order to do that, they needed to learn how to play the new game.

Yet, there was also a silver lining within this cloud. Being creative people, filmmakers and scriptwriters soon found very clever ways to "get around the code" by becoming subtler and more suggestive in their treatment of potentially controversial subjects. Sometimes this strategy could be highly effective. For example, killing a person off screen as we see exaggerated shadows of a struggle often gives viewers a very different experience from seeing the actual killing on screen. Simply put, it leaves more to the viewer's imagination, creating an even more chilling and disturbing effect. Rather than shown, the horror is suggested in a more artful and ultimately more satisfying way. The storytelling becomes richer and more fulfilling for the consumer.

As the code remained enforced from the 1930s until the 1960s, some of Hollywood's most gifted creative people found more and more ingenious ways to get provocative and sometimes very subversive stories past the censors. Along with Alfred Hitchcock, Billy Wilder, Fritz Lang, and others, Ford became quite good at this. His solution was often to set his films in rural locales or in other historical periods. That way he could comment on dicey contemporary issues such as the harshness of capitalism, American imperialism, and racism without seeming to be critical of contemporary attitudes and behaviors and risking a backlash of some kind. It's no coincidence, for example, that his films *The Searchers*, *Sergeant Rutledge*, and *Cheyenne Autumn*—all westerns that focus on racism—were made at the height of the civil rights struggles of the 1950s and 1960s.

The Whole Town's Talking is the third film that Ford directed in this new age of censorship and his first to subvert the code in significant ways. What seems at first to be a fast-paced farce with lots of snappy dialogue and a nice lesson about courage is really an indictment of a business and social system that rewards compliance and punishes individuality and personal expression. Based on a story by W.R. Burnett and an intricate and very adept script by Robert Riskin and Jo Swerling, and supported by cinematographer Joe August's often brooding, highly suggestive expressionistic camera work, the film is the fruit of a highly successful behind-the-camera collaboration.

In front of the camera, something very interesting was occurring too: audiences were seeing the unofficial "unveiling" of not one but two of the best film actors of the period: Edward G. Robinson and Jean Arthur. While both actors had been working in films for a long time, *The Whole Town's Talking* was crucial to establishing new and more luminous star personas for each, the personas they are best remembered for today.

Robinson had been active on stage as well as in films since the 1910s, and, after a long apprenticeship, finally broke through to stardom in Warner's gangster film *Little Caesar* in 1931. After *Little Caesar*, Robinson was repeatedly typecast in gangster roles. Then, with the enforcement of the Production Code, the available gangster roles became fewer and less interesting. His career had hit a snag. In *The Whole Town's Talking*, Robinson began to make the transition from typecast gangster to versatile and highly respected character actor.

Arthur, while not yet a star of Robinson's stature, had traveled a similar road. At 34, she had worked in films and on stage for more than a decade. Yet, even after making numerous silent films and surviving the transition to sound, she had still not been able to break through to the top tier of stardom. But in

Jean Arthur as the fearless Wilhelmina Clark and Edward G. Robinson as the meek and mild Arthur Ferguson Jones share a water cooler moment at the accounting firm where they both work in Ford's delightful but little known 1935 comedy *The Whole Town's Talking*. The role of Wilhelmina was key to establishing the Jean Arthur star persona, which would serve her well in such films as 1939's *Mr. Smith Goes to Washington*, 1942's *The Talk of the Town*, and 1943's *The More the Merrier*.

this film, she too found her niche, playing the first of many roles as a hard-boiled, sometimes cynical working woman with a keen intelligence, sharp wit, delightful sense of whimsy, and (we usually discover) big heart.[2]

While Arthur's role in *The Whole Town's Talking* (Miss Wilhelmina Clark) is secondary to Robinson's dual role (both Jones and Mannion), it is — considering her many flat and undistinguished roles up to that time — quite startling. Arthur inhabits Wilhelmina with an ease and an authority fans had only seen glimpses of in past performances. She also infuses her with that special Arthurian quality, her whimsical eccentricity, which audiences would grow to value more and more during the 1930s and 1940s. It's a fine performance by an actress on the verge of greatness.

* * *

The real Jean Arthur, however, was very different from the confident, feisty screen persona that's etched so clearly into so many filmgoers' minds. Born Gladys Greene in Plattsburgh, New York, in 1900, she lived a largely reclusive life and had intense struggles with stage and camera fright when she acted. Yet, she was still determined to perform. After dropping out of high school in her teens, she began working as a stenographer and then a commercial model when Fox Film Studios signed her to a contract in the early 1920s. As part of this career change, she took a new professional name, which paid homage to two of her personal heroes: Joan of Arc (Jeanne d'Arc) and King Arthur. She then made her debut in a small role in *Cameo Kirby*, a 1923 film starring silent screen heartthrob John Gilbert and directed by one of Fox's promising young directors, John Ford. She was, as she freely admitted about this and subsequent roles, not very good. But, she continued to work in a variety of films, including low-budget westerns, and she managed to make the transition to sound and also to make the most of her unique husky, sometimes quavering voice, turning it into one of her most effective acting tools. After a two-year stint honing her craft on Broadway between 1931 and 1933, she returned to Hollywood and was soon signed to a long-term contract by Columbia Pictures. Within a year, she was at work on *The Whole Town's Talking*.

The Perils of Mistaken Identity

The Whole Town's Talking is set in a major city in the present, something that, as mentioned earlier, would occur in fewer and fewer of Ford's films as his career progressed.

A compliant, mild-mannered accountant named Arthur Ferguson Jones, who works with Miss Wilhelmina Clark in a large accounting firm (and sheepishly longs for her), turns out to be an exact look-alike for "Killer" Mannion, a hardened bank robber who also has no qualms about living up to his notorious nickname. Jones is mistaken for Mannion and arrested, but soon his real identity is confirmed and he is quickly freed. As assurance that Jones won't be mistaken for Mannion again, the district attorney gives him a letter attesting to his identity. When the story becomes news, the evil Mannion hears about the letter, shows up in Jones' rented room, and announces that he will share the letter with Jones, using it only at night. Ever the accommodating one, Jones quickly acquiesces, and Mannion continues on his crime spree, using the letter as safe passage around town. Then, Mannion decides to take the letter for good, leading others to assume that Jones is really Mannion. For good measure, he also plots to have Jones bumped off and kidnaps — among others — Wilhelmina and Jones' aunt. For the meek and mild Jones, this is the last straw. By sheer good fortune, he avoids being killed and unwittingly leads police to Mannion's hideout. Once there, Mannion's henchmen mistake Jones for their boss, and the accountant learns he's been tapped to take the fall. Then, discovering that Wilhelmina and his aunt are being held captive, he summons his courage. When Mannion arrives, he orders the henchmen to kill Mannion, whom they naturally assume is Jones. Immediately, he rescues the captives. Mannion's henchmen try to escape but are immediately surrounded by the police. Finally, with the $25,000 reward for Mannion's capture, Jones and Wilhelmina, now married, head off on a cruise to Shanghai. At last, they can now have the kind of adventure they've long dreamed about.

* * *

When it opened a couple of months into 1935, *The Whole Town's Talking* was generally received with enthusiasm. "[I]t may be handsomely recommended as the best of the new year's screen comedies," noted *The New York Times*. "Usually the cinema is forced to struggle along in spite of its stories, but this time the tale is eminently worth the telling." The review also singled out Robinson for his "splendid" dual performance, Arthur for "separate applause," Riskin and Swerling for their "riotous script," and Ford for his "persuasive direction."[3] With such accolades, the film became an immediate hit and both Robinson and Arthur entered the most successful phases of their careers.

* * *

What's curious today is how far into obscurity this clever and well-produced film has fallen. People simply don't watch it anymore. While it's not one of Ford's most accomplished films, there is still much in it to enjoy and appreciate.

On the surface, it works well as an entertaining, fast-paced comedy with lots of plot twists, snappy dialogue, and pointed ironies. One fascinating dilemma occurs early in the film when the pompous head of the accounting firm tells the conscientious but dim-witted supervisor both to fire the next employee who comes in late to work and also give Jones, the company's most punctual employee, a raise. As it turns out, that very morning, Jones's new alarm clock doesn't work and he turns out to the be next employee to walk in late. Now, the poor supervisor must struggle. Does he give Jones a raise? Does he fire him? Or does he give him a raise and then fire him? Oh, the challenges of management!

As the case usually is in Ford's comedies, much is also brewing beneath the surface, with underlying tensions often being conveyed visually. The film's opening scenes bear a striking resemblance to the opening scenes of King Vidor's 1928 silent film masterpiece *The Crowd*, when the camera enters a large impersonal skyscraper and pans across rows and rows of anonymous clerks at their desks, depicting a sterile, oppressive environment that places a high value on regimentation, conformity, and compliance. In *The Whole Town's Talking*, the point is not made in such an obvious way. This is a comedy, after all. But the point is still made very clearly. Later in the film, Ford visually links the regimented office scenes to scenes within a prison. His point here is clear as well: there isn't much difference between working for a large company and being in prison. This connection harkens back to another under-appreciated Ford comedy from the era, 1930's *Up the River*, which is about two chronic criminals, who eventually learn that, for them at least, the world outside of prison is far less desirable than prison itself.

Another tension the film considers is between appearance and reality, a theme Ford will return to in a comic vain later that year in his *Steamboat Round the Bend*. Here, there is much to think about as well. Which one of these men (as other characters sometimes wonder) is the meek and mild Jones and which the thoroughly evil Mannion? Is Jones, a man who for most of the film is weak and frightened, really the good guy? Is Mannion the real villain of this piece? Or is the real villain the repressive society intent on stamping out individuality and personal expression?

The film also conveys added depth and complexity through Joe August's highly effective cinematography. A master of creating haunting expressionistic images to convey intense mood and feelings, August worked with Ford often during the 1930s and later did some of his most stunning work in Ford's *They Were Expendable* in 1945 and William Dieterle's *Portrait of Jennie* in 1948. Here, his camera does much to provide the story with added emotional texture. One scene that's particularly effective is when we see a succession of swirling images to show the chaos and distress within Jones's head as he endures this experience. Another scene is when Jones and Mannion first meet. As in a similar scene from Ford's 1962 western, *The Man Who Shot Liberty Valance*, an unsuspecting and vulnerable good man walks into a familiar dark room, lights a lamp, and is startled to come face to face with a dangerous bad man who has been waiting patiently for him in the dark. The way August lights Mannion's eyes in this scene is worth noting too. They are cold, mean, and shrouded in black. This is one scary man.

Brave Companion

Just as Mannion is Jones's identical twin and moral opposite, Wilhelmina Clark is Jones's kindred spirit and fearless counterpart. In fact, in the dark, fearful world depicted in the film, she is the freest spirit. When she also arrives at work late and is fired by the supervisor, she blithely sits at her desk and comments to a fellow employee: "Well, I've been canned. I feel like celebrating." She's a single working woman who's just lost her job in the depths of the Great Depression, and she doesn't seem a bit worried. "Oh well," she seems to be telling us. "It'll work out, and I'm not going to worry about it."

Later, when the police mistake Jones for Mannion and bring him in, she must also go through an interrogation.

"It was terribly embarrassing," Jones says afterward.

"Not for me," she responds. With a little bravado, she also likens the questioning to "a cross-country sleigh ride."

Nothing scares this woman, no one can intimidate her, and she has a great sense of the absurdity of things. It's easy to see why Jones is smitten with her. She has the kind of courage he desperately wants to have.

She genuinely likes Jones too and even sees some real potential in him. "I've always thought Rabbit had something," she tells a co-worker. "All he needs is courage." Yes, her nickname for him is "Rabbit," as in "scared rabbits."

Soon, she takes on the role of Jones's cheerleader. "Oh, stop being scared," she says when they are police custody. "Just growl at them, Killer. You'll scare them to death." Now, she's calling him by the name of his evil twin, both to mock his fear and to bolster his courage.

Afterward, as she sees Jones release himself somewhat from his fears, we see her feelings for him deepen. After he's cleared and released by the police, he has a few too many drinks with his boss (who's become quite impressed with him), returns to the office and — now bolstered by the alcohol too — forthrightly kisses Wilhelmina. She's surprised and delighted. We can see the "Wow!" in her eyes. She has been right: this man has something. "Jonesy, you need a caretaker, and I think I'm elected," she says. That's about as close to a statement of commitment as we — or Jones — is likely to get from her.

The Whole Town's Talking has two catalysts. Wilhelmina gives Jones the desire to want to be a more courageous person, and Mannion gives him the opportunity to force that courage to the surface. Each character — she in a very conscious, direct way and he in a much less conscious, more indirect way — makes a critical contribution to Jones's development.

Now that Wilhelmina has helped release Jones from his fears (and now that Jones also has $25,000 in reward money), the film's ending suggests that the world is now finally opening up for Jones. We assume that they have both quit their deadening jobs as we see them depart to fulfill a lifelong dream, traveling to Shanghai. The happy ending is well earned.

While the Riskin/Swerling script is key to making *The Whole Town's Talking* a very solid film and Wilhelmina a very credible and appealing character, both director and actress deserve major kudos too.

"Considering the heavy-handed horseplay that Ford often included in his films as comic relief, the deftness of his touch in this masterful farce comes as something of a surprise," critic Michael Costello has written. "Ford directs and cuts the scenes with uncharacteristic rapidity, seeming to enjoy playing off the meek clerk against the anarchic gangster."[4] We can certainly extend this praise to his handling of Arthur in this key role. Although the Jean Arthur persona was yet to fully blossom, Ford saw her unique qualities and allowed her to use them to full advantage — and to soar.

Arthur, too, was ready and more than able to make the big leap forward in her career. In every one of her scenes she is pitch-perfect with both her effective facial expressions and her beautifully timed line deliveries. But, most important, this actress who had faced so many career setbacks seemed to be, despite all that, oozing with confidence and conviction in this role. As Wilhelmina tackles life head on, Arthur tackled Wilhelmina, infusing her with the buoyant fearlessness that soon became a key component of the unique, multi-faceted Jean Arthur persona. This is a clear case of the actress and the role being ideal for each other.

* * *

After *The Whole Town's Talking*, Arthur quickly became the toast of Columbia Pictures and one of the most highly respected and sought-after actresses of the era. With a gift for giving a special depth to roles that blended comedy with serious moments, she starred in 24 more films before retiring and returning occasionally for television appearances. Among her most memorable films are Frank Capra's *Mr. Deeds Goes to Town* (1936), *You Can't Take It with You* (1938), and *Mr. Smith Goes to Washington* (1939). She has also been highly praised for work she did for director George Stevens in *The Talk of the Town* (1942), *The More the Merrier* (1943), and *Shane* (1953). She received one Best Actress Academy Award nomination during her career (for her role in *The More the Merrier*), which is a shame because she deserved several.

In his 1973 autobiography, *All My Yesterdays*, Arthur's co-star from *The Whole Town's Talking*, Edward G. Robinson, shared his thoughts about her. "She was whimsical without being silly, unique without being nutty, a theatrical personality who was an untheatrical person," Robinson wrote. "She was a delight to work with and to know."[5]

Arthur married twice but never had any children and remained reclusive for the rest of her life, once famously saying that she would rather have her throat cut than give an interview.[6] She died in 1991 at age 90.

After her death, Charles Champlin of *The Los Angeles Times* wrote: "To at least one teenager in a small town (though I'm sure we were a multitude), Jean Arthur suggested strongly that the ideal woman could be — ought to be — judged by her spirit as well as her beauty.... The notion of the woman as a friend and confidante, as well as someone you courted and were nuts about, someone whose true beauty was internal rather than external, became a full-blown possibility as we watched Jean Arthur."7

3

"Swamp Gal"

Anne Shirley's Fleety Belle in *Steamboat Round the Bend*

"Is there anything lovelier or more careless than the way Fleety Belle, her first time at the wheel, ... joyfully calls, 'Steamboat round the bend?'"—Tag Gallagher[1]

Ford's *Steamboat Round the Bend* (1935) is best known as the last film of Will Rogers, the legendary American wit, vaudevillian, newspaper columnist, and actor. Only six weeks after the film's shooting was completed, Rogers, who was just 55, and his friend, pilot Wiley Post, were killed in a plane crash near Nome, Alaska. Ford, who greatly liked and admired Rogers, was devastated. When *Steamboat* was released soon after Rogers' death, Fox studio executives even altered the ending hoping to diffuse the grief they assumed audiences would feel as they saw the last images of their beloved Will.

This is a sad story of course, and film scholars have often speculated about what Ford and Rogers might have done together if Rogers had lived. *Steamboat* was only their third collaboration (after 1933's *Dr. Bull* and 1934's *Judge Priest*), and the joint ventures had proven beneficial for both. Ford gave the films a level of complexity, moral shading, and visual power that Rogers' other films often lacked. Rogers gave the films a very natural, relaxed, unforced quality that Ford wasn't always able to convey. The pair apparently had great fun working together, too. It was a good match.

It's also a pity that *Steamboat*'s backstory often overshadows the actual achievement. It's more than an entertaining film; it's an extremely good one. The clever, crisply paced story is filled with sharp wit, quirky humor, and a great zest for life. The Ford-Rogers partnership is working extremely well. As critic Andrew Sarris notes: "[In *Steamboat*] Ford and Rogers had finally attained a marvelous rapport between their respective styles, thus achieving a mature exuberance that is virtually unique in American cinema."[2] In addition, the film is filled with colorful, eccentric characters. (Among them are the New Moses, a fiery evangelist played with great relish by Ford regular Berton Churchill, and Rufe Jeffers, a curiously indifferent local sheriff played with comic mastery by character actor Eugene Pallette.) And the film's climactic riverboat race down the Mississippi to Baton Rouge has both epic sweep and lots of fresh, inventive humor. Beneath the surface, the film also touches upon some interesting issues. One is the tension between appearance and reality. Throughout the story, things and people often aren't what they initially seem to be. In fact, they can be very different, and we constantly need to be aware, on the lookout, willing to learn and change our perspectives and personal stances. Linked to this is another familiar Ford theme: tolerance, the need to acknowledge and respect other kinds of people and their different points of view.

Among the film's strengths, one that's often overlooked is its main female character, a young "swamp gal" named Fleety Belle, played by a very talented 17-year-old actress named Anne Shirley.

Anne Shirley, as fans of the novel *Anne of the Green Gables* will know, is also the name of that story's young heroine. Believe it or not, this is not a coincidence. Shirley the actress, who was born Dawn Evelyeen Paris in 1918, began her film career at age five in the silent era using the name Dawn O'Day. Unlike both many child actors and many silent film actors, she managed to make a successful dual transition to adult roles and to talking pictures. Much in demand for supporting roles during the Pre-Code period of the early 1930s, she appeared in such notable films as *Three On a Match* with Bette Davis and Joan Blondell and *Rasputin and the Empress* with John, Ethel, and Lionel Barrymore. Then, in 1934, she received a major career break: she was cast in the lead of the film version of *Anne of the Green Gables*. As a tribute to her good fortune (and perhaps to distance herself from her child-star identity), she officially changed her name to the heroine's. For the remainder of her career, Anne Shirley was the name she went by.

In *Steamboat Round the Bend*, Shirley takes on the role of Fleety Belle, who may be the film's most complex and fully developed character. Raised and abused by the people Dr. John (Rogers) calls "swamp trash" and naïve about life outside the wetlands, Fleety Belle is nevertheless smart enough to see the goodness in Dr. John's nephew Duke (John McGuire) and courageous enough to run away with him and stand up to both Dr. John and her very unpleasant swamp relations. At the same time, she is a quick thinker with excellent instincts, often the smartest person in the story. In fact, if we look at *Steamboat* closely, it's not as much a story about Rogers' Dr. John as it is about Fleety Belle's coming of age under his wily, sometimes fumbling, always good-hearted tutelage. She is the one who experiences the most dramatic personal changes and growth,

In 1935's *Steamboat Round the Bend*, 17-year-old Anne Shirley more than held her own with legendary co-star Will Rogers, giving the film's leading female character, Fleety Belle, surprising depth and maturity. Shirley, a film actress since age five, had several memorable roles as a young adult in the late 1930s and early 1940s but eventually grew weary of the profession she had pursued from such an early age. After her 1944 hit, *Murder My Sweet*, with Dick Powell, she retired from acting. She was 26.

and she is the one who blossoms into a new maturity that at film's end will bring, we're assuming, added depth to her relationship with Duke.

"See that steamboat comin'..."

"See that steamboat comin'," the song that plays over the film's opening credits tells us, and the adventure begins.

The time is the early 1890s, and the place is Louisiana along the mighty Mississippi.

The story starts with a curious and ironic juxtaposition. In one scene we see the New Moses making a valiant effort to convince a scruffy old drunk (Francis Ford as he was so often cast) to find salvation by forsaking demon rum.

In the very next scene, Dr. John is selling his product. It's a different kind of salvation: a "restorative" elixir with a fairly high alcohol content. Immediately, the tension between perception and reality is in plain view. Is the New Moses really a prophet? Is Dr. John's remedy all that he says it is? Is he even a doctor? Is either of them really peddling anything resembling salvation? Are lots of people really just hucksters of one kind or another? How can the rest of us ever tell?

Back on board his riverboat, the *Claremore Queen*, Dr. John is reunited with his nephew Duke, who has picked up with a girl from the swamps named Fleety Belle. As well as being at odds with Fleety Belle's relatives, Duke has another problem: to protect Fleety Belle, he has — in self-defense — killed a man. He feels confident that this can be proven because there was a witness at the scene, none other than the New Moses. So, against Fleety Belle's objections — she fears what she's heard about the local jurist, "this hangin' judge" — Dr. John and Duke surrender to the sheriff, Rufe Jeffers (Eugene Pallette).

While he's in jail, Duke asks Dr. John to look after Fleety Belle, and his uncle agrees. But there's another problem: Dr. John doesn't like her. Not only does she come from "swamp trash," but, because of her, Duke is in serious trouble. In addition, they both have different plans for Duke. Dr. John wants him to help operate the *Claremore Queen*. Fleety Belle wants him as a husband. Right now this looks like an either/or situation.

Soon, however, initial perceptions change. Fleety Belle's father, former beau, and other swamp folk pay her and Dr. John a visit. They're a mean, unsavory lot. In fact, her father even threatens her with his whip. Fleety Belle stands her ground with them. Dr. John has to intervene, eventually telling them the lie that convinces them to leave — that Fleety Belle and Duke have already married. From this point, the bond is formed. With a new appreciation for each other's goodness and decency, Dr. John and Fleety Belle are now on the same side, allies committed to freeing Duke.

Still, the complications keep on coming. The New Moses can't be located, and without his testimony Duke is found guilty of murder and sentenced to hang. To raise money for Duke's appeal, Dr. John buys a wax museum and plans to go up and down the Mississippi offering shows to the locals in each port. Then the appeal fails too, Duke is sentenced to hang in Baton Rouge, and Dr. John decides to head there to appeal directly to the governor.

The wax museum is a fascinating addition to the proceedings. Again, perception and reality collide. To placate the Louisiana locals, Dr. John changes the identities of the wax figures. General Grant becomes General Lee. King George III is turned into George Washington. Two Old Testament prophets are transformed into the notorious outlaws Frank and Jesse James. Often wax figures are mistaken for real people and real people for wax figures. And, at one point, the mere presence of the wax James brothers stops an angry mob in its tracks. What's real and what's not? It's hard for the characters to know sometimes. Sometimes it's hard for any of us to know.

Then, on the way down to Baton Rouge, there's still another complication: the river has been closed down for a big riverboat race. Dr. John's archrival, Captain Eli (Irwin S. Cobb), owner of the fastest boat on the river, the *Pride of Paducah*, is competing. Since it's the only way that Dr. John and Fleety Belle can get to Baton Rouge in time to try to stop the hanging, they enter the *Claremore Queen*. Soon, we see a long row of steamboats at the starting line before a cheering crowd and the band playing *Dixie*. It's stirring stuff. By 1935 standards, it must have been spectacular on the big screen, and it's still impressive today. The cannon goes off; the race is on; and along the way Dr. John sees the New Moses preaching on the shore, lassos him with a rope, and brings him onboard.

"I've got souls to save," Moses says indignantly.

"You've got a life to save first," Dr. John tells him.

So, Moses joins the motley crew. Fleety Belle steers, and everyone else feverishly stokes the engine. When fuel runs out, they start tearing up the boat. Then they throw in the waxworks. Finally, they use Dr. John's elixir to power them into Baton Rouge for the happy ending at the gallows.

On the surface, the film is great fun. But Ford and his scriptwriters, Dudley Nichols and Lamar Trotti, have things to say here too. As we consider the tension between perception and reality and the need for greater tolerance between swamp people and river people, we are often reminded that we are in a truly segregated, truly divided society in the 1890s American South. African Americans and whites keep to themselves, the jailhouse is sharply divided along racial lines, and at one point we see a public restroom with "WHITE" painted boldly on the door. In fact, the only integrated society that's prominently featured is Dr. John's crew, which includes Jonah, played by Stepin Fetchit,[3] and another African American actor. It's interesting that this crew, in which everyone is treated as equals, is the group that works so well together in the end, everyone enthusiastically pitching in to get to Baton Rouge in time.

"Duke ain't blamin' you, Dr. John"

When we first meet Fleety Belle, she is frightened, lacks confidence, and looks more like an urchin than an ingénue. She can tell that Duke's Uncle John doesn't like her. She also doesn't like the way the conversation is going: if Duke turns himself in, what's to become of her? She seems very young, but she's also assertive enough to plead for Duke to go away with her and not get anywhere near that "hangin' judge." Even at this point, she is willing to trust her own instincts: instincts that we learn are usually quite sound.

The next time we see Fleety Belle, Ford puts her — literally — in a very different and positive light, and Shirley portrays her with great subtlety. It is evening. The last of the sunlight shines on the river and Fleety Belle as she stands next to the deck railing of the *Claremore Queen*. Both she and the scene are quite reflective and beautiful. We notice the badly frayed skirt she wears (which we soon learn was once a table cloth), and we are reminded of the poverty and abuse she has endured. We also sense that there is something more to her, something untapped and maybe quite substantial. We don't know what it is quite yet, but we are intrigued and curious to find out. The three brief shots of Shirley on the deck at dusk is a lovely, unexpected Ford touch: one of many that give this film its special character.

In the scene that immediately follows, which is a masterpiece of compressed storytelling, we learn a great deal about Fleety Belle and Dr. John while the plot takes several steps forward. First, as she and Dr. John bicker before dinner, we (along with Dr. John) see that she is smart and forthright, has integrity, wants to do her fair share, and sincerely loves Duke. Then the dreadful swamp relations arrive, Dr. John comes to her defense, and she slips him a big, nasty-looking knife to counter. The bond between them is forged. After that, Dr. John becomes the surrogate father, offering Fleety Belle a proper dress to wear to court for Duke's trial, the dress that once belonged to his sister, Duke's mother. The bond becomes stronger. They are now family.

On the way to the courthouse, we see the dress in full flower. It has a hoop skirt, and it seems hopelessly out of date even by 1890s fashion standards. Yet, Fleety Belle is thrilled to be wearing it and deeply touched that Dr. John has given it to her and treats her so respectfully. She is definitely not an entitled youth.

Another fascinating scene — an example of Ford's fondness for elliptical storytelling — is next. Ford has bypassed the trial, and Fleety Belle and Dr. John sit together in the otherwise empty courtroom. We learn that Duke has been found guilty and sentenced to hang. Dr. John is both crushed and angry with himself for not getting better counsel. Now it's her turn to support him.

"Duke ain't blamin' you, Dr. John," she says.

Saddened herself, she sees the complexity of the situation. Over her initial objections, Dr. John convinced Duke to turn himself in and appear before the "hangin' judge." Now, it's clear that the local lawyer Dr. John has retained has failed too. He has made two less-than-stellar calls that have seriously affected both Duke and her. Yet, she isn't angry or spiteful. She is simply aware that bad things can happen to good, well-intended people. Again, Shirley's acting is worth noting. As Rogers talks, we are drawn to her sad and very understanding face. Fleety Belle is undergoing the greatest test of her life, one that is quickly turning her into wiser, much more mature woman.

Later, when Fleety Belle visits Duke in jail, she is allowed to speak to him only from the other side of barred windows. The exchanges between both characters are sweet and tender. They are young and in love, but there's a very good chance Duke will soon be executed. Their life together could be over before it's really had a chance to start, and both understand this fully and deeply. Another poignant Ford touch in these scenes is the way Fleety Belle holds the window bars with her hands. She does it warmly and tenderly, the way she would, if she ever gets the chance again, hold Duke.

As Fleety Belle and Dr. John pursue their quest to raise money for the appeal, we see that they make a good team. She has the better instincts about things, and, while he fumbles from time to time, he is both kind and fearless. She sees all of this and is open in her appreciation. In the same scene when she calls "Steamboat round the bend," for example, she's concerned about where Dr. John has advised her to steer the *Claremore Queen*.

"You don't want me to run into that sandbar, do you, Captain John?" she asks gently.

Together, they make the course correction, and she adds: "I feel like the Lord is just shaming me for having hated you so."

Dr. John (or Captain John, since his title sometimes depends on what he is doing at the moment) may not be the world's best riverboat pilot, but that's a small shortcoming. What's far more important to her is his goodness and commitment to her. She has never known anyone quite like him, feels guilty for having judged him harshly at first, and is deeply grateful for what he has done for her and is trying to do for Duke.

Later on, another scene that shows Fleety Belle's growing maturity is the very understated and moving jailhouse wedding. The appeal has failed, and Duke will soon be taken to Baton Rouge to be hanged. Still, Fleety Belle and Duke would like to be married, and the sheriff agrees to perform the ceremony. The prisoners, both African American and white, are let out of their cells to attend the ceremony. The African American prisoners faintly sing a slow, mournful dirge: not what you'd expect at most weddings but entirely appropriate here. And Fleety Belle and Duke stand before the sheriff with great poise and dignity, both very aware of the joy and sadness of this occasion. In the face of death, they both humbly but boldly proclaim their love for each other. There is no self-pity. Neither breaks down from the emotional strain. They are both calm and in control. Once they have exchanged vows and are pronounced husband and wife, they simply kiss and hold one another. Then there's another curious Ford touch: instead of lining up to congratulate them, the prisoners and the others who are present—so moved by what they have witnessed—can only walk awkwardly about, not wanting to interrupt the couple's sublimely intimate moment.

At the end of the film, both Fleety Belle and Duke are together again but in a very different place from where they were when we first met them. Both have been tested, and both have prevailed. She, especially, has grown from a frightened, insecure girl to a confident, self-assured, and sensitive young woman enriched by experience and keenly aware of life's infinite complexities and ironies. She has become a woman much older than her years.

"Is there anything lovelier or more careless...?"

As the case almost always is with films, many people deserve credit for creating a memorable character. Certainly, Ben Lucien Burman, whose novel was the initial inspiration for the film, gets a nod. We can also see the contributions of the two very talented screenwriters, Dudley Nichols and Lamar Trotti, who each wrote several fine scripts for Ford during the 1930s. The director, famous for getting great performances from actors, uses Shirley's talents to great effect throughout, often enriching her portrayal with his trademark visual touches. Then there's 17-year-old Anne Shirley. In the end, she is the one who conveys the complex, quickly maturing character of Fleety Belle in such a credible and compelling way. As we read her face and hear her line delivery in scene after scene, we see how natural and effortless the portrayal seems and how absolutely at one she is with her character. "Is there anything lovelier or more careless...?" Ford scholar Tag Gallagher asks, and we find ourselves hard pressed to answer. Just as Fleety Belle becomes a woman older than her years, Anne Shirley clearly was an actress far more accomplished than her young age would suggest.

* * *

After *Steamboat Round the Bend*, Shirley appeared in more than 30 more films including 1941's *The Devil and Daniel Webster*, 1942's *Four Jills and a Jeep*, 1944's *Murder, My Sweet*, and 1937's *Stella Dallas*, for which she and the film's star, Barbara Stanwyck, were both nominated for Academy Awards.

Then, in 1944, immediately after completing *Murder, My Sweet*, Shirley abruptly retired. She was only 26 but, by her own admission, had grown tired of the very intense and competitive business she had been working in since she had been five. Her retirement also coincided with her decision — after ending a brief marriage to actor John Payne — to marry Adrian Scott, the producer of *Murder, My Sweet*. Her marriage to Scott, however, lasted only three years. In 1949, she married screenwriter Charles Lederer, and they were happily married until his death in 1976. Unlike other actresses who retired young, Shirley never tried to re-launch her career. A socialite who painted on the side, she was content to stay away from the studios and the spotlights for good. She died of lung cancer at age 75 in 1993.

Although Shirley never acted again, her daughter with John Payne, Julie, and Julie's daughter, Katharine Towne, pursued Hollywood careers. Julie appeared in guest roles on several television shows, including the 1960s' hits *The Wild Wild West* and *The Big Valley*. Granddaughter Katharine (born in 1978) has appeared frequently in both television shows and films, including David Lynch's much praised *Mulholland Drive* in 2001 and the 2007 Will Ferrell comedy, *Blades of Glory*.

Writing about Shirley, film historian Gary Brumburgh has noted: "Not as well remembered as an actress of her award-worthy caliber should be, perhaps had Anne Shirley given Hollywood a longer tryout and added a bit more bite to her rather benign, sweetly sentimental image, her star wouldn't be as dim today. Nevertheless, she has unarguably preserved herself quite well on film."[4]

4

The Innocent Turned Imperialist
Shirley Temple's Priscilla in *Wee Willie Winkie* and Philadelphia in *Fort Apache*

Shirley Temple and John Ford? The pairing seems surreal: the precocious child star who won our hearts by singing "The Good Ship Lollipop" and the tyrannical film director who could make John Wayne cry. Yet, the two worked together twice, their relations were amiable, and the results were two excellent films, 1937's *Wee Willie Winkie* and 1948's *Fort Apache*.

Initially, this odd coupling was the brainstorm of 20th Century–Fox's recently installed production head, Darryl F. Zanuck. According to Ford, Zanuck popped the idea on him by saying: "I'm going to give you something to scream about. I'm going to put you together with Shirley Temple."[1]

There was, however, a method to Zanuck's seeming madness.

At the time, the nine-year-old Temple was not only 20th Century–Fox's biggest star but also in the middle of her four-year run as America's top box-office attraction. Born in 1928, she began appearing in short films in 1932 and by 1933 was appearing in bit parts in films for Universal, Paramount, and Warner Brothers. In February 1934, two months before her sixth birthday, she signed with Fox. Then, just two months after that, she broke through to stardom in the film *Stand Up and Cheer!* By December of that year her name appeared above the title for the first time in *Bright Eyes*, the first film tailored specifically to her talents. When she made *Wee Willie Winkie* two years later, she was fresh off a string of nine highly successful films including such hits as *The Little Colonel*, *Curly Top*, and *The Littlest Rebel*. She was, indisputably, American's darling, and her box office was as golden as her curly blonde tresses.

While Temple's films were beloved by the public, however, critics usually dismissed them as little more than light, fluffy entertainments. Zanuck, ever the perfectionist, saw an opportunity to do more with his young superstar. During a story conference discussing *Wee Willie Winkie* in mid–1936, he said:

43

"My idea about doing this picture is to forget that it is a Shirley Temple picture. That is, not to forget that she is the star, but to write the story as if it were a *Little Woman* or a *David Copperfield*.... All the hokum must be thrown out. The characters must be made real, human, believable. Only then can we get a powerful, real story. The role must be written for Shirley as an actress and nothing sloughed over because Shirley is in it.... We don't want to depend on any of her tricks. She should not be doing things because she is Shirley Temple, but because the situations — sound and believable — call for them. In other words, write the role and let Shirley adapt herself to the picture.... And it must be told from the child's viewpoint, through her eyes."[2]

The other part of Zanuck's brainstorm of course was to bring in Ford, a director who had a reputation for taking mundane material and giving it freshness, immediacy, and emotional depth. Ford wasn't thrilled with the idea, but he went to work, methodically turning a Shirley Temple picture into a John Ford picture starring Shirley Temple.

When the two made *Fort Apache* 11 years later much had changed. Ford now had three directing Oscars under his belt, and Temple, just 20, was nearing the end of her film career. As happened (and still happens) with many child stars, her popularity began to fade as she reached adolescence and young adulthood and tried to transition into different kinds of roles. After two consecutive unsuccessful films at 20th Century–Fox in 1940, her parents bought up her contract and sent her to a boarding school. Then, during the 1940s, she attempted comebacks first with MGM and then with David Selznick's independent production company. Although she made several good films during this time (including 1944's *Since You Went Away* and 1947's *The Bachelor and the Bobby-Soxer* as well as *Fort Apache*) she could not successfully establish herself in romantic and other adult leading roles. She would soon retire from films, while Ford, 34 years her senior, would go on to make more than 20 additional feature films and remain a force in the industry for nearly two decades more.

The irony is that, while Ford was hesitant to work with Temple when she was at her height, he sought her out for *Fort Apache* when at her career was at a low ebb. While he could be a tyrant, Ford was also fiercely loyal to people he liked. And he grew to like Temple enormously.

* * *

Even though the stories of *Wee Willie Winkie* and *Fort Apache* take place on different continents, it's curious how similar the two films are. Both, for example, are set in remote military outposts, involve conflicts with alien people called "Indians," and focus on the impact of imperialist values and institutions on the various groups of people involved. One very intriguing element the two films also share is Ford's use of Temple the child and then Temple the young woman. In each, she plays a sweet, openhearted innocent who accompanies her one living parent to this remote military outpost. Initially, she questions traditions and systems that are fundamentally imperialist, racist, and repressive. In the process, she has a humanizing effect on those around her. Ultimately, though, she becomes a part of these systems. The innocent, now transformed by the values of the societies in which she now lives, becomes an active participant in those societies and supporter of those values.

Celebrating — or Subtly Subverting — British and American Imperialism

At first glance, several Ford films appear to be celebrations of what British writer and poet Rudyard Kipling famously — or infamously — coined as "the white man's burden," the moral imperative to bring the benefits of white man's civilization to "backward" or "savage" lands. It's easy to interpret these films in this way, too. The stories are usually told from the white world's perspective, and so many of the white men and women we get to know are so well intentioned and likable. If they're such nice people, we assume, then they can't really be doing bad things.

Yet, upon closer inspection, a very different and subtly subversive picture emerges, one that often gives these films much greater complexity and resonance. Are the people who dutifully bear the white man's burden performing a worthy service, or are they actually deluding themselves? If so, what do their delusions mean for all involved?

Wee Willie Winkie (inspired by a poem by none other than Kipling) and *Fort Apache* clearly fall into this category.

Wee Willie Winkie is set during the British occupation of India during the late 19th and early 20th centuries often referred to as the "British Raj." A destitute widow named Joyce Williams (June Lang) and her daughter Priscilla (Temple) travel to a remote British outpost in northern India to live with Joyce's father-in-law and the outpost commander, Colonel Williams (C. Aubrey Smith). Just before they arrive they watch as a much-feared local rebel leader named Khoda Khan (Cesar Romero) is captured. Soon, Priscilla befriends gruff but loveable Sergeant McDuff (Victor McLaglen); plays matchmaker for her mother; brings out the kindly, more sensitive side of her rigid, duty-driven grandfather; and even connects through prison bars with Khoda Khan. But local conflicts also rage. Khoda Khan's men help him escape from prison in a violent raid, McDuff is fatally wounded while on patrol, and it looks as if a major battle is inevitable. Believing that she can persuade Khoda Khan not to go to war, little Priscilla finds a way to get to his mountain fortress. Khoda Khan is delighted:

she will be the bait that brings the British soldiers into his stronghold and ensures their defeat. Colonel Williams and his forces arrive, but, knowing Priscilla is with Khoda Khan, he keeps his soldiers out of range and walks alone to the entrance. Several of Khan's men start shooting at Williams, and Priscilla rushes to her grandfather's side. Impressed by the colonel's courage and overcome with respect for the child, Khoda Khan orders his men to stop firing. He agrees to negotiate, war is averted, and the story ends with little Priscilla, now in a specially tailored British uniform, engaged in all the military pomp and ceremony.

While the tone of *Wee Willie Winkie* is usually light (the star is, after all, Shirley Temple), we are reminded constantly that empire can extract an enormous cost. Colonel Williams' weariness at having to shoulder Britain's perceived burden is apparent. Priscilla, her mother, and her grandfather have all lost Priscilla's father presumably in the defense of empire. During the film, many people on both sides of this conflict are killed. Of all these losses, perhaps the one most eloquently conveyed is McDuff's. After being wounded in battle, he is weak and lying on a hospital bed. Priscilla, not yet understanding that he will soon die, brings him a small bunch of flowers. In a two-shot, he asks her to sing "Auld Lang Syne." As she does, the camera slowly — almost imperceptibly — moves toward Priscilla as McDuff literally slips away from the scene as well as from life. Then, when all we can see of McDuff is his hand holding the flowers, we see the hand turn limp and the flowers fall. In a way, this beautiful, very moving scene sums up all the deaths that occur in the story. Each person's death is profound

In 1937's *Wee Willie Winkie*, Shirley Temple's Priscilla Williams makes fast friends with Victor McLaglen's Sergeant McDuff. The teaming of Temple and director Ford, perhaps Hollywood's oddest couple ever, was the brainstorm of 20th Century–Fox production head Darryl F. Zanuck, who believed that Ford could give the story a level of emotional depth that most of Temple's previous films lacked. Later in life Temple agreed, citing this as her favorite among the 40-plus films she made.

both for the individual and for all those who have been touched by that person. We have to wonder whether maintaining an empire justifies so much loss.

In her 1988 autobiography, *Child Star*, Temple speaks very highly of this whole experience. "Death scenes in movies are notorious booby traps," she notes. "One plucked heartstring too many and everything turns into discord and audience indifference. In this case, Ford's direction was unfaltering and supremely sensitive, memorable for both critics and audiences. McLaglen's last gasp did not drag on and my song was phrased and paced to support the action, not dominate it. With this brawny hero counter-posed with an innocent child under the encompassing shadow of death, every nuance of movement and sound coalesced in a scene of power and purity.... When the cameras had stopped, McLaglen raised on his elbow and placed one massive hand over mine. 'If I wasn't already dead,' he said, 'I'd be crying too....' [Afterward] Ford came over and put his arm around my shoulder, as he would have a boy. My grief had come across with perfect restraint, he said.... That we could be friends I had never doubted. But now we were colleagues."[3]

Fort Apache begins in a similar manner but then veers off into far more tragic territory. Young Philadelphia Thursday (Temple) accompanies her father, Colonel Owen Thursday (Henry Fonda in a superb performance) to Fort Apache, an isolated U.S. cavalry outpost in the American southwest shortly after the U.S. Civil War. Again, we see life mostly through the perspectives of the people at the fort: most of them good, caring people, some devoted to their own families, and all devoted to their common military family. Philadelphia works to make a home for her and her father. She also meets and falls for handsome young Lieutenant O'Rourke (John Agar). But Colonel Thursday disapproves of the match. He also turns out to be arrogant and harsh with his soldiers, and unreasonable, intolerant, and unnecessarily belligerent toward the Apaches. Foolishly, he insults the Apache chief, Cochise, and forces a needless, ill-conceived battle in which many of the characters we have grown close to during the film are, along with Thursday, slaughtered. Afterward, we see a surviving officer, Lieutenant-Colonel Kirby York (John Wayne), who now commands the regiment, meet with a group of journalists in Colonel Thursday's old office. In addition to learning that Philadelphia and Lieutenant O'Rourke are now married, we find out that Colonel Thursday is now a national hero, "the envy of every schoolboy in America." In fact, a painting showing "Thursday's Charge" now hangs in Washington, D.C. Yet, while York praises the sacrifices of Thursday and the others who died, his voice intonations and body language don't match up with his words. He talks without real emotion, as if he is just reciting the company line. His eyes seem detached as if he just doesn't fully believe what he is saying. Then, when the meeting is over, he puts on a cap reminiscent of Thursday's and leads the regiment out on patrol.

One of the most startling and unsettling endings in any Ford film, this scene has inspired discussion and argument for decades. What is really going on here? Does York believe that these sacrifices in the name of American territorial dominance are warranted? Or do his voice intonations and body language suggest something different? Is he merely masking his personal distaste for Thursday, Thursday's arrogance, and his ineptness as a leader? Or is he also questioning some of the imperialistic values that drove Thursday and the others to their doom? Or, if York isn't questioning them, is Ford? This is all very intriguing, and no doubt the arguments will continue.

The Innocent in Strange, Hostile Lands

While the story arcs in *Wee Willie Winkie* and *Fort Apache* are ultimately quite different, the main female characters, each played by Temple, are remarkably similar and undergo very similar journeys. Innocent and curious at first, they soon become humanizing influences on others they come into contact with. In the end, though, they succumb to their respective societies' imperial ways of life.

Their curiosity is especially fascinating not only because it suggests strong individualistic streaks but also because it often taps into key issues in the films. Before Priscilla arrives at the British outpost in India her grandfather commands, for example, she asks her mother that, if her grandfather were English, "why doesn't he live in England?" One answer would be that, if England weren't a colonial power, then, yes, he probably would live in England. Philadelphia has her share of questions too. She constantly asks what her role as "the colonel's lady" should be and what she needs to do to play it correctly. Of the two Temple characters, it's interesting that little Priscilla asks the bigger questions, questions about war and peace, questions that get to the heart of the story's core conflicts. In contrast, Philadelphia's main focus is domestic: she is angry that her father doesn't approve of her and Lieutenant O'Rourke and openly questions and occasionally defies fatherly judgments based on classism and prejudice.

Because they are genuinely kind and caring as well as inquisitive people, Priscilla and Philadelphia both do much to humanize their communities. Much has been written about Priscilla's relationship with the gruff but lovable Sergeant McDuff in *Wee Willie Winkie*. But Priscilla also has a great humanizing effect on her equally gruff grandfather, Colonel Williams. She charms him by telling him that the men call him "Old Boots," nudges him into taking her widowed mother to a dance, and gets him to change some of his assumptions about the native peoples under his jurisdiction. Her act of kindness to the "enemy" leader Khoda Khan — returning a talisman to him — has a major impact on his attitude

4. The Innocent Turned Imperialist

In 1948's *Fort Apache*, Temple's Philadelphia Thursday (right) joins Irene Rich's Mary O'Rourke (left) and Anna Lee's Emily Collingwood as they all watch the men in their lives leave for the film's climactic battle. Temple's love interest in the film, actor John Agar, was also her husband at the time. Unfortunately for Temple, though, both her marriage and her film career ended shortly afterward.

toward the British. Little Priscilla is remarkable at seeing through stereotypes and helping others to do the same, and her ability to transform both her grandfather and Khoda Khan directly results in the conflict's positive resolution. In *Fort Apache*, Philadelphia plays a similar role but nowhere near as successfully. From the beginning of the film she wins the hearts of Lieutenant O'Rourke and just about everyone else at the fort. Even before she reaches the fort, when she lets an old frontier women try on her big-city hat, we see how her kindness touches people. She is also the only one who can get underneath her stern father's hard shell. The scene when she shows Colonel Thursday how she has fixed up their quarters and he awkwardly kisses her on the forehead is both painful and moving. This arrogant, bigoted, self-centered man does have a tender side, and Philadelphia, it seems, is the only one who can bring it out. Sadly, though, Colonel Thursday is not nearly as balanced or reasonable as Colonel Williams. Try as she might, Philadelphia can't get her father to accept Lieutenant

O'Rourke as a potential son-in-law, O'Rourke's lower-class background, or even his Irish heritage (let alone accept Apaches). Here the ability to humanize is profoundly limited because her father adheres so fiercely to a rigid set of classist, racist, imperialist values. The tragedy at the film's end is inevitable.

Despite their shared ability to question and sometimes challenge the systems they must live within, however, both Priscilla and Philadelphia succumb to those systems. This is part of the essential — and very disturbing — irony at the heart of both films. At the end of *Wee Willie Winkie*, Priscilla now has her own soldier's uniform and toy rifle and, in a display of classic Temple cuteness, is marching around, enthusiastically embracing her new role. At the end of *Fort Apache*, Philadelphia has fully made the transition to by-the-book military wife and mother. The spirited young woman, once so oblivious to the military's rigidity and the way it can stifle self-determination, has now been fully integrated into the system. Her hair is tightly (almost unpleasantly) wound around her head. She doesn't smile. She is all duty. Here, she is so different from the way she is at the non-commissioned officers' dance that immediately precedes the last tragic battle. There, almost everyone dances with incredible stiffness, grim-faced and determined. This is more of a march than a dance. The exception is Philadelphia. Her movements are livelier, looser, easier. She smiles and seems endlessly curious. She is actually enjoying herself and seems light years away from the fully initiated military wife we see in her last scene.

The Toll of Empire

While quite different in tone, both *Wee Willie Winkie* and *Fort Apache* astutely examine the consequences of imperialist mindsets, showing how empire extracts an enormous human toll on the oppressors as well as the oppressed. We see this most obviously in all the deaths that occur in both films. We also see this in the people who remain, including Priscilla and Philadelphia. To survive in imperial systems, they must sacrifice something good and true of themselves. Especially in these remote outposts where options are few, there is little else these people can do.

As most would agree, Shirley Temple and John Ford make a true odd couple. But in both these films their collaborations work quite well. Temple has called *Wee Willie Winkie* a "watershed" in her career and her favorite among the 40-plus feature films she made.[4] And, in *Fort Apache*, Ford's casting of Temple — no longer box office gold by 1948 but still in full possession of the Temple persona of innocence, integrity, kindness, curious intelligence, and boundless spunk (the Temple "brand," if you will) — is inspired. This helps to make Philadelphia's change at the film's end to stiff, dutiful military wife all the more startling to watch.

Andrew Sarris has said that Temple "seems in retrospect to have been too much the performing prodigy ever to generate genuine emotional responses."[5] That may be true in many of her films, but in her two films with Ford her characters convey more vulnerability — and more emotional depth — than they usually do. In *Wee Willie Winkie*, Priscilla must come to grips with McDuff's violent death and, as she does, we glimpse her internal struggle. And in *Fort Apache*, Philadelphia's change from spirited to duty-burdened young woman is deftly handled. In both these cases, she ably gets the job done.

* * *

As affecting — and effective — as Temple is in *Fort Apache*, her work in this film did little to reignite her career. After making four undistinguished films in 1949, she retired from film acting in 1950 at the age of 22. After a few attempts to re-launch her show business career through television in the 1950s and 1960s, she turned to public service, first running unsuccessfully for the U.S. House of Representatives in 1967 and then serving as the U.S. ambassadors first to Ghana in the 1970s and then to Czechoslovakia from 1989 to 1992. She was the recipient of many honors, including an honorary Oscar and the Screen Actors Guild Lifetime Achievement Award.

Temple was married twice. At age 17, she married John Agar, her *Fort Apache* romantic interest. The couple had one daughter but then divorced in 1949. Soon afterward, she met businessman Charles Black. They were married in 1950, had a son in 1952 and a daughter in 1954, and remained married until his death in 2004. She died in 2014 at age 85.

Always keenly aware of how early stardom made her life very different from other people's, Temple once quipped: "I stopped believing in Santa Claus when I was six. Mother took me to see him in a department store and he asked for my autograph."[6]

5

All About Attitude

Claire Trevor's Dallas in *Stagecoach* and Joanne Dru's Denver in *Wagon Master*

If there were ever a perfect John Ford double bill, it would be 1939's *Stagecoach* followed by 1951's *Wagon Master*. Each film is a crisp 90 or so minutes, so the program would be a comfortable length. But, more important, these two great westerns seem to fit together in some curious, mystical way — a little like chocolate and orange sorbet. Critics, especially, enjoy playing one off against the other. That might be because the similarities and the differences between the two films are both so striking.

We see the similarities almost immediately. Both stories are about communities in motion. People from various walks of life, a veritable cross-section of society, must traverse perilous territory to get to a desired destination. Among these people are society's outcasts, those who must join the migration because they are not welcome where they have been. And figuring prominently are stunning Southwest landscapes, rousing music, and the mode of transportation, which itself becomes a character. Along with *The Iron Horse* and *Steamboat Round the Bend*, *Stagecoach* and *Wagon Master* have been called Ford's "conveyance" films. That's a very apt name. Perhaps we have a sub-genre in the making.

The differences jump out at us too. While Ford loved using the same actors again and again in his work, and, while both films include many of these actors, none of the featured players appears in both. In fact, the only actor to show up anywhere in both is Ford's brother Francis in bit parts. Another curious difference is the treatment of the Native Americans. In *Stagecoach*, they are fierce and violent. In *Wagon Master*, they are friendly and quite hospitable. Each film also offers a very different sensibility. *Stagecoach* is taut, fast-paced, and suspenseful: a well-made thriller. And *Wagon Master*, while it also moves quickly, seems more leisurely, lyrical, and evocative: a cinematic poem.

Among the most engaging characters in each film is its leading lady, Claire Trevor's Dallas in *Stagecoach* and Joanne Dru's Denver in *Wagon Master*. With them too, both the similarities and the differences stand out in a big way. On one hand, they are both frontier prostitutes driven out of "respectable" towns; they both fall in love with capable young cowboys with dubious backgrounds; and (in a bit of Fordian eccentricity) they are both named after major American cities. When we scratch the surface a bit, however, we see a number of fundamental differences between them. At heart, they are worlds apart in how they see themselves, their profession, their current situations, and the romantic relationships they are pursuing. With them, it's all about attitude.

* * *

Trevor and Dru, the two actresses Ford tapped for these roles, were both unlikely choices and highly effective ones, excellent examples of Ford's ability to see qualities in actresses that others often overlooked.

Born Claire Wemlinger in the Bensonhurst section of Brooklyn in 1910, Trevor was the only child of a merchant tailor and his wife, Noel and Betty Wemlinger. After graduating from high school, she took art classes at Columbia University and then acting classes at the American Academy of Dramatic Arts. This experience led her to acting roles in stock companies, and by 1932 she was both appearing in plays on Broadway and in Vitaphone short subject films shot in Brooklyn. Her first credited feature film was 1933's *Life in the Raw*, and, by the time she was cast in *Stagecoach*, she had made nearly 30 features and was considered an established leading lady. When Ford was first shopping *Stagecoach* around, Trevor was not any producer's first choice. In fact, there was a concerted effort to pressure Ford into casting Marlene Dietrich as Dallas along with Gary Cooper as Ringo, the role that ultimately went to the young John Wayne. Eventually, Ford prevailed and Trevor and Wayne were chosen.

Dru also came to films by way of theater. Born Joan Letitia LaCock in West Virginia in 1922, she moved to New York in 1940 at age 18, found work first as a model, and was quickly chosen by singer Al Jolson to appear in his Broadway show *Hold On to Your Hats*. She then moved to Hollywood, where she did more theatrical work before being cast in the 1946 film *Abie's Irish Rose*. Then, during the next few years, she performed in some of her best-remembered roles, including Tess, Montgomery Clift's love interest, in Howard Hawks' classic 1948 western *Red River*; a supporting turn in Robert Rossen's Academy Award–winning *All the King's Men* in 1949; and Olivia Dandridge, the manipulative ingénue in Ford's *She Wore a Yellow Ribbon*, also in 1949. Her work in Ford's film impressed the director enough to cast her in the more complex and interesting role of Denver in *Wagon Master*.

"You gotta live no matter what happens"

In *Stagecoach*, nine people travel by coach across the desert in the 1870s: a driver (Andy Devine), a local sheriff named Curley (George Bancroft) who's subbing as "shotgun," and seven passengers. They are going to a place called Lordsburg, and they all have their reasons. Lucy Mallory (Louise Platt) is joining her husband, a military officer. Gatewood (Berton Churchill) is absconding with $50,000 from his bank. Dallas is going because she really has no choice. For plying her trade, she has been run out of the town by members of the local Law and Order League. In Lordsburg, at least, she will be able to find work again. While other passengers snub Dallas, one passenger, the Ringo Kid (John Wayne) treats her with respect. She appreciates it, and it is soon clear that the two are smitten. But there are complications. Ringo has broken out of jail to avenge the deaths of his father and brother. He plans to have a reckoning with their killer, Luke Plummer (Tom Tyler). Afterward, he's agreed to go back to jail and serve out his time. And Dallas, who assumes Ringo is too naïve to realize what kind of woman she really is, can't believe that he would still want her when he finds out. During the journey, she helps Lucy give birth, considers Ringo's offer of marriage and life at his ranch in Mexico, and — during the film's thrilling attack sequence — dodges Apache arrows. Then, in Lordsburg, she tells Ringo about her profession and expects him to leave. He simply tells her to stay put. After he settles his score with Luke and gives himself up, Curley, who's been fond of Ringo all along, puts both Ringo and Dallas on a buckboard and throws rocks at the horses to get them galloping. As they ride off (into the moonlight instead of the sunset) presumably to that ranch in Mexico, Doc Boone (Thomas Mitchell) wishes them well, saying that they'll be "saved from the blessings of civilization." It's Ford's parting shot: his way of saying that, alone on Ringo's ranch, they will be spared the bigotry and hypocrisy they've both had to endure from supposedly civilized communities.

Stagecoach is one of the most influential Hollywood films ever made. Widely acclaimed in 1939 for its tight, well-crafted script; riveting action sequences; dramatic Monument Valley landscapes; and exuberant musical score, it resurrected the western as a prestige film, took the genre to new heights of sophistication, ushered in a 25-year "golden age" of westerns, and even served as a model of good filmmaking for Orson Welles when he made *Citizen Kane*. In fact, many of the innovations that Welles often gets credit for in *Kane* were borrowed straight from *Stagecoach*.

The film can creak a bit for viewers today, and one reason why is that it has been so relentlessly imitated. Elements of the film, which were quite striking and original in 1939, seem clichéd now because lesser filmmakers have been recycling them for decades.

Trevor's Dallas, the "whore with the heart of gold," often strikes people as one of those clichés, but she is a much more fully developed character than many people assume. From the first moments we see her, for example, we are struck by her sadness and her vulnerability. Dire circumstances have forced her into prostitution: her family was massacred when she was a child. Once more, she has never come to terms with her line of work. In fact, she feels shame and guilt and dislikes herself because of what she does. Add to this, she is thin-skinned, feeling genuinely hurt when the ladies of the Law and Order League, Lucy Mallory, and others refuse to treat her with respect. Life is painful for her. But, she also has a great capacity for caring and, in turn, is particularly touched by the kindnesses that Ringo and a few others accord her. She can be strong and assertive too. Her transformational moment comes when Lucy is about to give birth. Despite Lucy's snubs, Dallas sees her through the ordeal,

As Dallas, the banished prostitute in 1939's *Stagecoach*, Claire Trevor fit extremely well into a talented acting ensemble that included such pros as Thomas Mitchell, George Bancroft, Andy Devine, and a young John Wayne. Later, Trevor would earn the nickname the "Queen of Film Noir" in honor of all the roles she played in 1940s and 1950s noirs and thrillers.

staying up all night with her and the baby. From this point on, Lucy is won over. So is Ringo, when he sees how natural and loving Dallas is with Lucy's baby. Motherhood might be a much better fit for Dallas. Finally, she is supremely sensible, at one point urging Ringo to put aside his vendetta against Luke Plummer and simply go to his ranch in Mexico.

One highlight in the evolution of Dallas and Ringo's relationship is a brief scene in the yard outside the stage stop where Lucy gives birth.

They stand in the moonlight on different sides of a low fence. Ringo tells her what Luke has done to his family. She tells him about her family being massacred and alludes to her work, adding: "You gotta live no matter what happens."

Then he surprises her. He tells her about his ranch and, in a very heartfelt and touching line reading from Wayne, says: "A man could live there ... and a woman."

Joanne Dru's frontier prostitute Denver and Ben Johnson's horse trader Travis engage in some lusty verbal sparring that entertains Harry Carey's Sandy (center) as their wagon train slogs westward in 1950's *Wagon Master*. Spirited, independent, and absolutely without guilt, Denver is one of the more fascinating female characters in Ford's westerns.

As Dallas hears his offer — his proposal — she is shocked, deeply moved, and even a little embarrassed. Why would this good, decent man want her? In fact, does he really understand what kind of a woman she is? Trevor, too, is wonderful in this moment, her face beautifully conveying all these strong and conflicting feelings.

Awkwardly, she says that he doesn't really know anything about her. He answers, "I know all I want to know," suggesting that he may not be as naïve about her work as she's assumed.

There are still issues to resolve, but in this scene a bond is established. The two are, for all intents and purposes, a couple looking out for each other.

Some critics have found Trevor's Dallas to be too emotional and vulnerable to be a convincing frontier prostitute, and she's certainly not the brassy, sassy sort that we've come to expect in these roles. But these traits are part of what make her distinctive and interesting. Dallas is a deeply emotional, caring person in a profession where women must detach from their emotions if they want to survive, and she has real trouble doing this. The opinions of others, even narrow-minded bigots, also matter. She can't even detach herself from their negative feelings toward her. As a result, she doesn't like herself very much. But, when she finally gets the opportunities to do those things that come naturally to her — to care for a baby and receive a good man's love — she soars. One of the happiest aspects to the film's happy ending is that Dallas finally gets what she's wanted all along — not just a man but a career change.

Trevor is excellent at conveying all this too. There's a natural honesty — a lack of affectation — to her Dallas that we don't see in many of her later roles. The actress takes on a character that, in lesser hands, could become cloying and annoying and makes her very real and sympathetic.

"I've done nothing I need be ashamed of"

Wagon Master is set in 1849, making it almost a pre-western. It begins with a robbery and murder. The evil Clegg clan is to blame. Then the story shifts to two young horse traders, the smart, level-headed Travis Blue (Ben Johnson) and his good-natured but not-too-bright friend Sandy (Harry Carey, Jr.). The two soon meet a group of Mormons heading west in a wagon train. The Mormons have been told they're not welcome in town and must push on soon. But they need someone who knows the route through the desert, someone like Travis. At first, Travis is hesitant. He has doubts the group can get through. Sandy, however, has his eye on a cute redheaded Mormon woman, and Travis eventually agrees. Soon, they meet up with another group of outcasts, the members of what the Mormon leader, Elder Wiggs (Ward Bond), refers to as a "hootchy-kootchy" show. Among them is Denver (Joanne Dru), who specializes in entertaining the men folk. All push on together fairly amicably. Travis and Denver begin to show a curious and playful but tentative attraction toward one another. Then the Cleggs show up, take the group captive, and use it as cover from pursuing lawmen. Finally, as the group works to get its wagons over one last mountain, Uncle Shiloh Clegg (Charles Kemper) goes too far, shooting one of the Mormon men. Travis and Sandy jump into the fray, grabbing guns and handily dispatching the Cleggs. Now all is well, and the group continues on together: Travis now with Denver and Sandy now with his redheaded woman.

No one has ever made another film quite like *Wagon Master*. Ford once called it the "purest and simplest western"[1] he ever made, and he often referred to it as a personal favorite among his films. It's easy to understand why. The film isn't large in scope or ambitious in design. In fact, the plot is fairly straightforward: another story about outcasts thrown together who must overcome their own prejudices, get along, and collaborate to survive. And the characters are simply drawn. Travis, for example, is smart and exercises good judgment, Sandy is the impetuous one, and the Cleggs are just pure evil. But the film is exceptionally well realized, almost magical in its spirit. It's been called a story about youth, and indeed it is bursting with energy, exuberance, and optimism: much like the America that was founded and settled largely by outcasts. We see this youthfulness in many of the characters; in the numerous visual compositions bathed in brilliant, almost transcendent sunlight; and in the catchy, energetic tunes sung over the track by the western group The Sons of the Pioneers. Without a doubt, *Wagon Master* is one of Ford's most likeable and addictive films.

One of the most likeable parts of *Wagon Master* is the Travis-Denver relationship. Travis is the essence of calm, cool, and competent. Denver finds this very attractive, and she wants to get under his skin and get him a little hot and bothered, hopefully, over her.

In one unforgettable scene, Travis, in the midst of asking people to conserve water, is greeted by a pan full of water flying out from the back of one covered wagon. His horse is startled and bucks him off. Then popping out of the wagon we see Denver's head and bare shoulders. It appears she has been bathing. Their conversation is about conserving water. But it's the subtext of mutual attraction that matters. Travis is intrigued. Maybe he's never met a woman like Denver. Then after just enough teasing, Denver flips her dress top back up over her shoulders and rises just a bit. Along with Travis, we see that she is more fully dressed than we had assumed. It's clear now that the water that startled Travis' horse was thrown specifically to get his attention. A moment later, Denver asks Travis to help her down, beckoning him with her hands. He holds her for a brief, suggestive moment. Then he leaves to go about his work.

Now, we follow Denver. She walks in her slinky fashion around the wagon, presumably to watch this absolutely unflappable man leave.

Fleuretty (Ruth Clifford), the other woman from the "hootchy-kootchy" show, now passes, smiles, and says: "Looks like you've got yourself an admirer, Denver."

"That rube," Denver retorts, trying to appear dismissive. But her face tells us that she is quite interested.

Here and elsewhere in *Wagon Master*, Dru shows an unabashed sexual side that relatively few of Ford's females do. Sex isn't just a tool she uses to attract men, either. It's a natural part of her, and she's just fine with that.

The playing continues, too. When they reach the river and Denver can finally take her bath, she strolls provocatively into some bushes as Travis says he likes the idea of joining her. Then, curiously, Travis takes his horse into the river to cool off. Is Denver his next stop? We don't know, but we certainly are wondering.

In addition to enjoying her sexuality, Denver is also proud of her independence and (totally different from Dallas) has absolutely no guilt about what she does for a living. As she tells Travis before they join the Mormons at the film's first dance: "Look, you don't have to protect me.... And I don't need any sympathy either. I've done nothing I need be ashamed of no matter what you and your friends think."

While the Denver-Travis relationship evolves in a very different way from the Dallas-Ringo pairing, one scene clearly echoes an important moment from the earlier film. Walking by themselves, Travis makes Denver essentially the same offer that Ringo makes Dallas: a lonely but respectable life together on a ranch. Denver, we find out later, eventually decides to get together with Travis. Whether a ranch is still in the plan, we don't know. But, what's intriguing here is Denver's initial response to Travis. Instead of feeling unworthy as Dallas does, she is at first startled and then turns away from Travis so he doesn't see her enormous smile.

Then this scene dissolves to another of Denver slouching, in an almost post-coital pose, alone in the back of her wagon; showing continued delight in the thought of Travis' offer; and smoking a cigarette. In the indirect language of the film, Denver has made a conquest, and this time it's with someone she considers worth her while.

While Dallas is more traditional, Denver is utterly modern. She's fine with who she is, and, as far as she's concerned, everyone else should be too. She's also her own person, and everyone else had better understand that. It's this sense of inner strength, security, and fearlessness that gives her much of her playfulness, charm, and fascination. The more we learn about her, the more we want to learn.

Dru's portrayal is exceptional too. She inhabits Denver in a way she just isn't able to do with other roles such as her Tess in Howard Hawks' *Red River* and her Olivia in Ford's *She Wore a Yellow Ribbon*. Of course, Dru has a more interesting character to work with in *Wagon Master*, but she also rises to the occasion — and then some.

The Delight Is in the Differences

Dallas and Denver share fundamental similarities, but their differences are what we delight in. While one feels shame and guilt about her work, the other takes pride in knowing that this work has given her a degree of independence most frontier women don't have. While one is thrilled at the prospect of a husband and children, the other, while curious about such possibilities, values her free-spirited lifestyle at least as much. While one touches us with her deep sense of caring and compassion, the other tickles us with her spirit and spark. In fact, they are about as different two wild-west prostitutes can be.

Their distinctly different personalities are also a testament to Ford's own curiosity about female behavior and its infinite diversity. Unlike many of his directorial peers who showed the same kinds of women in film after film, Ford was always exploring. Dallas and Denver could easily have been two versions of Dallas. Ford was, after all, working in both a male-dominated industry and in the male-dominated western genre, and no one with any real power would have cared one way or the other how he characterized Denver. But, just as Denver is intent on being her own person, Ford was committed to assuring that she is a distinctive, memorable character. With directors too, it's all about attitude.

* * *

After their work in these films, Trevor and Dru, neither of whom ever worked again with Ford, continued their film careers.

Trevor, who had shown in *Stagecoach* that she had real chemistry with John Wayne, co-starred with him in two films soon afterward, 1940's *Allegheny Uprising* and *Dark Command,* and she kept working in films and then more frequently in television until the late 1980s. In addition to her Dallas in *Stagecoach*, she is best remembered for her bad girl roles in *Murder, My Sweet, Raw Deal, Born to Kill, Key Largo*, and many other films noir in the 1940s and 1950s. She acted in so many of these roles, in fact, that she was nicknamed the "Queen of Film Noir." During her career she received three Academy Award nominations, all for Best Supporting Actress. She won in 1948 for her role as Edward G. Robinson's alcoholic mistress in *Key Largo*. She was married three times and had one son. After suffering the twin deaths of her son in 1978 and her third husband in 1979, Trevor, who had been living in New York at the time, returned to Hollywood and became an active supporter of the arts. She died exactly one month after her 90th birthday in 2000.

Dru, unfortunately, did not have as long or full a film career as Trevor. After co-starring in such roles as the wife of baseball star Dizzy Dean in 1952's *The Pride of St. Louis* and James Stewart's love interest in 1953's *Thunder Bay*, she began to appear less frequently in films. In the early 1960s, she tried to re-launch her acting career on television, starring in the ABC sitcom *Guestward Ho!*, the adventures of an urban family that decides to run a guest ranch in New Mexico. The show lasted only one season. Dru was married four times. Her first two husbands were singer Dick Haymes, with whom she had three children, and actor John Ireland, who she met when they were both making *Red River*. She died in 1996 at age 74.

While probably best known today for her roles in westerns, Dru revealed later in life that there were aspects about working in this genre that she didn't particularly like. At the top of her list were her costumes. "[T]hose long gingham dresses with boned bodices," she said, "are miserable things to wear."[2]

6

Colonial Spunk

Claudette Colbert's Lana and
Edna May Oliver's Mrs. McKlennar
in *Drums Along the Mohawk*

For centuries, people have used the Latin term "annus mirabilis" (roughly translated "the wonderful year" or "the year of miracles") to describe yearlong periods of remarkable achievement — often by individuals — in politics, science, the arts, and other arenas. For Isaac Newton, for example, the great year was 1666, when he made revolutionary discoveries in calculus, motion, optics, and gravitation. For the poet John Keats, it was 1819, when he wrote his great cycle of odes. And for Hollywood, it was 1939 — often called "the movies' greatest year" — when studios churned out perhaps more film classics than any other year before or since.

Within this highly energized and inspired film environment, one of the most remarkable stories is John Ford's. During an extraordinarily creative 11-month stretch between February 1939 and January 1940 four new Ford films were released: *Stagecoach, Young Mr. Lincoln, Drums Along the Mohawk,* and *The Grapes of Wrath*. In the midst of Hollywood's "annus mirabilis," Ford was having his own. All four of these films were nominated for Academy Awards (*Grapes* in the 1940 competition). And three — *Stagecoach, Young Mr. Lincoln,* and *Grapes* — are widely recognized film classics.

Surrounded by all these widely praised films, *Drums* can now sometimes seem lost in the shuffle. Ford's first foray into Technicolor as well as his only film set during America's Revolutionary War, it contains elements that, by today's standards, are clearly dated. One is its political point of view. Mainly, it is about American Manifest Destiny but without the subversive undercurrents and ironies we see in later and far more complex Ford films such as *Fort Apache* and *The Man Who Shot Liberty Valance*. Homesteading in the Mohawk Valley in particular and expanding American presence across the continent in general are never really questioned in the film. It is simply implied to be our God-given right. Another is the film's racial stereotyping. The white settlers, for example, are all good; the film's one African American is happy, loyal, and compliant; the one "good" Native American is a converted Christian; and the rest of the Native Americans (who've hooked up with the evil British) are brutally savage.

Yet, if we can acknowledge these issues and put them aside, *Drums* also has numerous strengths that make it an engaging and often very gripping experience. Among these are its beautiful Technicolor compositions; its moving love story focusing on young marrieds Gil and Lana Martin (Henry Fonda and Claudette Colbert); its well-staged battle scenes; a heart-thumping sequence when Gil is pursued by three Mohawks as he runs through forests, across streams, and over hills to Fort Dayton to seek help; and an exquisite Ford visual moment when Lana watches alone from a distant hilltop as Gil and others march off to war.

Ford's first color film and his only film set during America's Revolutionary War, 1939's *Drums Along the Mohawk* features fine performances by Claudette Colbert (left) as Lana Martin and Edna May Oliver as Mrs. Mc-Klennar, two women who endure the trials of pioneer life and war in New York's Mohawk Valley. For her work in the film, Oliver received an Academy Award nomination for Best Supporting Actress.

In addition, *Drums* distinguishes itself in another and quite novel way for its time: it is an action-adventure film in which two of its three most prominent characters are women. Film historian Jim Kitses has even gone so far as to call it "a matriarchal western" and "a tribute to women, to their endurance and grit and vitality."[1] We see this "tribute" expressed in numerous ways, including the opening credits and inter-titles, all of which are rendered in the traditionally female art of needlepoint.

These two female characters are Colbert's Lana, fresh to the wilds of the

Mohawk Valley from Albany and civilization, and Edna May Oliver's Mrs. McKlennar, a crusty old Yankee widow who becomes a surrogate mother to both Gil and Lana. Together, the two women combine to form a kind of relationship unusual in Ford films, a strong mother-daughter bond. Throughout the story, Mrs. McKlennar mentors the young Lana, helping her acquire both the skills and emotional toughness she will need in the Mohawk Valley, here a metaphor for the entire American frontier. As a good American woman should also do, Lana rises to the occasion, dealing with the hardship of losing her and Gil's farm, tending to a wounded Gil, bearing a child, and even donning a blue colonial soldier's uniform and dispatching a Mohawk with a musket. As the story progresses, both women show their colonial spunk.

* * *

The two actresses were also unusual choices for a Ford film. On loan from Paramount for this project, Colbert was best known for her roles in light, frantically paced screwball comedies. And Oliver, a veteran of both stage and screen, seemed to specialize in playing well-bred and sharp-tongued English spinsters. Neither had worked with Ford before, and neither would again. Reportedly, Colbert and Ford clashed frequently over how she should be photographed. For Oliver, *Drums* would be her third-to-last film before her untimely death in 1942.

Born Emilie Chauchoin in a suburb of Paris, France, in 1903, Colbert came to the U.S. in 1906, settling with her family in a fifth-floor walk-up in Manhattan. Quickly learning English, she went to Washington Irving High School, where she wanted to pursue a career as an artist, and then the Arts Students League of New York, where she intended to prepare to work as a fashion designer. Instead, she accepted an invitation to appear in a bit part in a 1923 Broadway play *The Wild Westcotts*, caught the attention of theatrical producer Al Woods, signed a contract with him, and worked consistently, playing mostly ingénue roles, throughout the 1920s.

With the coming of sound films, she traveled to Hollywood, auditioned with studios, was quickly signed to a long-term contract with Paramount, and became one of the top box-office stars of the 1930s. Early in the decade she created stirs in sexually overt roles such as the Roman Empress Poppaea in Cecil B. DeMille's 1932 epic *The Sign of the Cross* and the title role in his 1934 *Cleopatra*. Then, she transitioned to playing romantic leads in both screwball comedies and dramas for the rest of the decade. Perhaps her most famous role during this time was Ellie Andrews in Frank Capra's 1934 comedy *It Happened One Night* co-starring Clark Gable. To the surprise of all involved, the film swept the Academy Awards that year, winning for best picture, best director, best actor (Gable), and actress (Colbert). Other notable roles during this time were in

1935's *Private Worlds*, which netted Colbert a second Academy Award nomination (but no Oscar this time), 1938's *Bluebeard's Eighth Wife* (directed by Ernst Lubitsch) and 1939's *Midnight* (directed by Mitchell Leisen with a very witty script by Billy Wilder and Charles Brackett). When she appeared in *Drums*, Colbert was at the height of her stardom.

As Colbert was a much-sought-after star of the period, Edna May Oliver was often in demand to bring her own particular brand of intelligence and eccentricity to quirky character roles. Born Edna May Nutter in Malden, Massachusetts, in 1883, she was a descendent of U.S. presidents John and John Quincy Adams. At 14, she quit school to pursue a career on the stage, but it wasn't until 1917 when she finally achieved success in Jerome Kern's musical *Oh, Boy!*, playing the hero's comically tedious aunt.

She made her film debut in 1923 but continued to enjoy working on the stage and alternated between the two mediums for many years. Perhaps her best-known stage role is Parthy, the wife of Captain Andy Hawks, in both the 1927 Broadway premiere of the landmark Kern and Hammerstein musical, *Showboat*, and in its 1932 revival. In 1936, she signed a long-term contract with MGM and played in several of its polished, big-screen adaptations of classic works of literature such as 1935's *A Tale of Two Cities* and *David Copperfield* and 1936's *Romeo and Juliet*. When she began work on *Drums*, she had appeared in 45 films.

"Every generation must make its own way ... in one place or another"

It is 1776 as *Drums Along the Mohawk* begins, and we are at the elegant Borst family home in Albany, New York. The story begins in a very Ford-like way with a close-up of a wedding bouquet in the bride's hands. The camera moves back and we quickly learn that Mr. and Mrs. Borst's daughter Lana is marrying young Gil Martin, an enterprising young man with a farm in New York's beautiful but wild Mohawk Valley.

As they leave the Borst home after the ceremony (with a cow in tow), the minister comforts a weeping Mrs. Borst, saying: "Every generation must make its own way ... in one place or another." Gil and Lana's adventure together is beginning.

Lana quickly questions her decision, however, becoming hysterical when they arrive at Gil's rustic farmhouse and she encounters (probably) her first Native American. Fortunately, he's Blue Blood (Chief John Big Tree), the one friendly Mohawk in the story. Gil calms her, she stays, and they work the farm. Then, stirred up by British agent Caldwell (John Carradine with an evil-looking eye patch), the Mohawks go on the warpath, burning Gil and Lana's farm. Lana, now pregnant, is overwrought and miscarries. Now homeless, the two find work with Mrs. McKlennar, a feisty but well-to-do Yankee widow.

Soon, participation in the Revolutionary War is unavoidable, and Gil must leave to fight. In their own ways, both Mrs. McKlennar and Lana feel great pain to see Gil and the others leave, and the waiting until the men come back seems unbearable. Although more than half of the 600 men Gil fought along side don't return, Gil does. He recovers from wounds. Again Lana is pregnant, and again they move ahead with their lives. Their child is born, a son. The community seems stable. In fact, another couple gets married. After the ceremony, Gil goes to watch his young son sleep. Lana follows him, sees them, and then leaves the two together. By herself now, she says: "Please, God, please let it go on like this forever."

Soon, however, the community is again under siege. This time Mrs. McKlennar's house is burned, and everyone must retreat to the nearby fort, where the Mohawks, aided by the British, are soon attacking. Now, the seemingly unsinkable Mrs. McKlennar is fatally wounded and dies. Desperately in need of help, Gil volunteers to run to Fort Dayton for reinforcements. He gets through enemy lines, but now he has three very athletic Mohawks pursuing him. Then, when it seems inevitable that the fort will fall, Gil and the reinforcements arrive. The community is saved.

The film's final scene is particularly intriguing. Local peace has been restored, and soldiers arrive at the fort to announce that the war is over and to show off the flag of the new nation, complete with its 13 stripes and 13 stars united in a circle. The men quickly place the flag at the fort's topmost point and carefully selected characters (including the film's one African American and one friendly Native American) look up at it with wonder and hope. Then Gil says: "Well, I reckon we'd better get back to work. There's goin' to be a heap to do from now on."

At first, the scene appears to be merely some jingoistic patriotism. Everyone seems to revere the flag; even the African American and Native American seem solidly behind the program. Considering that the film was made when Ford and other Americans knew they would soon be involved in another great war, the unabashedly pro–American message is not all that unreasonable here.

What's especially curious is Gil's line. The "heap" of work he refers to can be Ford's sly reference to the fact that a U.S. with true racial and social equality was still a long way off, not just in 1783, but even in 1939. If the promise of liberty and justice for all were ever to become a pervasive reality, we can infer, much more hard work lay ahead. Certainly since the early 1930s, Ford had been making both subtle and not-so-subtle comments in his films about racial and social inequality in the U.S. It's not unreasonable to assume that — despite this film's propagandistic leanings — this is another one of those comments.

* * *

When reviewing the film for *The New York Times* in 1939, Frank Nugent called *Drums* "a first-rate historical film, as rich atmospherically as it is in action," and specifically praising "its humor, its sentiment, its full complement of blood and thunder."[2] Looking at *Drums* three quarters of a century later, we are certainly more conscious of (and critical toward) its racial stereotypes and propagandistic components. Otherwise, Nugent is right on the money: this is a superbly made action-adventure film with a highly appealing romance at its center.

Visually, *Drums* has many stunning moments. As Gil and others march off to a major battle, for example, the camera cuts between him, Lana, and Mrs. McKlennar as they all experience the moment and the loss and anxiety that come with it. Most of our attention is on Lana as she moves from spot to spot trying again and again to get a last glimpse of Gil. Finally, she stands atop a hill watching the column of soldiers become smaller and smaller in the distance. Photographed in long shot, she is herself little more than a speck on an enormous landscape. Then, burdened by sadness and anxiety, her body simply crumbles, falling to the ground. Another magnificent sequence is when Gil runs to Dayton as three Mohawks pursue him. It lasts for several minutes of screen time, and in different ways each scene is riveting. One amazing moment shows a dramatic sunrise. Then out of the lower right-hand corner of the screen we see the tiny, silhouetted figure of a lone man, Gil, running over a hill. A moment later we see silhouettes of the three Mohawks in hot pursuit. It's great stuff.

Another reason why *Drums* works so well as an action-adventure saga is that we care deeply about several of the people in harm's way, most notably the two principal characters. "Be sure and preserve the wonderful domestic relationship between Gil and Lana," 20th Century–Fox studio head Darryl F. Zanuck stressed in a script conference in early 1939.[3] And it's clear that Ford and the film's scriptwriters took this advice to heart. "They are the ideal couple," Kitses writes, "a perfect match in their courage and passion."[4] After Gil and Lana, there's the marvelous Mrs. McKlennar. We greatly admire her big heart, fearlessness, keen intelligence, sharp wit, and other qualities.

"I'm not the only woman who's going through this"

Drums Along the Mohawk is primarily Gil and Lana's story. Their marriage — their new union — symbolizes the new union among the 13 former

British colonies, and their struggles mirror the young nation's struggles to repel its enemies and establish itself and its way of life in this bountiful new world.

Strictly in terms of character development, however, *Drums* is more Lana's story than Gil's. Personally, she must travel the longest journey and make the most dramatic accommodations, and in the process she experiences the most sweeping growth of anyone in the story. While the film is populated with many colorful characters, she is the only truly dynamic one.

Lana's journey begins in Albany, where she has lived a privileged and probably pampered life. Yet, while money has been a part of her life, it isn't everything to her. She's deeply in love with young Gil, a good man but not yet a prosperous one. When she and Gil ascend the stairs on their wedding night, we can sense both sexual anticipation and the depth of their emotion. "I was just wondering if you love me as much as I love you," Lana says with great feeling. She is acutely aware of the commitment she is now making to this man, a commitment she considers profound and unbreakable.

Once Lana enters the Mohawk Valley and Gil's rustic farmhouse, however, her emotions head in a far more negative direction. The very sight of the friendly Blue Blood sends her into hysterics. "I'm no frontier woman," she frantically tells Gil. "I didn't know it was like this. I hate it!"

But, after Gil calms her down, she decides she'll tough it out because she loves Gil and chooses to be with him.

In many ways, *Drums* is the story of Lana's adapting to one grim reality after another: the loss of her refined life in Albany and adjustment to life in the rough frontier community, the loss of their farm, her miscarriage, the prospect of losing Gil in battle, and even the prospect of losing her own life in the story's final battle. Through it all, though, she bears each new challenge with increasing grace, composure and resilience. In the process, she develops a special presence of mind. "I'm not the only woman who's going through this," she says to Gil at one point when he frets about the difficulties of this life for her.

One often-repeated pattern throughout the story is how both Gil and Lana pick the other up when they need to. As Gil convinces Lana to stay with him early on, for example, Lana convinces him that they should both hire on with Mrs. McKlennar until they can get themselves back on their feet again. As Gil is tender with Lana after her miscarriage, Lana is tender with Gil when he returns from battle wounded and spent. Clearly, they both draw their strength directly from each other. One very moving instance of this is just before Gil makes his run to Fort Dayton. The man who has just tried to do it has been killed. Gil knows that he is the one who must go now, and he is understandably fearful. He knows Lana is too, and he goes to her and asks her to repeat these words: "I'm not afraid, and I want you to go." Dutifully, as if this is part of a ritual, she does. It's an especially powerful moment, one that excellently captures how far this relationship has evolved over the course of the story.

Some critics have found Colbert too urban and frothy for the part of Lana, and Colbert herself fretted that the role might damage her glamorous screen image. While this casting might be jarring to some, it is actually inspired. As Lana is initially a fish out of water in the Mohawk Valley, Claudette Colbert is clearly a fish out of water playing a frontier wife in a John Ford film. This casting against type, this displacement of actress as well as character, works especially well here. We easily accept Colbert as the privileged young woman in Albany, and to see her have to adapt and adapt and adapt to the challenges of life in the Mohawk Valley is much more interesting than seeing an actress more easily suited to this kind of role.

Colbert does a fine job too. As many critics have noted, she is heavily made up, but that was the convention of the time. What's far most interesting is how she establishes the right emotional pitch in scene after scene. When she goes into hysterics on her first night in Gil's farmhouse, for example, her fear is far more real than theatrical. In fact, it's so real that it's uncomfortable, even painful to watch. Much later, when she sees a happy Gil looking at their tiny son in his cradle and says, "Please, God, please let it go on like this forever," we feel both her great joy and her keen awareness that the happiest moments can often be the most fleeting. Requiring the ability to convey great sensitivity and great strength (sometimes simultaneously), Lana is a difficult role to bring off credibly, and Colbert delivers.

"I've got a long face, and I poke it where I please"

"Structurally," Jim Kitses writes, "the curmudgeonly (Mrs.) McKlennar ... stands behind Lana, bequeathing her not only her home but her feisty pioneer spirit as well."[5] But, in terms of prominence in the story, the larger-than-life Mrs. McKlennar clearly earns the right to stand beside her and Gil (and well ahead of everyone else in the film).

Mrs. McKlennar is a tough, formidable force of nature. You'll not trifle with her if you know what's good for you. She doesn't suffer fools or drunkards gladly, but, if you are good and hard working, she has a big, generous heart. Her sharp, witty remarks are also great fun. "I've got a long face," she tells Gil and Lana when she first meets them, "and I poke it where I please." Later, when she confronts an old man who needs to expel some phlegm from his mouth and doesn't know quite what to do in her presence, she loses patience and says: "Go on, man, spit. Spit and get it over with."

Everything about Mrs. McKlennar is eccentric and very appealing. Even her most poignant scene, when she bids Gil farewell before he goes off to battle, has an offbeat edge to it. "Gil Martin, I'm going to kiss you," she says. "So I'm going to do it now so you don't go off with the taste of a widow in your mouth."

While critics have been mixed about Colbert's Lana, they have generally praised Oliver's Mrs. McKlennar. "Miss Oliver could not have been bettered as the warlike Widow McKlennar, with a tongue sharper than a tomahawk and a soft spot in her heart for a handsome man,"[6] Frank Nugent wrote in his 1939 review of *Drums*. Soon after the film's release, Oliver received an Academy Award nomination for Best Supporting Actress for the role, losing to the equally charismatic Hattie McDaniel, who that year was nominated for her portrayal of the spirited, no-nonsense mammy in *Gone with the Wind*.

From the first moments we meet her, Oliver's Mrs. McKlennar is a delight to watch. This is a variation of some of Oliver's fussy old maiden aunt roles, but, when we look closely at Mrs. McKlennar's many facets, we see that she is also different from all these other characters, an original creation. Impressive too are Oliver's command of her craft and the fearless authority she brings to this part. She goes all out, and, as Nugent noted, she "could not have been bettered."

"You've been like my own flesh and blood"

As Mrs. McKlennar lay dying in the besieged fort before Gil makes his run to Fort Dayton, she tells Gil and Lana that she would like to give them her home. "You've been like my own flesh and blood," she says. Though not genetically related to her, they are, in her mind, her rightful heirs — her true family and the ones best suited to carry her spirit forward.

Two facets of this moment are especially worth noting. The first is Ford's attitude toward family, a subject he explores in many of his films. For him, family is much more than mere genetic relationships. People must earn the right to be members in good standing of a family, whether it's a literal one, a communal one (as in *Drums*), a national one, or even the entire human race. When they have proven themselves worthy, then they can assume greater responsibility and eventually perhaps the right to lead in the name of the family. The second facet is the scene's highly female emphasis. The dying woman is passing on both her property and the torch of de-facto communal leadership not just to the young man but also to the young woman. Together, they will carry on as equals. For a 1939 film about the American Revolutionary War, that is a very feminist message. Ford's nod to women here clearly goes well beyond credits and inter-titles done in needlepoint. He valued and respected women highly, and *Drums* presents ample proof of this.

* * *

Just as they were very different kinds of actresses, Colbert and Oliver's lives took very different paths after they completed *Drums Along the Mohawk*.

Colbert remained a major Hollywood star throughout the 1940s and into the early 1950s. She received a third acting Academy Award nomination in 1944 for her work in David O. Selsnick's World War II homefront drama *Since You Went Away*. During these years, she is also remembered for comedies such as Preston Sturges' 1942 hit *The Palm Beach Story* and 1947's *The Egg and I* with Fred MacMurray. She was the original choice to play aging Broadway diva Margo Channing in Joseph L. Mankiewicz' 1950 film classic, *All About Eve*, but, because of severe back problems at the time, she had to bow out. The role, and much acclaim, eventually went to Bette Davis.

While Colbert made a few film appearances after the mid–1950s, her work focused increasingly on the stage and television. She received a Tony Award nomination in 1959 for her starring role in the Broadway comedy *Marriage-Go-Round*. And, she worked periodically for the next 30 years, rounding out her career with an Emmy nomination and Golden Globe Award win for her supporting role in the 1987 television miniseries, *The Two Mrs. Glenvilles*. She was 84 at the time.

Married briefly to character actor Norman Foster (who was featured in Ford's film, *Pilgrimage*) in the 1930s, Colbert later married Dr. Joel Pressman, a UCLA throat specialist. This union lasted until his death in 1968. She never had children.

In a 1981 interview with *Time*, Colbert discussed both her pleasure at playing comedy and her frustration at not being offered a wider range of roles. "I love to play comedy and I can say immodestly that I'm a very good comedienne," she noted. "But I was always fighting that image, too. I just never had the luck to play bitches."[7]

Colbert died at her home in Barbados in 1996. She was 92.

Edna May Oliver, unfortunately, did not have as long or as full a career. After film appearances in 1940's *Pride and Prejudice* with Laurence Olivier and Greer Garson and 1941's *Lydia* with Merle Oberon, Oliver died of an intestinal ailment in her sleep at a Los Angeles hospital on November 9, 1942. It was her 59th birthday. Her good friend, actress Virginia Hammond, who flew out from New York to be at Oliver's bedside, was with her and said: "She died without ever being aware of the gravity of her condition. She just went peacefully asleep."[8]

In 1931, Oliver revealed another side to her usually comic persona. Recalling her shock when reading that a critic had compared her long face to a horse's, she said: "Oh yes, I'm grateful in a way for this face, now that I've gotten used to it. I know it's brought me this success. I know it's given me the chance to make and save enough money so I won't spend the end of my days in an old lady's home somewhere. But all the same I'm a woman, and what woman doesn't long to be beautiful?"[9]

7

Family First

Jane Darwell's Ma Joad in *The Grapes of Wrath* and Sara Allgood's Beth Morgan in *How Green Was My Valley*

Filmed just a year and a half apart, Ford's two great social dramas, 1940's *The Grapes of Wrath* and 1941's *How Green Was My Valley*, share many similarities. Both, for example, are emotionally wrenching stories about the effects of extreme economic hardship on close-knit working-class families. Both are among the director's most honored films, netting Ford back-to-back Best Director Oscars and New York Film Critics Awards. And both are the results of highly collaborative production teams dominated by a producer — in both cases, the brilliant Darryl F. Zanuck — at least as much as by Ford.

Another similarity many people also point to are the film's prominent mother figures, Jane Darwell's Ma Joad in *The Grapes of Wrath* and Sara Allgood's Beth Morgan in *How Green Was My Valley*. These two women clearly share some readily recognizable traits. Each, for example, is committed — first and foremost — to her family. Each is strong willed, persevering, and able to confront outside threats to the family. Each also has a favorite son, who just happens to be the film's main character. These similarities have often led people to lump the two characters together both with each other and with the saintly, long-suffering, and overly sentimental mothers that sometimes pop up in Ford films.

Upon closer inspection, though, this isn't the case at all. First, Ma Joad and Beth Morgan are both far more fully developed and complex than most of Ford's mothers. Second, the two characters are really quite different from one other. While both are deeply committed to preserving and protecting their besieged families, each brings decidedly different personalities, attitudes, and

7. Family First

As Ma Joad in 1940's *The Grapes of Wrath*, Jane Darwell nabbed an Oscar for Best Supporting Actress. Here, Ma quizzes her son Tom, played by Henry Fonda, who's just been released from prison. She's concerned, and rightfully so, about what jail may have done to his psyche.

strategies to the task. One is utterly realistic, practical, and ultimately selfless in her love. Adversity only makes her stronger. The other doesn't have near the coping skills. As her story progresses, she has more and more trouble accepting reality, adapting to change, and loving selflessly.

As a result, the efforts of these two mothers produce strikingly different outcomes, and in each instance no other character is affected more profoundly than each of these favorite sons. One of them will lead his life as he chooses with his mother's full support, if not her full understanding. The other will squander his life and, like his mother before him, retreat into memories of the past to avoid the realities of the present.

* * *

Something comparable can be said about the women who played these roles, Darwell and Allgood. At first glance, they seem very similar. Both were veteran stage and screen actresses; both specialized in character roles; both were recipients of Best Supporting Actress Academy Award nominations for their roles in these two Ford films (Darwell winning); and both were even born on the very same day, October 15, 1879. Upon closer inspection, however, two very distinct careers and people emerge.

Darwell was about as American as they come. Born Patti Woodard, the daughter of a railroad president, in Missouri, she at first wanted to become a rider in the circus. Later, she set her sights on becoming an opera singer. Finally, though, she settled on becoming an actress, and, to spare the family name from disgrace, she changed her name to Darwell. After studying voice culture and dramatics, she began acting in stage productions in Chicago in 1913. Then, for the next two years, she shifted gears and acted in nearly 20 silent films. But, in 1915, she returned to the stage and worked there exclusively until 1930, when she accepted the role as the Widow Douglas in the 1930 film version of *Tom Sawyer* starring Jackie Coogan, and her long career as a Hollywood character actress began. In the 1930s, she appeared in numerous films, often playing a kindly elder of some kind. During this time, she was often cast in Shirley Temple films, usually as a housekeeper or a grandmother.

While Darwell was born in Missouri, Allgood was born in Dublin, Ireland. A featured actress at the Dublin's fabled Abbey Theatre for many years, she was also the sister of Maire O'Neill, an actress who was romantically involved with the Irish playwright John Millington Synge and reportedly the inspiration for his widely performed play, *The Playboy of the Western World*. Allgood was briefly married to another stage actor, Gerald Henson. After just two years, however, he and their newborn daughter died from influenza in the epidemic of 1917, and she never remarried. In the 1920s, she began to work in British films and worked for a young Alfred Hitchcock in such efforts as 1929's *Blackmail*, 1930's *Juno and the Peacock*, and 1936's *Sabotage*. In 1941, she relocated to Hollywood to make *How Green Was My Valley*.

"We ain't the kissin' kind"

Based on John Steinbeck's Pulitzer Prize winning novel, *The Grapes of Wrath*, Ford's film focuses on the Joads, a family of sharecroppers who are evicted from their farm in Oklahoma, travel to California as part of the great "Okie" migration of the 1930s, and move from one migrant camp to another looking for whatever farm work they can find. Along what seems to be a never-ending journey, they are treated with both kindness and cruelty, lose several family members, and meet scores of people who are even worse off than they are. While Pa Joad (Russell Simpson) is officially the head of the family, Ma is the one who seems to run things. Just as the Joads are about to leave Oklahoma, the family also gets a surprise. Tom (Henry Fonda), the oldest child, has come back from prison and agrees to join the group on their journey. In their travels, Tom learns about unions and eventually leaves to find a better way: not only for the Joads, but also for everyone in a similarly desperate situation. Then, the film ends in many ways as it begins, with the family on the road looking for the next job. By now, Pa is tired and spent. But Ma continues to push on, because that's what people do and, as she proudly affirms, "we're the people."

There's a widespread belief in the film industry that it's next to impossible to make a great film from a great novel. That's probably true. But it's not always impossible, and *The Grapes of Wrath* is one of those rare and inspiring exceptions. The film could have easily become an anti-capitalist polemic or sentimental melodrama. Instead, it rises above such temptations and stands as a stunning work of art in its own right: one that sometimes (such as in the flashback showing the eviction of another sharecropper named Muley) leverages the assets of the film medium to surpass even Steinbeck's novel. The film's strengths are numerous. There is the great sensitivity with which Ford directs his characters as well as the starkly poetic visual compositions that hit us one right after the other. There is cinematographer Gregg Toland's utterly breathtaking lighting and camera work. There is Nunnally Johnson's earnest, deeply felt script, which even the finicky Steinbeck praised. Finally, there is the superb acting, especially by Henry Fonda, who delivers one of the most honest, probing, and subtly nuanced performances of Hollywood's classic era. In just about every respect, this is a phenomenal film.

An instant popular hit despite its disturbing subject matter, the film also received wide critical approval. Amid the praise, perhaps the highest compliments came from the uncompromising Steinbeck, who had initially feared that Zanuck and 20th Century–Fox might soften his story and lessen its impact. In a letter to his literary agent, Elizabeth Otis, shortly after seeing the completed film, the novelist wrote: "Zanuck has more than kept his word. He has a hard, straight picture in which the actors are submerged so completely that it looks and feels like a documentary film, and certainly it has a hard, truthful ring. No punches are pulled...."[1]

While Pa Joad, Tom, and most of the other Joads are by no means slackers, Ma is both the head and the heart of the family. She has assumed this position because she has several valuable qualities.

One is her calm authority, practicality, and resourcefulness when facing difficult situations. She can, in fact, even resort to trickery to do what needs to be done. When the Joads reach the California state line and Ma knows that Grandma has died, for example, she lies to a state inspector, telling him that Grandma is sick and needs a doctor. The inspector sees what's actually happened but goes along with her story probably because he doesn't want the hassle of dealing with a dead old woman. Both play the charade, and the family gets across.

Another quality, which is especially important when it comes to Tom, is Ma's ability to understand and empathize with others on a deeply emotional level. She is especially dear to Tom, for example, because she both knows who he is and feels for him in a way no one else does. We see this when they first reunite in the film. Tom tells everyone he's fresh from jail. Grandpa's excited because he thinks that Tom's "busted out" and takes great delight in living out this fantasy. For Ma, however, the main concern is Tom's state of mind. She's already aware that Tom's inability to control his anger landed him in jail in the first place. Now she's worried that the prison experience has made him "mean" as well. More than anyone, she sees and values Tom's gentle side, and he loves her for this.

One of Ma's defining qualities is her ability to love selflessly and to let go in a healthy way. Again, we see this with Tom. Through his friend, Casy (John Carradine), Tom has come to understand the importance of working together to fight for better working conditions. The law is after him again too, this time for a crime he didn't commit. He knows that he will burden the family and that he needs to separate. If this has to be, he figures, he will go and work to find a better way for the rest of the Joads and all the people like them. In one of the great speeches in any Ford film (with help from Steinbeck and Johnson, of course), Fonda's Tom tells Ma about his new understanding of things — how we're all part of a larger consciousness. She listens, wanting to understand and not quite being able to. But, while she doesn't understand, she realizes that Tom must now go his own way and fully supports his decision. Although the Joads "ain't the kissin' kind," she asks for a kiss from Tom. He tenderly obliges her. Then, without further ado, he is on his way — to find his way.

Again, Ma is a realist. She may see Tom again. She may not. She has no fantasies, and it is not her nature to hold him back for her own selfish reasons. With Pa beginning to slow down, she needs Tom more than ever, but she won't pressure him to stay. Somehow, she'll find a way to manage without him. As the saying goes: she loves with an open hand.

Like Tom and Casy, Ma's willingness to face new realities and adapt also allows her to be a dynamic character. In fact, while the hardships take their toll on other characters, they only seem to make her stronger. Early in the film, we often see pain and fear in her eyes. She feels great sadness at leaving their home, and she is often frightened about what the future may bring. By the very end of the film, however, she is at an almost Zen-like place. She knows there will be more pain and hardship ahead, but she is more confident now, better prepared to tackle challenges head on.

Some critics have found Darwell's performance too soft, especially in such

Playing Beth Morgan in 1941's *How Green Was My Valley* was a highlight of Sara Allgood's 10-year Hollywood career. Here she shares a happy moment with co-star Donald Crisp, who played her husband Gwilym. Although Beth is sometimes dismissed as simply another idealized mother in a Ford film, she is anything but. While well meaning, her inability to acknowledge and adjust to change ultimately damages her family.

an uncompromising and hard-edged film. But she is actually quite effective, doing a very honest, intelligent job with a difficult role that could have easily have become maudlin. In addition, she ably serves as the perfect counterpoint to Fonda's Tom: the mother whose patience, empathy, practicality, and even-tempered realism squarely balance his bottled-up anger, restlessness, and idealism. There's a reason why "Ma Joad" has become a synonym for women who bear great hardship with great dignity, and it has as much to do with Darwell's stirring portrayal as with Steinbeck's original character or Ford's direction.

"He spoke to me and told me of the glory he had seen"

Based on the best-selling 1939 novel by Richard Llewellyn, *How Green Was My Valley* is the story of the Morgans, a family that lives and works in a South

Wales coal mining village in the late 1800s. In the film, this story is told through the eyes of Huw Morgan (Roddy McDowell), by many years the youngest of Gwilym (Donald Crisp) and Beth Morgan's seven children. As the film begins, Huw, now well into middle age, tells us in narration (the voice of Irving Pichel) that, after 50 years, he is finally leaving the valley he has always called home. The few shots we see reveal a depressed, decrepit place: a pitiful slum. Then, in flashback, Huw takes us back to the world of his boyhood. We meet his family members as they were when they all enjoyed better times. Huw's father and five older brothers all work in the local colliery. His mother and sister Angharad (Maureen O'Hara) tend the home. But, almost immediately, changes come. Some are good. Huw's oldest brother Ivor (Patric Knowles) marries Bronwyn (Anna Lee), a sweet, modest woman from a neighboring valley. But most of the changes are painful. Wages are cut at the mine. Huw's older brothers argue with their father over forming a union (Gwilym's opposed to the idea), become frustrated, and move out. Eventually, the miners strike. After several months, the strike is resolved, but conditions are never as good as they once were. Soon two of Huw's brothers are laid off and leave the valley to find work. Later, two more must do the same. In the meantime, Ivor, the oldest, is killed in a mine accident, leaving Bronwyn a widow with a newborn. And Angharad also marries, but very unhappily. Encouraged by a local minister, Mr. Gruffydd (Walter Pidgeon), Huw is accepted to a state school. Over time, he excels and has the opportunity to go to the university in Cardiff. He declines, though, preferring to work, as his father and brothers have done, in the colliery. Then his father is also killed in a mine accident. Along with Gruffydd and others, Huw retrieves him, his young face blank-eyed, spent, desolated as he and others bring Gwilym's body up to the surface on the lift. The film's final images amount to a curtain call filled with happy images and Huw's heartfelt narration about his father and others being as "real in memory as they were in flesh."

For anyone who has experienced economic hardship and/or the dissolution of a close, loving family, *How Green Was My Valley* can be a wrenching experience. Like young Huw, we want the good times to continue, and the pain of so much loss can be unbearable. We almost can't blame the adult Huw for giving fond memories a status equal to (or even greater than) reality.

An enormous commercial and critical hit in its day, *How Green* was declared "a beautiful and affecting film achievement"[2] by the *New York Times* and went on to receive 10 Academy Award nominations and win five, including Best Picture and Best Direction — more Academy acclaim than any other Ford film.

Its reputation, however, has taken some hits over the years. One reason, oddly enough, is the ascendance of Orson Welles' *Citizen Kane* as a darling of the film criticism establishment. Ever since *Citizen Kane* was "rediscovered" in the late 1950s and hailed far and wide as "the greatest film ever made," *How Green* has been belittled as the lesser film that deprived *Citizen Kane* of its rightful Best Picture and Best Direction Oscars for 1941. Every year at Oscar time, it seems, film critics and buffs alike write articles to express their feeling about this "travesty" and, to reinforce their point, criticize *How Green* for everything they can think of. This is unfortunate because it's so needless. Both are brilliant films deserving of continuing study, and, as nearly all of these critics will agree, relatively few of the very best American films ever won the Best Picture or Best Direction Oscars anyway. In other words, when it comes to serious film study, the Oscars shouldn't mean that much. The second reason, which often comes into play during these annual pre–Oscar bashings, is the way most people (including many critics) interpret *How Green*. Basically, they see it as a sentimental slobber-fest. This is also unfortunate. The film is actually the very complex and subtle story of young Huw Morgan's failure to adapt to a changing world and his growing reliance on old (and increasingly romanticized) memories to sustain himself through a bleak existence. Like Ford's *The Man Who Shot Liberty Valance*, *How Green* is a story told mostly in flashback by a very subjective and probably very unreliable narrator with a vested interest in defending, rationalizing, or at least glossing over tragic life choices. To dismiss the film as maudlin mush is simply to miss the point.[3]

A key player in Huw's tragedy is, sadly and ironically, his mother, Beth. While she is a loving, dutiful wife and mother, she has serious—and as the story continues—deepening flaws. They, in turn, help lay the groundwork for Huw's tragedy.

First, Beth is incapable of seeing new possibilities and understanding the importance of adapting to change. In this respect, she is at odds with her husband Gwilym, who more readily accepts new realities and the need to adjust to them. This is especially true when it comes to Huw, and we see Beth's lack of vision (and perhaps her insecurity and fear) in several scenes involving her young son's education. One is when Mr. Gruffydd and Gwilym work with Huw on a hypothetical math problem. She finds it silly that they are considering the rate of water pouring out of a bathtub with holes. Even after Gwilym tries to tell her that it is just a problem "for the mind," she still dismisses the whole idea as foolish and not worth anyone's time. Later, she doesn't understand why Huw should study Latin. "Why not Welsh or even English?" she asks disdainfully. Not only does she find little value in Huw's scholarly pursuits, but she also seems to be trying to subvert them.

Beth's conflict with Gwilym over Huw's education climaxes in one of the most tragic scenes in the film: when Huw chooses to work in the colliery rather than attend the university in Cardiff.

Gwilym urges him to go to where he can study to be a doctor or a lawyer.

He sees the young man's potential and genuinely wants a better life for him, calling these professions "respectable."

"Respectable?" Beth counters. "Are you and his brothers all jailbirds then...? If he is as good a man as you and his brothers, I will rest happy."

"Why take brains down a coal mine?" Gwilym pleads.

But, by now, Huw has made up his mind. It will be the colliery, and misplaced loyalty to his mother and the family's tradition triumphs. In despair, Gwilym leaves to get a drink. He knows his son has made a terrible decision, but at this point there is nothing he can really do about it.

Beth, however, is pleased. By this time, she has lost all her children except Huw. Perhaps she is happy simply because she will not be losing him too. Perhaps she is also threatened by the prospect of Huw getting an education and eventually looking down on her and the rest of the Morgans — another kind of loss. Whichever the case, it is a selfish, shortsighted position to take.

To emphasize her quiet power over Huw in this scene, Ford places Beth directly between him and Gwilym in the shot and has her look at the boy sternly throughout, clearly tipping the scales. It's a lot of pressure for a loyal son Huw's age to take, and Huw responds just as she wants him to.

To supplement for her many losses, Beth also starts living more in memory, a behavior that also has an enormous impact on Huw. When Huw shows her a map of the world and talks about his various siblings being in South Africa, Canada, and New Zealand, for example, Beth becomes agitated. "I know where they are," she proclaims. "They are in the house." In other words, they are with her in memory just as they once were in real life.

Another fascinating moment is when Beth learns of Gwilym's death. Her face is very peaceful, almost transported. She stands in radiant light, and the uplifting music swells. "He came to me just now," she says to Bronwyn and Angharad. "Ivor [her dead son] was with him. He spoke to me and told me of the glory he had seen."

Most viewers interpret this moment as a bit of Hollywood hokum, something akin to the our-spirits-will-live-on ending of William Wyler's *Wuthering Heights* two years before. But this is not Ford's point of view; it is Huw's, and it comes to us decades after the fact.

As communicated through Huw, this is also further proof of Beth retreating into memory (and perhaps delusion) for comfort and solace from the many losses she's sustained. Undoubtedly, she will have more "visions" of Gwilym and Ivor as the grim years grind on. In fact, her memories and visions could likely become intertwined and indistinguishable from one another.

Immediately following this scene, the older Huw returns to tell us in narration: "Men like my father cannot die. They are with me still, real in memory as they were in flesh, loving and beloved still. How green was my valley then."

What's startling is that he is essentially echoing Beth's words. For both mother and son, life in the present is becoming less important and memories of the past more so. And eventually all that either person will have is memories. They share an unusually strong bond, this mother and son, but it is not a healthy one.

In the film, it's unclear why Huw finally leaves the valley. Maybe he has spent years caring for Beth and then for Bronwyn and/or Angharad. Maybe he can no longer find work there either. We don't know for sure. We assume, though, that he is alone. We know that he is taking books with him — perhaps the books Mr. Gruffydd introduced to him decades before — and we know that they are wrapped in his beloved mother's shawl. It's a curious contradiction: the trappings of education wrapped in the venerated shawl of the person who pressured him against pursuing education. Clearly, Huw is still deeply conflicted. Like his mother, he has spent many sad years trying to keep alive a world and people that have long since passed away.

Throughout the film, Allgood's portrayal is quite effective. She communicates Beth's love for her family and their life as it once was so convincingly that we're almost willing to forgive Beth for nudging Huw into the coal mines. Almost but not quite. And, although Beth rarely speaks openly of the pain she feels with each one of her losses, Allgood makes sure that we clearly understand, and empathize with, the immense sadness Beth is experiencing.

Worlds Apart

While sharing many similarities, including strong mother figures, *The Grapes of Wrath* and *How Green Was My Valley* end quite differently. One leaves us with a glimmer of real hope, the other with romanticized memories of ghosts born out of despair. In both, a key reason why is the mother involved: one who accepts reality and becomes stronger and more confident and another who retreats more and more into her memories and visions. In the end, too, we see the consequences of their attitudes and behaviors manifested most dramatically with their favorite sons. Although both Tom and Huw are very different from their mothers, the two young men are also the recipients of maternal attitudes and behaviors that deeply affect them and ultimately determine their destinies. Tom remains an idealist, but he is also tempered by Ma's realism. He will try to change the world, but now he is armed with more of her ability to see things as they are, remain calm, and devise practical solutions. But, Huw, always a bit of a dreamer himself, takes his cues from a mother who refuses to face harsh realities or adapt to change. As she retreats into memory as a coping mechanism, so does he.

Certainly, both Ma Joad and Beth Morgan believe in putting family first, but they are worlds apart in understanding what this task means.

* * *

While Darwell and Allgood both continued to act in Hollywood regularly during the 1940s, their lives took different paths too.

Darwell had memorable turns in numerous films and then television shows for many years. One of them is a fascinating role in William Wellman's 1943 film of *The Ox-Bow Incident*. The antithesis of her Ma Joad and the many kindly old lady characters she often played, she was the bloodthirsty Jenny Grier, the only woman to participate in the film's notorious lynching. She also became a favorite of Ford's, playing roles in several more films for him including 1946's *My Darling Clementine*, 1948's *3 Godfathers*, and 1953's *The Sun Shines Bright*. Today, she is considered a member in good standing of the director's famous "stock company" of actors. In the 1950s, Darwell turned increasingly to television, playing, among many roles, Walter Brennan's mother in an episode of the series, *The Real McCoys*. Her last role is, along with Ma Joad, one of her best remembered — the bird woman in Disney's 1964 film, *Mary Poppins*. Reportedly, Walt Disney asked her personally to do the part. Often cast in films with Henry Fonda during her career, Darwell once quipped: "I've played Henry Fonda's mother so often that, whenever we run into each other, I call him 'Son' and he calls me 'Ma,' just to save time."[4] Darwell never married, and she died in 1967 at age 87.

Although Allgood's work in *How Green Was My Valley* earned her much critical praise and her only Academy Award nomination, it was not a good experience for her. Reportedly, she and Ford clashed often during production, and, unlike Darwell, Allgood never worked with Ford again. She stayed in Hollywood, though, and worked consistently during the 1940s, playing other memorable roles in such films as the 1943 version of *Jane Eyre*, 1944's *The Keys of the Kingdom*, 1945's *The Spiral Staircase*, 1947's *Mourning Becomes Electra*, and 1950's *Cheaper by the Dozen*. In 1945, she decided to stay in the U.S. for good, becoming a naturalized citizen. In 1950, she died of a heart attack. She was a month short of 71.

8

More Than the Sum of Her Parts

Mildred Natwick's Four Small Gems for John Ford

Creating an indelible screen character is no small feat. First, all the key ingredients for an original but immediately recognizable, complex, and at least somewhat conflicted person have to be there. Second, the person playing the part needs to infuse the character with an extra, sometimes indescribable, something that's unique and captivating. Finally, the film's director has to successfully orchestrate the portrayal, assuring that the role and performer are not only fused together but also fully integrated with the rest of the story. With all these prerequisites, it's easy to see why most film characters, even those with lots of on-screen time to develop, fall flat. By the same token, it's all the more remarkable when an actor or actress creates indelible characters in a matter of minutes — or even seconds — the way veteran stage actress Mildred Natwick does in the four films she made with John Ford.

* * *

Mildred Natwick is not a household name to many film fans today, but within the stage and screen communities in her day she was a highly respected pro.

Born in Baltimore in 1905, she was the descendent of some of the first Norwegian immigrants to the U.S. and the first cousin of Myron "Grim" Natwick, the creator of the Betty Boop cartoon character and one of the main animators of 1937 Disney classic, *Snow White and the Seven Dwarfs*. After graduating from New York's Bennett College in theater arts, she began performing with the Vagabonds, a non-professional company in the area, and soon joined the celebrated University Players on Cape Cod in Massachusetts. During the

1930s, she was constantly working in featured roles on Broadway and elsewhere and often collaborated with widely respected theater (and later film) director Joshua Logan. She also achieved wide notice and praise for a role in a Broadway production of George Bernard Shaw's comedy, *Candida*, which starred the legendary stage actress Katharine Cornell.

While preparing for his screen adaptation of three Eugene O'Neill one-act plays, *The Long Voyage Home*, in 1940, Ford mentioned to a friend that he wished he could find a young version of the character actress Una O'Connor to play the small but very important role of a Cockney prostitute in the film. The friend, probably thinking of the sharp, birdlike facial features the two actresses shared, suggested Natwick. Ford hired her for the film, her first ever.[1] They would also work together in 1948's *3 Godfathers*, 1949's *She Wore a Yellow Ribbon*, and 1952's *The Quiet Man*.

* * *

The experience in *The Long Voyage Home* established not only an ongoing professional relationship between the director and the actress but a very specific working pattern. In each of the four films Ford uses Natwick the way a good writer uses an exclamation point: sparingly but to great effect. In each, she plays a small but critical role that supplies the story with a major turning point, added emotional texture, or both. And in each, she delivers a superb performance, which, despite her character's limited screen time, adds greatly to the film's richness and to the impact her character, and her character's distinct female perspective, has on the viewer. She was one of those very resourceful and gifted actresses who could get to the essence of a role, however small, and give us a gold mine.

Mildred Natwick never starred in a film for John Ford, but she left an indelible mark on the four in which she appeared. Here, as veteran cavalry wife Abby Allshard who at one point refers to herself as "Old Ironpants," she poses with actor George O'Brien, who plays her husband Mac in 1949's *She Wore a Yellow Ribbon*. Natwick's other Ford films include 1940's *The Long Voyage Home*, 1948's *3 Godfathers*, and 1952's *The Quiet Man*.

Her presence also suggests something often overlooked in Ford: although female roles in his films are often small, female characters and their perspectives are still extremely important to him. While the role might not have a lot of screen time, the impact of the role on the story often looms large. Perhaps nowhere in Ford's work do we see this illustrated better than in his films with Natwick.

Natwick admitted years later that she was frightened of the new medium (and she had undoubtedly heard stories about Ford's treatment of actors too), but, according to Ford biographer Scott Eyman, "Ford sensed that this was a true, gifted actress, and always treated her with the greatest respect."[2]

"He told me everything to do," Natwick recalled. "It was like marvelous coaching.... He just made me so comfortable and easy, that it was a wonderful way to do one's first movie.... He could bark at people. I always thought it was to bring out an effect, to make an effect."[3]

* * *

In *The Long Voyage Home*, Natwick plays Freda, a Cockney prostitute who conspires with two shady characters to drug and abduct a young seaman named Ole (John Wayne). In her scenes, which, when combined, take only about four minutes of screen time, we see her own tragic story unfold.

As she enters the pub and eyes her mark, young Ole, we can see that she is already a little drunk. After a moment or so, he decides to leave. She follows him out and begs him to "have a pint" with her. She underscores this with a quietly desperate "Please."

They both re-enter the pub, and she asks Ole to tell her something about himself. After learning that he's Swedish, she says: "I was born there too." Listening to her thick Cockney accent, this sounds both dishonest and foolish. But her desperation is what is paramount here: she needs to get him to buy drinks for them both so the bartender can slip a drug into Ole's. Ole agrees and she asks for "a drop of gin" and quickly adds a "beer chaser," underscoring that drinking is indeed a regular thing with her—something that's necessary to numb her self-loathing.

When the drinks arrive and Ole gulps his down, she gets him to talk. As he speaks, we can see the drug taking effect. We can also see her, sitting silently and looking with revulsion at what is happening. More than anything else we see, it is her troubled, conflicted face that dominates these few moments.

Finally, after Ole collapses from the drug, is taken away, and several other characters leave, we see Freda for one last time. She is alone at a corner of the bar, her entire body crumpled over in self-hatred and defeat.

Echoing Gypo Nolan in Ford's 1935 *The Informer*, Freda earns her money by betraying another's trust. Unlike her two co-conspirators, she hates what she does and hates herself for doing it. Yet, she's also frightened and desperate for money. Hardly any of this is in the dialogue, of course. It's in Natwick's spectacular body language and voice intonations. Every pained expression, every twitch, every word that doesn't ring true is disturbingly real. Freda is a bit part, but Natwick turns it into a powerful bit.

* * *

Ford uses Natwick just as sparingly — and effectively — in 1948's *3 Godfathers*. Here, she is a woman alone and stranded in a covered wagon in the desert. Three outlaws who have found her by chance have just helped her give birth to a boy. Now, she is dying and is painfully aware that she may just have moments left.

"Will you save my baby?" she asks the three men.

When they agree, she is relieved for a moment. Then she looks at her infant again and is struck by the realization that merely saving him will not be enough. "Poor little son," she says to her baby, "you'll be all alone in the world ... when Mother leaves you. And you'll miss me so. Nobody to tuck you into bed at night. Nobody to teach you your prayers. Nobody to kiss the little sore spots when you fall and hurt yourself. Nobody to tell your little secrets to."

She turns away, overwhelmed by her grief. We see that a tear has run down one cheek. Then she smiles as if she's just had a revelation and asks the three men to jointly be her son's godfathers. All are deeply moved and, without hesitation, agree. "You tell him about his mother," she adds, "who so wanted to live ... for him."

Gently, she kisses the baby, smiles again, says, "We must be moving on," and dies. As the three men look at her, the night wind blows, and the lantern perched on the back of the wagon flickers out. All we see through the wagon's opening is a gnarled dead tree trunk in the night.

The scene is great Ford poetry: simple, eloquent, and moving. Once again it's Natwick who elevates the few moments, here by communicating so beautifully the intense mixture of happiness and sadness her character feels, her resigned stoicism, her clear-thinking practicality, and her hope that her baby will be all right. Her scene (again just four minutes long) is the film's key turning point. From this moment on, the outlaws have all become surrogate fathers. Her character's baby has given their lives a new, and much nobler, purpose.

"I've never forgotten," Natwick said later, "that Ford seemed pleased with the scene and pleased that I'd done it. I guess because I knew my lines and got through it in [one] morning.... I don't know, you get things by osmosis from a wonderful director, I think. His feeling about what the woman was thinking and feeling."[4]

* * *

8. More Than the Sum of Her Parts

In 1949's *She Wore a Yellow Ribbon*, Ford asks Natwick to go in an entirely different direction. As Abby — the wife of fort commander Major Allshard (George O'Brien) and a hearty, opinionated, good-natured veteran of army life — she is in a number of scenes and her actions are not pivotal to the story's main action. Instead, she is a "texture" character who gives perspective, dimension, and great humanity to the community of characters in the film. Again, here as the self-described "Old Ironpants," Natwick excels, this time often moving from drama to broad comedy with great ease and economy.

One of these scenes occurs as a cavalry patrol led by Captain Brittles (John Wayne) is retreating. The mood is tense; one of the soldiers, Corporal Quayne (Tom Tyler) has been wounded and the bullet in him must be removed; and then, to intensify the mood, a storm, complete with thunder and lightning, arrives on the scene. The doctor (Arthur Shields) pleads with Brittles to slow the retreat just enough so he can remove the bullet. Reluctantly, Brittles agrees. Inside the retreating wagon, Abby, acting as nurse, wants to give Quayne "another slug" of liquor to numb the pain he will soon feel as the bullet is removed.

But, ever the gentleman, Quayne insists that the lady imbibe first. "After you, Mam, if you please," he says gallantly.

To oblige him, she takes a big swig herself, something she is clearly not used to doing. Then, when Quayne in his liquor-induced joviality, starts up with a chorus of "She Wore a Yellow Ribbon," Abby, now feeling pretty relaxed herself, soon joins in with rip-roaring enthusiasm. When Quayne is sufficiently numbed, the doctor begins to operate. As he does, Abby keeps singing.

Later, Captain Brittles comes up to the back of the wagon to get a report from the doctor, learns that Quayne will be fine, and sees a very hung over Abby holding a bedpan. "Thanks, Soldier," he says with good humor.

She sits with the bedpan on her lap and tries to steady herself so she doesn't have to use it.

It's a nice comic sequence in the midst of the drama, but throughout *She Wore a Yellow Ribbon*, Natwick always serves a more important purpose: to show Abby — the only strong, mature female voice in the film — to be credible, memorable, and as much a trooper as any of the men.

* * *

In Natwick's final Ford film, 1952's *The Quiet Man*, she again provides a strong, dignified, mature female presence. This time, though, her character, Sarah Tillane, is a wealthy Irish widow with eyes for Victor McLaglan's lovable lug, Squire Will Danaher.

Sarah is not especially demonstrative, but, when we first meet her in her study, Natwick takes us almost instantly to her character's core.

At first, Sarah hears the request of the newcomer to town, Sean Thornton (John Wayne), to sell him back his family home, White O'Morn. Sean says how his mother had always made their town of Innisfree sound like heaven. But, she cautions him, saying: "Innisfree is far from being heaven, Mr. Thornton." Her message is clear — it's simply another place with people and all the flaws and foibles that come with them. Then, she has a little fun with him, saying that she's not quite comfortable with him trying to make a family monument out of the old home. He doesn't know whether to take her seriously or not.

Soon Squire Will arrives, blustering with annoyance because he's heard that she's sold White o'Morn to Thornton and not to him. She says she hasn't, but she's also miffed at Will's tendency to assume and presume, behaviors she's clearly seen before.

Will is relieved at this news. He says that he recently argued with another man at the pub about that very subject and that he had defended Sarah, noting that she would never do such a thing without Will's knowledge, especially, as he puts it, "and us so close to an understanding, you might say." Again, Will is being presumptuous, both about Sarah's willingness to confer with him about such matters and about their "understanding," or impending betrothal.

Sarah turns livid, saying: "So you told him all that, did you, ... down at the pub, I suppose, in front of all those big ears with pints in their fists and pipes in their hands?"

When Will nods, she turns to Thornton and with great authority says: "You may have the land, Mr. Thornton." She even suggests a price lower than his original offer.

This scene firmly establishes Sarah Tillane's character in the film. Here and throughout, she's smart, confident, dignified, practical, proud, prickly, and definitely not to be trifled with. She knows how to hold her own with any man and won't, in any way, be bettered. If Will has hopes of marrying her, he is going to have to learn a few things. Slowly, as the story proceeds, he gets the point and we see her interest in him develop in brief but punctuated moments.

Again, Natwick brings her special intelligence and talent to a very small role. In doing so, she turns what could easily have been a routine performance into something quite subtle, complex, and memorable.

* * *

When the subject turns to the John Ford Stock Company — the group of actors now famous for working with Ford again and again — Mildred Natwick is a name that comes to mind for many Ford buffs as quickly and automatically as does Jane Darwell, Ben Johnson, Anna Lee, Ward Bond, or Harry Carey, Jr. What's amazing is how little screen time she has in Ford films compared to these and literally dozens of other Ford regulars. Her four characters, as briefly as they are all onscreen, are all deeply etched into people's minds.

This is undoubtedly to Natwick's great credit. But the success of these characters also suggests both Ford's genuine interest in their distinctively female points of view and his commitment to telling their stories as effectively as possible. He knew he could count on Natwick to make these characters memorable, and he capitalized on her talents.

Including the four films she made with Ford, Natwick made fewer than 20 films in all, preferring to work on stage and in later years on television. She was twice nominated for Tony Awards for her theater work, in 1957 for *The Waltz of the Toreadors* and in 1970 for the musical *70 Girls 70*. In 1974, she received an Emmy Award for her work playing opposite her good friend Helen Hayes in the limited-run television series *The Snoop Sisters*. During that time, she also had a recurring role as Rock Hudson's eccentric mother in the 1970s series *McMillan & Wife*.

Natwick received her only Academy Award nomination in the Best Supporting Actress category for her turn as Jane Fonda's mother in 1967's film version of the play *Barefoot in the Park*. In addition to her roles for Ford, she is probably best known today for other small but unforgettable roles she played in such films as Walter Lang's 1950 version of *Cheaper by the Dozen* (as Mrs. Mebane, the birth control advocate) and Alfred Hitchcock's 1955 *The Trouble with Harry* (as Miss Ivy Gravely).

In an interview late in life Natwick discussed the importance, when creating a role, of constantly experimenting. Just about everything, she noted, "is hit or miss for a while, until it all comes together." She added that her advice to aspiring young performers was to "act every time you get a chance. At least in the beginning, go wherever acting is."[5]

Natwick never married and died in New York City in 1994. She was 89.

9

"On the very edge of eternity"
Donna Reed's Sandy Davyss in *They Were Expendable*

In the understated dialogue that deftly weaves its way through John Ford's remarkable World War II film, *They Were Expendable*, the 1940s slang term "swell" has a special meaning. Instead of merely "nice" or "good," it's a way of saying "magnificent" or even "extraordinary." The sailors and soldiers use it often to describe each other, and, along with every mention of the word, we hear their deeply felt respect and affection. "Swell" is the ultimate compliment, the greatest tribute.

It's also the word Navy Lieutenant Rusty Ryan (John Wayne), repeatedly uses to describe Sandy Davyss, the Army nurse with whom he falls in love as the world around them is falling apart—and as they both may be, as critic Andrew Sarris puts it, "on the very edge of eternity."[1] Played with great intelligence and authority by the luminous Donna Reed, Sandy is much more than the film's requisite romantic interest. She is a counterpoint to the brutality that exists elsewhere in the story: a courageous, humanizing presence that reaffirms the best in life while also reminding us of life's fleeting, fragile nature. In terms of screen time, her role is small; she's in only a handful of scenes. Yet, her impact on Rusty and other men in the story, and by extension the film's viewers, is immense.

* * *

At the time, the 24-year-old Reed was a curious choice to play the critical part of Sandy. Casting the young actress with only four years of film experience, and mostly in minor roles in insignificant films, was a gamble both for Ford and for MGM, the film's studio. But, as often happened when Ford took a casting risk, it paid off handsomely.

Born Donna Belle Mullenger in 1921 on a farm near Denison, Iowa, Reed grew up the eldest in a family of five children. After graduating from Denison High School, she wanted to go to college and become a teacher, but money was a problem. So, with her aunt's encouragement, she moved to Southern California and, while working part time, enrolled in Los Angeles City College, began appearing in local stage plays, and soon began receiving offers to do screen tests for studios. Eventually, she signed with MGM, but she insisted on completing her degree first.

Beginning in 1941, she appeared frequently

As the world about them is falling apart, Sandy and Rusty (Donna Reed and John Wayne) realize that they've fallen in love in 1945's World War II drama *They Were Expendable*. In only a handful of scenes, Reed gives this brilliant film — one of Ford's most under-appreciated — added poignancy and dimension. This role also launched Reed, then a minor MGM contract player, toward stardom, which she achieved the following year in Frank Capra's *It's a Wonderful Life*.

in MGM films. While most of the films were forgotten quickly, Reed wasn't. Her intelligence, warmth, and wholesome beauty made her a favorite and a popular "pinup" girl of American soldiers serving in World War II. She took this role very seriously, too, spending hours answering fan letters from soldiers overseas.[2]

"If the manager says 'sacrifice...'"

Filmed in 1945 as World War II was winding down, *They Were Expendable* is about one of the U.S. military's great defeats in that war, the loss of the Philippines in 1942. Specifically, it's about a small group of PT-boat pioneers led by Lieutenant John Brickley (Robert Montgomery in perhaps his finest film performance) and his executive officer, Wayne's Rusty Ryan.

Shortly after the film begins, the characters learn that Pearl Harbor has been bombed and war declared. The Japanese are advancing on the Philippines, the Americans and Filipino forces must retreat, and help, at least in the near term, will probably not be coming. In a calm but very sobering scene, the admiral (Charles Trowbridge) spells the situation out to Brickley. "Listen, son," he says. "You and I are professionals. If the manager says 'sacrifice,' we lay down a bunt and let somebody else hit the home runs.... Our job is to lay down that sacrifice."

As the days go by, the PT squadron does what it can, but even in its small victories there are always casualties. Boats are damaged or destroyed. Men are wounded or killed. Pulling back, as frustrating and painful as it is to everyone, becomes a way of life.

Early in the story, Rusty receives treatment for a wound at a military hospital where he meets Sandy. They are involved only briefly. Then he must leave for Mindanao, while she remains on Bataan. The last time we see her (and Rusty hears her voice) is when she and Rusty talk briefly on the phone hookup. As often happens in the film, however, pressing military business takes precedence. Their line is abruptly cut.

Later, after still more setbacks and retreats, Rusty and Brickley find out that they are two of only 30 servicemen who have been "ordered out" and will soon be airlifted away from what will undoubtedly be a holocaust. Feeling enormous sadness and guilt, they say goodbye to their men. Rusty feels the added burden of having to leave Sandy behind, even though he has no idea where she might be or even if she is still alive.

Yet, as the plane lifts off and the men left behind look up, there is hope in their eyes and the confidence that these and other Americans will someday return. Whether those left behind will be around for that day is another matter. For the moment, though, they are happy to see a few of their friends get out.

Simply put, *They Were Expendable* is one of John Ford's most emotionally powerful and beautifully rendered films. Every major element — from Spig Wead's understated, utterly dignified script; to Joe August's gorgeous, often haunting black-and-white cinematography; to the low-key but deeply felt performances by Montgomery, Wayne, Reed, Ward Bond, Russell Simpson, and others; to the abundance of highly effective directorial touches (or "grace notes" as Ford liked to call them) — makes a sizable contribution to the film's overall effect.

In terms of its setting and action, *They Were Expendable* is a war story. But it is far from typical, steering clear of the jingoistic propaganda found in so many war films and the scathing indictments of the military and governments found in so many others. It focuses on Americans, but its point of view is universal. The Japanese soldiers and sailors — who we never see — are never judged or criticized. In fact, the only Japanese person to appear in the film is a mature woman (perhaps a mother with a son old enough to serve *his* country) listening with growing distress and sadness to a radio report describing the attack on

Pearl Harbor. We see Filipinos, too, most notably one woman standing on a dock watching her loved one being evacuated after an attack. Here, there is no political agenda, just the acknowledgement that a sequence of events has brought all these people to this very unfortunate time and place: the acknowledgement that, in wartime, people on both sides suffer.

Film director and critic Lindsay Anderson has called *They Were Expendable* "a heroic poem,"[3] and it's hard to disagree. This is a film about the tragedy of war; the dissolution of a family (in this case a military family); the precious, fragile nature of life; and many other facets of human experience. But this is ultimately a film about heroism: about ordinary people summoning up the best in themselves to face the worst of times. Partly this means having the courage to face the very real and imminent prospect of death, and partly this means facing our greatest fears without surrendering our integrity, generosity, compassion, and those other "noble" attributes that make us fully human. In addition to being about heroism, the film is also the work of a poet, and, like great poetry, it is deeply felt and highly suggestive throughout. The blend of strong emotion and personal restraint is remarkable. Characters rarely speak directly of death, for example, because they don't want to make others feel uncomfortable. Yet, we know that it weighs on everyone's minds. In the film too, the slightest smile, nod of the head, or other small gesture can often convey enormous sentiment. And, yes, "swell" always means much more than simply "nice" or "good." What's left unsaid is often so much more important — and affecting — than what's said.

"The torch held steady"

We first meet Lieutenant Sandy Davyss just after a grumpy Rusty has checked into the hospital, and we see immediately that she is a professional and an adult: smart, assertive, down-to-business, and not about to take nonsense from Rusty or anyone. He tries to pull rank, and she immediately tells him that she's the one in charge here. Rusty backs down; he is impressed.

A little later, Rusty's estimation of her grows even more. As he plays cards with another patient, Carter, bombs begin to fall around the makeshift hospital. Patients huddled in corners smoke cigarettes to try to ease their fears. Rusty and Carter, however, are focused on Sandy assisting the doctor as he operates on patient after patient. No one says a word. No one needs to. Ford simply holds his camera on Sandy's face as she works underneath the shining lamp, as the light flickers, as darkness consumes the scene, then as she uses a flashlight to help the doctor continue to work. The bombs keep falling, but Sandy remains, "the torch held steady," as Lindsay Anderson has written, "the image of unwavering humane devotion."[4]

Rusty, deeply moved by her quiet toughness and professionalism, tells Carter: "That's a nice kind of gal to have around in wartime."

"Anytime," Carter tells him.

Afterward, Sandy plays a central role in two remarkable scenes. In both, precious but fleeting moments are shown in the midst of daily horror and death. And, in both, vintage Ford poetry — deep shadows, actors often in silhouette, soft voices, strains of gentle music, and familiar homey settings such as a hammock on a porch and a candlelit dinner table — gives these moments immense emotional power.

The first is at a dance that's been arranged near the hospital. Rusty and Sandy take a turn inside with the others and — as the same lush, evocative melody plays on — find themselves outside on the veranda dancing in eerie silhouette. It's sweet and exhilarating and chilling all at the same time. As Andrew Sarris observes: "The shadowy images of Wayne and Reed as they ritualistically seek each other out are among the most intensely romantic images of love and death in American cinema."[5]

Soon, Rusty and Sandy sit on a hammock and talk of their homes. She is from Iowa: "You know, tall corn." He is from upstate New York: "You know, apples." They hear guns in the distance, guns, Sandy says, that are coming closer each night. The reflection from the gunfire flickers across their faces. Ford's camera, never too intrusive, moves closer to give us a more intimate glimpse of these faces. As when she assisted the doctor, Sandy is associated with light. This time, however, the light is ominous, not benign. It literally intrudes upon their intimate moment, telling them that the joy they are feeling will indeed be brief. They both sense this too, realizing that this moment of sublime connection — their moment — is already passing.

Another intrusion follows almost immediately. Brickley has come. He hates to interrupt, but he needs to talk to Rusty about pressing matters. Again, Ford's camera lingers on Sandy, who takes all this stoically. These are definitely the times that try men's — and women's — souls.

The second scene is a dinner party Brickley, Rusty, and the other officers under Brickley's small command give for Sandy.

Sandy gets out of a jeep in the rain and enters wet and dripping. Brickley wants to introduce her to the others, but, before this happens, she insists on a moment to herself. She takes off her wet hat and coat, fixes and combs her hair, and, in a wonderful touch, pulls out a string of pearls (supplied by Ford just before the scene was shot), and puts it on. In just moments, and as the men watch in awe, she is transformed and radiant.

At the dinner table she is again associated with light, this time with a bright candle in the foreground — a warm, comforting light. For that evening she isn't just the light in Rusty's life but the light in the lives of all the men at the table.

Three of the enlisted men serenade them with a sweet song. Eventually, Brickley and the other officers excuse themselves. As he leaves, one of the junior officers tells Sandy that her visit "meant a great deal to all of us." It certainly has. As Rusty and Sandy sit alone, the cook returns to blow out the candles. Again, a brief, exquisite moment is ending. This time, however, the light, so closely associated with Sandy, does not return.

As they did at the dance, Rusty and Sandy go outside to talk. Now, she starts to cry. He asks her why. She denies she is crying and, wiping away her tears, says in a sad voice: "It's just that they're such nice guys." Again, grim reality breaks the mood, and the beautiful, joyful moment of seconds before is gone.

We don't know it when we see the film for the first time, but this is the last time we ever see Sandy and Rusty together. The scene doesn't merely cut or dissolve to another scene; it fades to black the way a scene might darken when a candle is blown out. We know that a chapter has ended. Except for the brief, interrupted phone conversation with Rusty later on, Sandy is gone, perhaps forever.

Although Sandy isn't present in the film, however, her presence continues to be felt, especially by Rusty.

Later, as he and what remains of his crew continue to retreat, he sits in a soon-to-be-abandoned bar and hears a radio report that the Japanese have captured Bataan. After the report, the radio plays the same melody he and Sandy once danced to, and he (and we) cannot help but wonder about her. Is she alive or dead? If she's alive, where is she and is she safe? If safe, how long will she be safe?

Eventually, when Rusty and Brickley are "ordered out" and wait for their plane, Rusty runs into Carter from the hospital. He asks about Sandy, but Carter has no information. She may have been taken prisoner, he tells Rusty. Or she may be in the hills, trying to evade capture. Although no one says the words, another possibility is that she may have already been killed. Neither man knows, and neither may ever know.

Then, as the men are called to board the plane, two junior officers ordered to go with Rusty and Brickley don't answer. They can't be found. In their place, two other names — Morton and Rusty's friend Carter — are called. Both men board the plane. The plane revs its engines. Then there is a knock on the door. The two junior officers have now arrived. Morton and Carter must get off. Rusty, overwhelmed with guilt by now, tries to get off in the place of one of these men and look for Sandy. Brickley, orders him back, saying, "Who are you working for, Rusty — yourself?" Then, with great, understated gallantry, Morton and Carter climb out of the plane. It isn't until after the door is closed and the plane readies for takeoff that one of the junior officers realizes what nearly everyone else already knows: that the two men they have replaced will likely die or be taken prisoner. Again, it's what is left unsaid that says it all.

"A nice kind of gal to have around"

In films such as *The Lost Patrol* and the aptly named *Men Without Women*, Ford tells engaging war stories without any female characters. And, considering that he was fresh from three years of direct involvement in World War II when he made *They Were Expendable*, it is likely that, even without Sandy, the film would still have been a fine and very moving experience.

Sandy's presence, however, gives the film dimension and emotional depth it clearly wouldn't have had without her.

First, she provides a strong, confident, and independent female point of view in a world where female points of view of any kind are in very short supply. This helps to enrich the family of characters in the film, giving it more variety and texture.

Second, she draws the kind of sweetness and gentleness out of the men we might not otherwise see. We notice this first with Rusty. As he interacts with her, this gruff, impulsive, and self-centered character becomes more thoughtful, mature, and tender. Then we notice this with the other men in the dinner party scene from the sailors who serenade her to the junior officer who asks if Sandy can bring some other women with her the next time she comes. In Ford's view, good women — just by being present and involved — can do a great deal to give men happiness and to humanize them. And in his films, we often see the stark differences between men with good women at their side (Sam Collingwood in *Fort Apache*, Mac Allshard in *She Wore a Yellow Ribbon*, etc.) and men without women (Ethan Edwards in *The Searchers*, Tom Doniphon in *The Man Who Shot Liberty Valance*, etc.). In *They Were Expendable*, Sandy serves a similar function. With her, Rusty is (maybe for the first time in his life) fully alive and happy. Without her, he struggles.

Third, Sandy raises the stakes. Both her growing importance in Rusty's life and then their abrupt (and perhaps permanent) separation makes the tragedy that is unfolding, and the sacrifices their characters must make, all the more wrenching. Not only are Rusty and Sandy's lives at great risk, but so is what could be their one opportunity for love.

Like Robert Montgomery's Brickley, Donna Reed's Sandy is a fascinating — and highly effective — mix of the ideal and the real. On one hand, she seems incredibly noble and good. On the other, she is entirely credible as a strong, mature, respectful, compassionate, grounded person trying to work her way through a terrible situation and, in the process, to hold on to her humanity.

Her character, extraordinarily moving without ever being sentimentalized, is exquisitely conceived and conveyed. Ford and scriptwriter Spig Wead deserve much of the credit for this. But it is Reed's special blend of intelligence, maturity (despite her youth), inner strength, and immense sensitivity that make her Sandy a real standout in a film filled with fine performances. Every word, facial expression, and gesture is just right. She is, as Rusty says about Sandy, "swell."

* * *

Playing Sandy, Reed quickly won Ford's respect too. Soon afterward, the director tried unsuccessfully to get her to play Clementine in his next project, *My Darling Clementine* for 20th Century–Fox (1946). The role eventually went to newcomer Cathy Downs.

After *They Were Expendable*, Reed's film career flourished for more than a decade. In 1946, she co-starred with James Stewart in Frank Capra's 1946 film and perennial Christmas favorite, *It's a Wonderful Life*, playing Mary, the film role for which she is probably best remembered today. And, in 1953, she took a risk of her own that paid off in a big way, going against type and playing a prostitute in Frank Zinnemann's 1953 film, *From Here to Eternity*. For her work, she received that year's best supporting actress Academy Award, her only Oscar.

In the mid–1950s, however, the quality of roles coming Reed's way began to decline. One low point was being miscast in Rudolph Maté's *The Far Horizons* (1955) as Sacajawea, the Native American woman who guides Lewis and Clark across the American continent between 1804 and 1806. While Reed brought her usual warmth, intelligence, and integrity to the role, it was clearly the wrong fit for her.

Like many film stars at the time, Reed turned to television in the late 1950s and, between 1958 and 1966, starred in the popular TV sitcom *The Donna Reed Show*. For her work, she received four Emmy nominations and a Golden Globe Award. As well as accolades, she also received the great respect of her co-stars. "[Donna Reed] definitely became my second mother," Shelley Fabares, who played Reed's TV daughter on *The Donna Reed Show*, noted decades after working with Reed. "She was a role model and remains so to this day. I still periodically hear her voice in my head when I am making a decision about doing something, I hear her urging me on to make the stronger decision of the two."[6]

After working occasionally in television (in roles which included a brief stint as Miss Ellie, the matriarch on the hit prime time soap opera *Dallas* in 1984 and 1985), Reed died in 1986 of pancreatic cancer just a few days short of her 65th birthday. The actress had been married three times, most notably to producer Tony Owen for 26 years, and had four children.

The town of Denison, Iowa, also remains proud of its homegrown star. Each year, the Denison-based Donna Reed Foundation for the Performing Arts hosts a Donna Reed Festival dedicated to performing arts education. Also, the street where Reed's childhood home once stood has been renamed Donna Reed Drive.

10

Ford's Wild Irish Rose

Maureen O'Hara's Kathleen in *Rio Grande* and Mary Kate in *The Quiet Man*

No actress is more closely associated both with John Ford and with the director's frequent on-screen alter ego, John Wayne, than Maureen O'Hara, and people are often surprised when they learn that the three made only three films together. Of these, the trio's legendary, if not iconic, reputation rests almost entirely on two: 1950's *Rio Grande*, the last of Ford's cavalry trilogy, and 1952's *The Quiet Man*, one of Ford's most popular films.

Much of the success of both films, just about everyone agrees, is due to O'Hara and Wayne's on-screen chemistry. The pair, as the Hollywood folk love to say, had "it." Other on-screen couples — Astaire and Rogers, Tracy and Hepburn, and William Powell and Myrna Loy — had "it" too. But, with Wayne and O'Hara, there's a repressed, smoldering, and ultimately uncontainable sexuality, which (especially for the era) is in a class by itself. When we see them together, we absolutely know that, at some point, something's gotta give.

In her 2004 autobiography, *'Tis Herself*, O'Hara offered her take on the subject with characteristic self-confidence. "Why were Duke and I so electric in our love scenes together?" she wrote. "I was the only leading lady big enough and tough enough for John Wayne. Duke's presence was so strong that when audiences saw him finally meet a woman of equal hell and fire, it was exciting and thrilling. Other actresses looked as though they would cower and break if Duke raised a hand or even hollered. Not me. I always gave as good as I got, and it was believable."[1]

This dynamic isn't just about sex and battling for supremacy, of course. In both films, the characters who feel all this passion are also smart, very caring, sensitive, proud, stubborn, strong willed, lonely, and usually quite conflicted. They sincerely want to be together and happy, but there are big issues to sort through first.

As Ford liked to do with many actors, he used O'Hara in very specific ways. Usually, she was his intensely passionate, intensely proud wild Irish rose. In particular, he capitalized on her riveting screen presence, fiery personality (to match her brilliant red hair), strong personality, and keen intelligence to play women whose consuming love for a man is thwarted by some complication. In *Rio Grande* and *The Quiet Man* the problems are resolved happily. But in two of her other Ford films, *How Green Was My Valley* and *The Wings of Eagles*, the outcomes are much darker, both women succumbing to depression and one also to alcohol.

Some critics have viewed this as a Ford shortcoming, a bit of unintended sexism suggesting he believed that women cannot be happy without a man in their lives. When we give the matter a closer look, however, this view seems oversimplified. Ford repeatedly puts men in similar situations, most notably Tom Doniphon in *The Man Who Shot Liberty Valance*. Without Hallie, Tom languishes and dies a forgotten, beaten man. Ford also portrays women who appear to be just fine without a man. A good example is Ava Gardner's Honey Bear Kelly near the end of *Mogambo*. If she can't find the right man, or, if the right man won't clean up his act, she seems to be telling us, she's probably better off without *any* man, at least for a while. It's probably more accurate to say that, in Ford films, there are no absolutes when it comes to male-female relationships but that there *is* great variety. While other actresses played different kinds of women for Ford, O'Hara played women who need passionate relationships with men in their lives. She was, he obviously felt, an actress who could convey that need — and the negative consequences when that need is not fulfilled — extremely well. As usual, he was right.

* * *

Born Maureen FitzSimons in a suburb of Dublin, Ireland, in 1920, Maureen O'Hara was the second of six siblings born to Charles Stewart Parnell FitzSimons, a clothier, and Marguerita Lilburn FitzSimons, a former operatic contralto. As a teen, she aspired to act on the stage and received training at, among other places, Dublin's famed Abbey Theater. She impressed her teachers at the Abbey enough for them to recommend her for a screen test, which eventually caught the attention of actor Charles Laughton and his business partner, producer Erich Pommer. The two signed the 18-year-old to a seven-year contract with their newly formed independent company, Mayflower Pictures, and cast her in their 1939 film *Jamaica Inn*, which was directed by Alfred Hitchcock. Delighted with O'Hara's work in *Jamaica Inn*, Laughton made sure she was cast as Esmeralda opposite his Quasimodo in *The Hunchback of Notre Dame*, which was made soon afterward at RKO in Hollywood. But, when World War II broke out and Laughton realized that film opportunities in England would be extremely limited in the short term, he sold O'Hara's contract to RKO.

At RKO, she made mostly low-budget films for the next two years. Most were forgettable. But one comedy, *Dance, Girl, Dance*, is a curious concoction that pairs O'Hara and Lucille Ball as two aspiring dancers — O'Hara, an idealistic ballerina, and Ball, an opportunistic showgirl — and gives both actresses the chance to showcase their talents. *Dance, Girl, Dance* is also notable as being one of the best-known films of its director, Dorothy Arzner, the only woman directing for any Hollywood studio at the time.

Then, in 1941, after such better-known actresses as Greer Garson and Gene Tierney[2] were considered for the part of the passionate young Anghard in 20th Century–Fox's *How Green Was My Valley*, the role eventually went to the 21-year-old O'Hara. This was the first of the five films she made with Ford and the film that made her a star.

During the 1940s, she worked steadily in various kinds of films from comedies to westerns. Perhaps her best-known film during this period was 1947's *Miracle on 34th Street* with Natalie Wood, which has become an audience favorite during the holiday season. Here playing a head-strong mother who must learn to accommodate both her child and the man in her life, we see a vivid earlier version of the kind of character O'Hara would play three years later for her old mentor Ford — Kathleen York in *Rio Grande*.

"Take me home again, Kathleen"

Most of *Rio Grande* takes place at the aptly named Fort Stark, a bleak, remote U.S. Cavalry post in Texas in 1879. Its commander is Colonel Kirby York (Wayne), who has been estranged from his wife, Kathleen (O'Hara), since General Sheridan ordered him to burn down her family's home in Virginia's Shenandoah Valley some 15 years earlier during the American Civil War. Early in the film, Kirby learns that his son Jeff (Claude Jarman, Jr.), whom he hasn't seen in those 15 years, has flunked out of West Point, joined the Army as an enlisted man, and been assigned to Fort Stark. Soon, Kathleen arrives too. She wants to "buy" Jeff out of the Army (a common practice at the time) and enroll him in another military academy so he can still become an officer. Initially, the three clash over this issue. Eventually, however, Kathleen realizes that Jeff needs to find his own way, and both she and Kirby reaffirm the love that they've never lost. Being a Ford cavalry film, *Rio Grande* also has skirmishes with Native Americans, Victor McLaglen comic relief scenes, gorgeous visual compositions, and lots of manly men singing. But mainly this is a film about an estranged family — a handy symbol for the U.S. after the Civil War — whose members

In 1950's *Rio Grande*, Ford teamed John Wayne and Maureen O'Hara for the first time and realized that he had caught, as O'Hara once put it, "lightning in a bottle." In this film, they play the Yorks, Kirby and Kathleen, a cavalry officer and his estranged wife who are reunited after 15 years and find they must work through many issues before they have even a chance at rekindled happiness. As Kathleen, O'Hara gives an intense, complex performance, one of her best.

must find ways to work through their personal differences and grievances, reunite, and move forward together.

At the center of these family struggles is Kathleen. While Kirby and Jeff come to terms early on, she takes much longer both to accept Jeff's decision to serve as an enlisted man and to fully reconcile with Kirby and again be part Kirby's military life. It's not difficult to understand why. She's seen the wreckage — both physical (her family's home and probably much more) and emotional (her marriage) — that can result from war. As she tells Jeff, "What makes soldiers great is hateful to me."

Yet, despite all these issues, Kathleen and Kirby have never stopped loving each other, and it is in the scenes when these feelings are expressed that *Rio Grande* shines most brightly. One exquisite moment is when the regimental singers serenade Kathleen and Kirby with "Take Me Home Again, Kathleen" as the pair stands just outside Kirby's tent. Ford's camera simply holds on Kathleen and Kirby in a medium two-shot for most of the song. Both are surprised by the musical selection and feel very awkward. After all, they parted in anger and haven't seen each other for 15 years. They twitch and fidget and exchange tentative, sometimes embarrassed glances. Both are also deeply moved.

Eventually, a slightly blushing Kirby says: "This music is not of my choosing."

"I'm sorry, Kirby," Kathleen replies. "I wish it had been."

There's nothing subtle about this scene. We know all along that we're being manipulated big time. But it's also beautifully done, and a big part of why it works so well is the range of conflicting feelings both O'Hara and Wayne are able to convey so convincingly without speaking. In their glances and awkward movements, we see their whole relationship unfold before us: the intense longing, the mutual love and respect, and the ongoing conflict all existing — as the two actors are shown on the screen — side by side.

Another wonderful moment comes at the very end of the film. Now, all is right with the world. In a grand gesture of reconciliation, General Sheridan (J. Carroll Naish) has asked the regimental musicians to play the Southern anthem, "Dixie," in honor of Kathleen. Again, both she and Kirby are surprised by the selection. Yet, this time, instead of feeling awkward and tentative, they are delighted. In fact, she is so delighted that, in an outburst of exuberance, she starts spinning her parasol and acting flirtatious — a striking expression of delight and attraction conveyed in a very clever, witty manner. The York family — and the nation — are united again.

When compared with Ford's two earlier cavalry films, *Fort Apache* and *She Wore a Yellow Ribbon*, *Rio Grande* is often viewed (and rather harshly) as the runt of the litter. There's no denying that it lacks *Fort Apache's* searing condemnation of imperialist values and *She Wore a Yellow Ribbon's* stunning Technicolor compositions. But, it's also a very different kind of story, a domestic drama rather than an epic. It's also the only one of the three to tackle (and quite successfully) a complex, mature love story. Add to that, it's the only one that pairs John Wayne with Maureen O'Hara. In some ways, it may not be quite the film that the other two are, but O'Hara's presence in it is more than adequate compensation.

"There are some things a man doesn't get over so easily"

The Quiet Man takes place in the fictional Irish village of Innisfree in the early 1950s. Sean Thornton (Wayne), an Irish-born American boxer, returns to his hometown after he accidentally kills a man in the ring and is haunted by the experience. He wants to put this nightmare behind him and begin life anew.

Caught up in emotions as fierce as the wind that swirls about them, John Wayne's Sean Thornton and Maureen O'Hara's Mary Kate Danaher prepare to share the first of many passionate kisses in 1952's *The Quiet Man*. As with 1950's *Rio Grande*, the heart of *The Quiet Man* is the O'Hara-Wayne romance, one that's filled with passion and fraught with complications.

He even buys back his family's modest ancestral cottage and finds himself passionately drawn to the beautiful Mary Kate Danaher (O'Hara). Unfortunately, though, Mary Kate's older brother and guardian, Will (Victor McLaglen), doesn't take kindly to Sean and objects to the union. The townsfolk get involved and trick Will into agreeing, and Sean and Mary Kate are finally married. At the wedding reception, however, Will finds out he's been tricked and refuses to give Mary Kate and Sean her "fortune" or dowry. Sean doesn't particularly care, but Mary Kate's fortune means the world to her. Sean must get it from Will, even if it means fighting for it. But Sean, fearing that he could once again kill a man with his fists, won't do it and won't tell Mary Kate why. So, the couple is stuck and the marriage unconsummated. Eventually, though, Sean and Will have their reckoning, Mary Kate's wishes are met, and peace is restored.

As with *Rio Grande*, the undeniable highlight of *The Quiet Man* is the O'Hara-Wayne relationship. Both have some nice moments when they are apart.

For example, O'Hara is excellent at showing both her strength and her vulnerability when she must deal with her overbearing brother. Wayne is also very touching when he talks with the Reverend Mr. Playfair (Arthur Shields) about killing the other boxer in the ring. Yet, it is a handful of magical scenes with the two actors together that are seared into our memories.

The first is when Sean and Mary Kate first set eyes upon one another. He has just arrived in Innisfree. She is herding sheep across a field. He looks at nothing in particular, spots her, and then can't help but stare at her. She knows that she has caught this handsome stranger's attention and reacts in a shy but somewhat flattered way. The mere sight of each other has been a jolt. Mary Kate especially, dressed in primary colors with a brilliant red skirt to match her hair, has moved Sean very deeply. Something very primal and powerful is in the making.

Years later, O'Hara discussed this scene with great fondness, saying:

> I loved Mary Kate Danaher. I loved the hell and fire in her. She was a terrific dame, though, and didn't let herself get walked on. As I readied to begin playing her, I believed that my most important scene in the picture was when Mary Kate is in the field herding the sheep and Sean Thornton sees her for the very first time. It's a moment captured in time, and it's love at first sight. I felt very strongly that if the audience believed it was love at first sight, then we would have lightning in a bottle. But if they didn't, we would have just another lovely romantic comedy on our hands.... The scene comes off beautifully. Mr. Ford brilliantly kept the camera stationary and had me walk slowly down and out of the frame instead of following me as I walked away. It's one of my favorite shots in the movie....[3]

The next wonderful scene between them is when they—though they barely know each other at this point—kiss for the first time. It is dusk. Outside, a fierce wind is blowing. Mary Kate has secretly come to Sean's cottage to make a fire for his arrival. He enters unexpectedly, surprising her. She doesn't want to be spotted and tries to sneak out the door. He sees her, grabs her hand, pulls her back into the cottage (accompanied by that fierce wind), and kisses her tenderly but with great passion and authority. The moment is both startling and grand in its primal qualities. Like the fierce wind, the passion that now grips them is a formidable, elemental force of nature, something that's much larger and more powerful than either of them, something that can't be denied.

This is also the scene when Sean says a line that reverberates throughout the film, "There are some things a man doesn't get over so easily." Here, he means the sight and touch of Mary Kate, the woman with whom he already senses a mystical bond. In addition, the line suggests Sean's traumatic boxing experience (which we learn about later) and his fear of doing harm again, a fear that, as the story unfolds, presents serious problems for both him and Mary Kate.

A third (and the most poignant scene so far) takes place soon after Sean and Mary Kate have run away from their chaperone (Barry Fitzgerald) during an official round of courting. They stop at some churchlike ruins in the middle of an ancient cemetery. The sky has turned dark. There is thunder, then rain. Sean gives Mary Kate his coat. Then they hold each other and kiss before the ruins. As the rain drenches them, they continue to hold each other and realize almost simultaneously that a profound change has just occurred: that they have now become — and will forever be — one. We don't hear a word; we simply see it all in their expressive faces. They are deeply moved, awestruck, and humbled by the power of this love. As before, their feelings exist beside other powerful, primal, unstoppable forces of nature, this time thunder and rain. It is fascinating too that they are standing in front of a church-like structure. They will soon go through the formal marriage ceremony before the community. We never see this in the film because we don't need to. In Ford's view, here is where the two have really become husband and wife.

Unfortunately, marriage brings more challenges with it for Sean and Mary Kate. When she is denied her dowry, her "fortune," she refuses to consummate their union and tensions build. Later on, both confide to different local clergymen and then tell each other as they sit by the fire in their cottage that night. Again, we see it in their faces — both the great love they have for one another and the great sadness they feel because they can't get beyond what divides them. It's another very poignant scene, and we feel deeply for them both.

O'Hara is so compelling in the romantic scenes that it might be easy to overlook the other facets of Mary Kate's complex character. One, for example, is her proud, stubborn, and strong-willed disposition. Another is her fearsome temper, which she even warns Sean about. Still another is her no-nonsense practicality, which we see when she tells Sean that it makes more sense to plant turnips rather than roses. There is also the deep connection she feels for her past and its importance on her present happiness, a connection Sean can scarcely understand. As she tells him when she stresses the importance of having her fortune, "There's 300 years of happy dreaming in those things of mine. And I'll have them. I'll have my dream." As we clearly see, there are many sides to this very complicated and engaging woman.

The subject of the "fortune" is also worth touching upon from a feminist perspective, especially because some film historians have looked at *The Quiet Man* as anything but a feminist film. In her landmark book about the treatment of women in American film, *From Reverence to Rape*, critic Molly Haskell comments on how the film's attitude toward Mary Kate and her needs as an individual is, in this respect, far ahead of its time. As Haskell writes: "In marrying John Wayne, the American who has come back to live in Ireland, Maureen O'Hara's redhead Irish firebrand insists on recovering her dowry from her father:

a £350 'fortune' and her furniture. Wayne is indignant. In characteristic American fashion, he feels his masculinity and ability to provide for her impugned until she finally makes him understand that it isn't the money, but what it stands for: the dowry and furniture are her identity, her independence. The furniture, particularly, is part of her personality—like a maiden name—and the money enables her not to be completely dependent on her husband and 'absorbed' by him."[4]

Just as it's impossible to imagine any other actor playing Tom Joad better than Henry Fonda or Ethan Edwards better than John Wayne, it's impossible to imagine any other actress playing Mary Kate anywhere near as well as O'Hara does. This is one of those indelible performances—a fascinating character fully fleshed out by an actress absolutely worthy of the task. While parts of *The Quiet Man*—in particular, the lovable drunks, all the other Irish stereotypes, and the interminable fight at the end—seem more and more tedious with repeated viewings, the parts with O'Hara and Wayne remain as fresh and vital as ever. They are as timeless as any moments in Ford's work.

In her autobiography, O'Hara concludes her reminiscence of *The Quiet Man* with an anecdote about the final moments of the film, one that captures both her great pride and delight in working on this project and Ford's great fondness for teasing his films' audiences with ambiguity—for keeping his stories alive and vital by keeping people guessing. This is what she had to say:

> There is only one way to end our discussion of *The Quiet Man*, and that's with a whisper. No matter what part of the world I'm in, the question I am always asked is: "What did you whisper into John Wayne's ear at the end of *The Quiet Man*?" It was John Ford's idea: it was the ending he wanted. I was told by Mr. Ford exactly what I was to say. At first I refused. I said, "No, I can't. I can't say that to Duke." But Mr. Ford wanted a very shocked reaction from Duke, and he said, "I'm telling you, you *are* to say it." I had no choice, and so I agreed, but with a catch: "I'll say it on one condition—that it is never repeated or revealed to anyone." So we made a deal. After the scene was over, we told Duke about our agreement and the three of us made a pact. There are those who claim that they were told and know what I said. They don't and are lying. John Ford took it to his grave—so did Duke—and the answer will die with me. Curiosity about the whisper has become a great part of the *Quiet Man* legend. I have no doubt that as long as the film endures, so will the speculation.... That little piece of *The Quiet Man* belongs to just us....[5]

"You may search everywhere, but none can compare..."

While the trio of Ford, O'Hara, and Wayne made one more film together, 1957's *The Wings of Eagles*, and while O'Hara worked with Ford and then Wayne separately on other films, none of these efforts succeeded in anywhere the same ways that *Rio Grande* and *The Quiet Man* did. These certainly aren't Ford's most complex films, but they could be his most resoundingly romantic. For that, we have O'Hara to thank. She clearly brought out something in the crusty old director that made him want to click his heels and act like a young man again.

* * *

In addition to her work with Ford and Wayne, O'Hara continued to act steadily in film and make television appearances (as a singer as well as an actress) until the late 1960s. Some of her better known roles during this time were the female leads in 1959's *Our Man in Havana*, 1961's *The Parent Trap*, and 1962's *Mr. Hobbs Takes a Vacation*. Then, in 1968, after two unsuccessful marriages, she married Charles Blair, a former Air Force general and a pioneer in transatlantic aviation, and eased into retirement. In 1978, however, Blair was killed when the engine of a plane he was flying exploded, and O'Hara was asked to assume his role as CEO and president of Antilles Airboats, making her the first female president of a scheduled airline in the U.S.

Eventually selling the airline, she remained retired from acting until 1991, when, at 71, she returned to co-star with comedian John Candy in the bittersweet *Only the Lonely*, playing — once again — a headstrong mother. Writing about Candy years later, she remarked: "The depth of John Candy's talent did surprise me.... He reminded me a great deal of Charles Laughton."[6]

During the 1990s, O'Hara worked occasionally in television films before retiring from acting for good in 2000. During her career, she acted in more than 60 films.

In 2012, O'Hara appeared in the Irish-made documentary, *John Ford: Dreaming The Quiet Man*, and reminisced about the film and the experience of working with Ford. "I knew what great directors and great actors were like," O'Hara said. "But I have to honestly say he [Ford] was the best, really the best." Then she paused for just a beat and added with a little emotional emphasis, "The meanest." A moment later, she also noted: "Believe me, I would rather work with the — pardon me — the old bastard than not."[7]

11

Female Supremacy

Ava Gardner's Honey Bear and Grace Kelly's Linda in *Mogambo*

"It is a pity Ford did not direct 'sex goddesses' more often." — Tag Gallagher on *Mogambo*[1]

By nearly all accounts, no one involved with John Ford's *Mogambo* (1953) saw the film as deathless art. Conceived by MGM executives as a comeback vehicle for an aging Clark Gable (who hadn't made a good film in years), it's an unabashed remake of *Red Dust*, another Gable-centered love triangle made all the way back in 1932. Ford, who considered the project little more than journeyman work, signed on mainly because filming would take him to parts of Africa he had never seen. To top it all off, Ford, who'd argued fiercely for Maureen O'Hara to play one of the female leads, had to settle for Ava Gardner, an actress he didn't think was all that good.

Then, as often happened with projects Ford initially seemed to care little about, the film turned into something quite special.

The finished piece, while by no means perfect, has many impressive elements. One, for example, is the complete absence of non-diegetic music, something highly unusual for films at that time. For nearly two hours, all the music we hear, from the African tribal chanting to Gardner's rendition of "Comin' Through the Rye," emanates directly from the story and gives the film an unusually authentic sense of place. Another is the film's lush, sensuous look. Photographed mostly by Robert Surtees (and under Ford's watchful eye), the film is filled with bold, rich, strongly contrasting colors that suggest primal experience and emotions. Associated with this is the striking use of color in the costuming choices for the two female leads, Gardner and Grace Kelly. Depending on what Ford wants to convey and when, we see yellow to suggest withdrawal, tentativeness, and even cowardice; green for openness, honesty, and a desire to connect; red for aggression; and so on. It's an intriguing addition to the story, one that enhances and intensifies its already rich visual texture.

Among the film's many impressive elements, perhaps the most fascinating is the depth and complexity of the two main female characters — Gardner's Eloise "Honey Bear" Kelly and (not to be confused with this Kelly) Grace Kelly's Linda Nordley. Although Gable's Vic Marswell is the apex of *Mogambo's* love triangle, it is the two females, and the actresses playing them, who reign supreme. Under Ford's direction, Gardner, then far better known for her sex appeal than her acting ability, delivers probably the best performance of her career. In fact, on numerous occasions she steals the scene outright. Ford, who fought to get Grace Kelly for the film, also got a remarkable performance from her, one that helped to make her a major star/sex goddess in her own right. For their work in the film, both actresses also received well-deserved Academy Award nominations: Kelly's first and Gardner's one and only. In addition, Kelly received that year's Golden Globe Award in the best supporting actress category. As Ford scholar Tag Gallagher suggests in the quote that begins this chapter, the multifaceted Ford may have had a special talent directing certain kinds of actresses: a talent that, except for this film, remained largely untapped.

* * *

While both actresses were known for their physical beauty, the two could not have led more different lives.

Born in the farming community of Smithfield, North Carolina, in 1922, Gardner was the youngest of seven children in a family that constantly struggled to make ends meet. After losing their property, her father worked in a sawmill while her mother worked as a cook and a housekeeper in a dormitory for teachers. When Ava was 15, her father died of bronchitis, and her mother soldiered on, eventually running another boarding house for teachers. In the meantime, Ava graduated from high school and began to take secretarial classes at Atlantic Christian College in Wilson, North Carolina.

While Ava was visiting one of her sisters in New York in 1941, her sister's husband, a professional photographer, took her portrait and displayed it in the front window of his shop. Several people were impressed by it, and soon Ava — just 18 — had a screen test directed by Al Altman, the head of MGM's New York talent department. Although Altman was struck by Ava's beauty, he felt that the test had gone horribly. When he saw her on film in the screening room, however, he was completely won over: on camera, she was captivating. After Altman sent this test to Hollywood, Louis B. Mayer, the head of the studio, sent him back a telegram. "She can't sing, she can't act, she can't talk," it read. "She's terrific!" Ava was on her way.[2]

After signing a long-term contract with MGM (and taking voice lessons to reduce her hard-to-understand North Carolina drawl), she appeared, mostly as an un-credited extra, in numerous films throughout the early and mid–1940s. Then, in 1946, she was cast as the female lead opposite a charismatic newcomer named Burt Lancaster in Robert Siodmak's film noir classic, *The Killers*. The role of *femme fatale* Kitty Collins made her a star. Although she still did not impress audiences with her acting, her beauty more than compensated. In the next few years, she was cast frequently in big-budget MGM films from 1947's *The Hucksters* with Clark Gable to the 1951 film version of *Show Boat*.

During these early years, her personal life was often much discussed. When she made *Mogambo*, she had married and divorced both actor Mickey Rooney and bandleader Artie Shaw and

Grace Kelly's Linda Nordley (left) and Ava Gardner's Eloise "Honey Bear" Kelly compete for the same man, Clark Gable's Vic Marswell, in 1953's *Mogambo*. While Gable is officially the film's star, both Kelly and Gardner turn in exceptional performances, Gardner often stealing her scenes outright. *Mogambo* made Kelly a star and convinced Hollywood that Gardner was much more than just another sex goddess.

she was in the midst of a rocky marriage to Frank Sinatra. During the 1940s and 1950s, she also had an on-again, off-again relationship with recluse billionaire Howard Hughes. Among friends, she was also known for her edgy wit and salty language. "All I ever got out of my marriages," she once said, "was the two years Artie Shaw financed on an analyst's couch." And, commenting on her skill at using foul language, one Australian reporter said that her swearing was "like a sailor and a truck driver were having a competition."[3]

In stark contrast to Gardner's impoverished rural North Carolina upbringing, Grace Kelly was the daughter of well-to-do parents in Philadelphia. Her father, Jack Kelly, was an Olympic triple gold medal winner in rowing who went on to head one of the largest construction companies on the East Coast, run as the 1935 Democratic candidate for mayor of Philadelphia, and serve as Franklyn Roosevelt's National Director of Physical Fitness during World War II. And, before her marriage, her mother, Margaret, became the first woman to head the Physical Education Department at the University of Pennsylvania.

Drawn to acting from childhood, Kelly appeared frequently in school plays and was insistent on pursuing acting as a profession. This was not to her parents' liking, however, her father reportedly seeing an actress as "a slim cut above streetwalker."[4]

But Kelly persisted, eventually getting roles in stage plays and on television. In addition to several Broadway appearances in the late 1940s and early 1950s, she acted in more than 60 television shows. Her television work led to her being cast in a small role in a little-known 1951 Henry Hathaway film called *Fourteen Hours*. To Kelly's good fortune, one visitor on the set of that film was actor Gary Cooper, who was impressed with her work and instrumental in getting her cast in another small role opposite him as his bride in Fred Zinnemann's 1952 western *High Noon*.

Yet, while *High Noon* put Kelly on the map, it was, as writer Laura Jacobs notes, "more of a spotlight than a spark." The real spark, Jacobs continues, "was a little black-and-white screen test she shot for 20th Century–Fox in early 1950 for a movie called *Taxi*, the part of a poor Irish girl. Grace didn't get the role, but the test hung around."[5]

When Ford, always up for a good western, first saw Kelly in *High Noon*, he was unimpressed. "All she did," he said, "was shoot a guy in the back. Cooper should have given her a boot in the pants and sent her back east."[6]

When he saw the test for *Taxi* in 1952, however, he saw potential he hadn't noticed before in Kelly, famously telling MGM executive Dore Schary: "[T]his dame has breeding, quality, class. I want to make a test of her — in color. I bet she'll knock us on our asses."[7]

As usual, Ford's instincts were correct, and Kelly was cast as Linda in *Mogambo*.

When Three's a Crowd

Mogambo, which means "passion" in Swahili, is an unusual yet highly effective mix of adventure story, romance, and drawing room comedy. Its main character, Vic Marswell, is an American alpha-male who lives in the wilds of Africa leading safaris and capturing wild animals for zoos. Early in the story, he meets Eloise "Honey Bear" Kelly, a "playgirl" (as Vic calls her) who has come at the invitation of a rich maharishi friend. The maharishi in turn has skipped out and effectively left her stranded. She and Vic make the best of it, starting a brief affair. Kelly, or "Miss Kelly" as several of the other characters call her, quickly grows accustomed to the place and wouldn't mind staying. A week later, however, when the boat back to civilization arrives, Vic wants her on it. Before she leaves, she sees two new arrivals, a British anthropologist and his wife, Donald (Donald Sinden) and Linda Nordley, who have come to see and study gorillas. As fate would have it, the boat breaks down and Kelly returns, but by now Vic has moved on and toward the beautiful, well-bred, and responsive Linda. At first, Vic delegates the safari to gorilla country to one of his employees. Then, as a pretext to be with Linda, he agrees to lead the party himself. Along the way, Kelly will be dropped off at a local official's and, from there, procure passage home. So, off they all go, and in their travels they visit a kind priest named Father Josef (Denis O'Dea), are threatened by hostile natives (forcing Kelly to stay with the group), encounter the gorillas, and play out various personal dramas. In the end, Vic is willing to be "found out" as the unconscionable cad (thus preserving Linda's reputation), the Nordleys remain together, and Vic and Kelly decide to try it again.

While similar to the plot of *Red Dust*, two changes are especially significant in *Mogambo*. First, the setting is shifted from Indochina (Vietnam) to Africa, where the chattering of the wild animals is ever-present and often seems to be functioning as a counterpoint to the verbal sparring between the humans. And second, the occupation of the straying wife's husband is changed from an engineer to an anthropologist who wants to study gorillas — to "get inside their heads," as Donald says — in their natural habitat. Both these changes — along with the constant linkages between the characters and animals (e.g. "Honey Bear" and Kelly's term for Vic, "that two-legged boa constrictor") — suggest a strong interest in examining not merely these characters but also the basic nature of human beings. Perhaps these linkages are even inviting us to ask: What, if anything really significant, separates human beings from the rest of the animal kingdom? Are we simply creatures driven by biological instincts? Or do we have higher capacities? And, if so, what, ultimately, is their value?

As the case often is in Ford films, the questions, while intriguingly suggested, are never fully answered. In the end, the equally intriguing ambiguities remain.

Honey Bear

Of the story's main characters, the most sympathetically drawn is Eloise Kelly, or Honey Bear, as she enjoys calling herself. She's definitely had a hard time of it. When we first meet her, she learns that the maharishi has essentially abandoned her at Vic's outpost. Later on, we also learn that she was once briefly married to, and deeply in love with, a young flyer killed in the war and has spent the interim looking for love with men who aren't necessarily looking for love with her. As Brownie (Philip Stainton), Vic's wise and good employee, remarks, she has emotional "scars." At the outpost, she also shows many appealing qualities: personal charm, curiosity, wit, frankness, and warmth for the people there as well as a genuine feeling and affinity for the animals in Vic's cages. As Vic says, she's "all right." We readily agree.

While vulnerable and still nursing her scars, she is also open to taking risks, in this case exploring the possibilities with Vic.

"I'm searching," she tells him just before they begin their affair.

"I'll look with you," Vic replies, "for a while."

Yes, here we go again!

Kelly, however, is not just a naïve, kind-hearted victim. She has a fighting side too. The first hint we get of this is when she identifies herself as Honey Bear. It's an interesting nickname, mixing the sweetness of honey with the ferocious nature of a bear, and we see this instinctive ferocity rise up several times in the film.

One of the most subtle and fascinating instances of this occurs fairly early on. Linda has just arrived, and Kelly has just returned after the boat has broken down. Her instincts tell her that Vic ("that two-legged boa constrictor") will soon be turning his attentions toward Linda. She and Linda chat briefly. Linda, clueless about the dangers in the animal kingdom that exists just outside the compound, announces that she is taking a walk. Kelly, who by now certainly knows about those dangers, lets Linda go without any advice or warning. Then, in two very revealing shots, we see Kelly peering, eyes narrowed with perhaps the slightest hint of malice, through window blinds as the innocent Linda blithely strolls out into the wild.[8] Later, Vic scolds Kelly for not warning Linda, Linda is put in imminent peril, Vic saves her, and they realize their deep attraction to each other. The irony is that Kelly's little plot has backfired: by putting Linda into peril because she is jealous of a potential involvement with Vic, she has unwittingly put her into Vic's arms.

Another facet of Kelly's fighting side is her sharp tongue. Once she knows that something is percolating between Vic and Linda, she takes great delight in taunting them, especially in front of Linda's husband and others. At the Nordley's first dinner at Vic's outpost, for example, she's in fine form, joking that: "These animal catching characters [i.e., Vic] don't have very many nerves — just one big one."

In Kelly's defense, however, she has good reason to lash out at Vic. He has dismissed her as a playgirl without "an honest feeling from her neck to her kneecap," but he really isn't much more than the male equivalent of this himself. He's callously dumped Kelly, not because she is unfeeling, but because he believes she is just not good enough for him. He's also moved on to Linda, at least in part, because he perceives her as woman of breeding and refinement: a woman more worthy of him.

Of the characters in the film, Kelly is also the only one who experiences substantial personal growth. When we first meet her she is still the playgirl, content to quickly pick up with Vic. When he drops her, she becomes the embittered jilted woman, happily dispensing cutting one-liners about Vic's womanizing in general and Vic and Linda's hypocrisy in particular. Then, once they meet the priest, Father Josef, Kelly undergoes her most profound change. We don't know precisely why. Perhaps Vic and Linda's behavior reminds her too much of her own playgirl past, and she decides that it's finally time to change her ways. In any case, she spends a few extra moments in Father Josef's church praying. Later, she asks Father Josef to hear her confession, indicating that she has been a practicing Catholic at some point in her life. We don't know exactly what she confesses, but we can reasonably guess that she's confessing her indiscretions with Vic, the maharishi, and others. Kelly clearly wants a fresh start in life. Once she feels that she has been forgiven, she acts in a stronger, more mature, more compassionate manner. The jabbing one-liners stop. She reaches out to Linda, trying to get her to see how damaging her actions can potentially be for both her and Donald. She even seems to forgive Vic his trespasses, treating him more sympathetically, more like an old lover who has now become a fond friend.

Vic too has had to make a change of sorts. A man accustomed to getting his way in female and just about all other matters, he finally acknowledges that, as much as he might want Linda, she is ultimately far better off returning to "home and Devonshire" with Donald. As Kelly tells him, "You went noble."

Seeing Vic's change, Kelly improvises with Vic to engineer the break-up with Linda. He's made out to be a cad, Linda is appropriately horrified, and she and Donald can both save face and go on together. Now, the playgirl has come full circle, becoming the co-savior of the story's real playgirl, Linda.

Vic's "sacrifice" is also important beyond solving the immediate problem. It opens the door for a new kind of relationship with Kelly. The new Vic is presumably wiser, less selfish, kinder, and more responsible. He is now the kind of man that the new Kelly can consider accepting.

There are many sides to Kelly, and in the story she goes through a series of major personal shifts. It's not an easy role for an actress to play. Before *Mogambo*, Gardner had never taken on as complex or as completely human a character, but here she makes the most of a great opportunity. Freed from the constrictions of playing one- and two-dimensional vamps, she tackles this character squarely, taking us through every step of Kelly's personal journey with the clarity and authority of an accomplished actress. Just as Kelly reaches a new level personally, Gardner, in playing her, reached a new level professionally.

The Anthropologist's Wayward Wife

Much that has been written about Linda Nordley focuses on Grace Kelly's ability to show her character's lust for Gable's Vic beneath her ultra-civilized veneer. But Linda's entire character is far more fascinating. Like Gardner's Kelly, she too is searching. She is, however, not nearly as self-aware. Linda, we learn, has known Donald since she was five, has been married to him for seven years, and, by all outward appearances, seems to be the happy help-mate of the aspiring young anthropologist. Yet, she is clearly not entirely happy or fulfilled, and Vic, ever the predator, senses this right away and wastes no time pouncing.

Their big sequence together begins when Linda, without proper warning from Kelly, walks naively into the jungle. Her initial impressions are thrilling and wonderful: the beautiful sky, the birds in the trees. Within moments, however, she sees two large, fierce beasts fighting and is frightened. Then, the nightmare occurs: she falls into a trap set for a black leopard and is about to be attacked by that very leopard. Vic arrives just in time to kill the leopard and rescue her. Almost immediately, she is drawn to Vic who she now sees (the way Ford also photographs him) as bigger than life, super-human, the master of the wild, the man to whom she now owes her life. Her attraction is immense, and Vic's seeming power is her aphrodisiac. Vic immediately takes advantage of her vulnerability too. When he leaves her at her door at the outpost, he pulls off her scarf (leaving her head and neck exposed, naked) in an almost-violent manner. It feels too much like a symbolic rape to be anything but, and, with Gable involved, it's hard not to think of Rhett carrying Scarlett up the stairs in *Gone with the Wind*.

From that moment until the very end of *Mogambo*, Linda is Vic's woman. By the jungle's law, he has won her. It's interesting too how quickly both Linda and Vic discount poor Donald, who's bright and likable but definitely not the alpha type. For them, he's usually little more than the nice guy who's in the way. (In fact, the only two characters who consistently show concern for Donald are Kelly and Brownie.)

Why does Linda act this way? On one level, danger — the danger of the jungle, Vic, and their illicit love — might arouse her, might make her feel a kind of excitement she has never felt with Donald. Deeper down, there's a more fundamental issue: Linda really has no core, no strong sense of self. She lives almost exclusively through the man she is with. In many respects, she is also unformed, like a child. And she acts like a child often in the film: refusing even to acknowledge her feelings about Vic to Kelly, lying to Donald, and even shooting a gun at Vic when she thinks he has been using her.

In the end, Kelly and Vic have fixed it so Linda can go back to England with Donald, her reputation intact. But are her problems over? One suspects not. Like Kelly, Linda may be searching. Yet, she lacks Kelly's self-awareness, her capacity to be honest with herself and others, and — certainly at this point — her strong desire to make a serious personal change. Linda may be searching in the dark for a long time, and in the meantime there will probably be other Vics.

Linda is another difficult character to portray successfully. She's lovely, young, and vulnerable. But she's also quite dishonest (with herself as well as others), selfish, irresponsible, and thoughtless. It's hard to connect with her. Facing these challenges, Grace Kelly also makes the most of her opportunity. Her Linda is also well meaning, impressionable, and conflicted. Her adventure with Vic may be thrilling for her, but it is also frightening. She's aware that the results can be disastrous. She's clearly concerned. And Grace Kelly makes us care enough about Linda so that we feel concern for her too.

The Ceremony of Courage

Before venturing into gorilla country, Vic and his party need to procure men and canoes from local tribesmen. To seal the deal, Vic must undergo the tribe's "Ceremony of Courage," an ordeal in which he is required to act much like a knife thrower's assistant. Standing in front of a target-like backdrop, he remains still as a statue as ten tribesman throw spears all around him, sometimes very close. Needless to say, he passes the test.

In the larger story, both Kelly and Linda have their courage tested too. In several respects, we can see the entire story arc as their respective ceremonies of courage. Kelly of course passes, and Linda fails. Kelly faces her fears and other demons, accepts the consequences, and — with or without Vic — is ready to move to a new phase in her life at peace with herself and the world. Linda cannot do this. She can't own up to her part of her relationship with Vic, let alone confess her affair to Donald. In her mind, she is, and may forever be, the victim and Vic the villain. As the film ends, it seems unlikely that she will be facing her own fears and demons anytime soon. Throughout *Mogambo* our sympathies are usually with Kelly, but ultimately the character who fares far worse — the truly tragic character — is Linda.

Speaking of courage, director Ford should also be commended for taking a big chance with *Mogambo*. He was nearing 60 when he made this film, and it's clearly not a typical Ford outing. The project would probably have been a more natural fit for a director such as John Huston. Although Ford originally wanted Maureen O'Hara to play Honey Bear and his brother, Francis, to play the small part of the boat captain, he made the film with only one member of his beloved Stock Company, Denis O'Dea, who plays Father Josef. Africa, a long way and several climate zones removed from Monument Valley, was definitely unfamiliar territory. And, while he generally felt much more comfortable in his role as a man's director, he joined forces with two actresses he had never worked with before, attempting to bring to life a pair of very complex female characters.

Fortunately, the risk paid off. *Mogambo* was successful both with the critics at the time and at the box office. (Financially, it was Ford's most successful film, netting approximately $5 million at the box office.) Over time, it has also continued to intrigue audiences with its many assets, including its witty, engaging, well-paced story; bold and beautiful cinematography; and fine acting, especially by Ava Gardner and Grace Kelly.

Yes, it *is* a pity Ford didn't direct sex goddesses more often.

* * *

After *Mogambo* brought critical acclaim to both Gardner and Kelly, the two enjoyed stardom for several years and then their lives went in decidedly different directions.

Gardner remained a major star, acting in 23 more films until the early 1980s before turning mainly to television roles. Among her better known films are 1954's *The Barefoot Contessa*, 1959's *On the Beach*, 1962's *Seven Days in May*, 1964's *The Night of the Iguana*, and 1968's *Mayerling*. Many of her roles, notably her portrayal of the earthy Maxine Faulk in *The Night of the Iguana*, received critical praise and industry recognition.

While her personal life never reached the tabloid heights of Elizabeth Taylor's, Gardner's off-screen life continued to be reported in the news. After ending her turbulent marriage to Frank Sinatra in 1957, she became close friends with writer Ernest Hemingway. Among her lovers was the legendary Spanish bullfighter Miguel Dominguin.

A lifetime smoker, Gardner suffered from emphysema in later years and died of pneumonia at age 67 in early 1990. While there were many men in her life, she was buried beside her parents and siblings in a family plot in Smithfield, North Carolina.

Writing about her many years later, her friend and one-time co-star, actor Joseph Cotton, commented: "Ava, besides being beautiful and glamorous, was straightforward and definite.... The pattern of life seemed clear and sharp to her, which probably increased her heartache when she was unable to make it work.... She believed that mornings were made for sleeping, and the clause in her contract that allowed her not to be disturbed until noon was the envy of all actors. 'Acting is simply not a daytime job,' she once said. 'No wonder all actors hate matinees.'"[9]

After *Mogambo* literally catapulted Grace Kelly to stardom, she was the toast of Hollywood for the next few years. She won 1954's Best Actress Academy

Award for her portrayal of Georgie Elgin, the long-suffering wife in George Seaton's drama, *The Country Girl*, with Bing Crosby and William Holden. Soon afterward, she starred in three very successful films for Alfred Hitchcock: 1954's *Dial M for Murder* and *Rear Window* and 1955's *To Catch a Thief* with, respectively, Ray Milland, James Stewart, and Cary Grant. Her star couldn't have been brighter.

Then, as head of the U.S. delegation to the Cannes Film Festival in 1955, she met Prince Rainier III, the ruler of the principality of Monaco. The next year, Kelly quit the movies (after only 11 films) and married the prince in what many newspapers billed as "The Wedding of the Century." Over the next several years, the couple had three children, two daughters, princesses Caroline and Stephanie, and a son, Prince Albert.

Then, while driving with her younger daughter to Monaco from their country home one day in September 1982, Princess Grace suffered a stroke and the car drove off the road and crashed. She never recovered consciousness and died the next day. She was just 52. After Prince Rainier died in 2005, their son Albert became Monaco's ruler.

Though Gardner and Kelly's lives went in different directions soon after *Mogambo*, Kelly did remain close friends both with Gardner and Gardner's then-husband Frank Sinatra. Notes Kelly biographer James Spada: "Ava seemed an odd choice by Grace for a friend; their public images could not have been less alike. But Ava's personality appealed to the earthy, sexy, private Grace; she enjoyed Ava's ribald sense of humor, admired her open sexuality and frank, often profane, outspokenness — something Grace's sense of propriety did not allow her."[10]

To illustrate this dynamic, Spada then shared an intriguing story from the filming of *Mogambo* that came to him by way of Gore Vidal who in turn heard it from the film's producer, Sam Zimbalist: "The location was full of these tall Watusis, beautiful warriors, who had been hired as extras, wearing their breechclouts. The girls were walking along, and Ava said to Grace, 'I wonder if their cocks are as big as people say? Have you ever seen a black cock?' Grace turned purple, of course, and said, 'Stop that! Don't talk like that!' Ava said, 'That's funny ... neither have I'— and with that she reached over and pulled up the breechclout of one of the Watusis, who gave a big grin as this huge cock flopped out. By then Grace had turned absolutely blue. Ava let go of the breechclout, turned to Grace, and said, 'Frank's bigger than that.'"[11]

12

"Way out on a limb"

The Women Who Trigger Ethan's Quest in *The Searchers* and the Women Who Must Face Its Consequences

In an interview he once gave for the American Film Institute Archive, Steven Spielberg made a statement that clearly expressed his feelings about both Ford's work and one Ford film in particular. "I try to run a John Ford film — one or two — before I start any movie simply because he inspires me," Spielberg said. "I have to look at *The Searchers*— have to — almost every time."[1]

In the interview, Spielberg also mentioned several other Ford films he greatly admired. But he left no doubt that Ford's 1956 western about the obsessive quest of Ethan Edwards (John Wayne) to find and perhaps kill his kidnapped niece has, even among Ford's best work, a special place in his heart.

Today, Spielberg has plenty of company. In 2007, the American Film Institute (AFI) ranked *The Searchers* number 12 on its list of the *Greatest American Movies of All Time* and the following year named it number one among the *Greatest American Westerns of All Time*. In 2012, the British Film Institute's (BFI) *Sight & Sound* magazine published the results of a survey it conducts every ten years among film critics, scholars, and directors around the world, and *The Searchers* placed number seven on its list of the best 250 films ever made. This was also the fourth time in the BFI's last five once-a-decade surveys that *The Searchers* has been ranked in its top 20. Add to all these accolades, J. Hoberman writing for *The New York Times* in 2013, made the confident pronouncement: "There are a few Hollywood movies so thematically rich and so historically resonant they may be considered part of American literature. *The Searchers* is one."[2]

All this adulation did not come immediately. In fact, appraisals of the film have fluctuated greatly over the years. When *The Searchers* premiered in March of 1956, for example, it was greeted with mixed reviews. Writing for *The New York Times*, Bosley Crowther was mildly enthusiastic, calling it a "ripsnorting western" and crediting Frank Nugent's "pungent" screenplay and Ford's production team for giving the story its "gusto."[3] The Hollywood trade publication *Variety* was a bit harsher, however, calling it "somewhat disappointing" because of its length and repetitiveness. "The John Ford directorial stamp is unmistakable," *Variety* noted. "It concentrates on the characters and establishes a definite mood. It's not sufficient, however, to overcome many of the weaknesses of the story."[4] The film was a hit, making $4.8 million in the U.S. and finishing number 11 in U.S. box office receipts for 1956. But there was no rapturous praise, and the film wasn't a contender for any of the movie industry's numerous awards that year.

Then, with each passing year during the 1960s, a growing number of critics and filmmakers started to view *The Searchers* very differently. More people frequently used the word "masterpiece" to describe it, and it began to exert an enormous influence over some of the best and the brightest young film directors of the day. Beginning in the 1970s, audiences started to see this influence in such films as Martin Scorsese's *Taxi Driver* (1975) Paul Schrader's *Hard Core* (1979) George Lucas' *Star Wars* (1977), Spielberg's own *Close Encounters of the Third Kind* (1977), and many, many others.

Yet, while *The Searchers*' influence is undisputed, admiration for it remains far from universal. Two very articulate "contrarians," for example, have been filmmaker and Ford authority Lindsay Anderson and critic Roger Ebert, both of whom — while admiring the film's mastery of composition and other strengths — faulted it on several levels including its clumsy comic relief scenes, lack of narrative cohesion, and uneven acting. "There is a lot of John Ford in *The Searchers*, a lot of his splendid craft and his ambiguous, divided personality," wrote Anderson. "But the sense of harmony, of resolution, and of faith which gives his work at his best a special grace is not there."[5] Ebert has expressed particular concern about what he also sees as a lack of harmony and cohesion. "*The Searchers* indeed seems to be two films," he noted. "The Ethan Edwards story is stark and lonely, a story of obsession.... [Then] the film within this film involves a silly romantic subplot and characters hauled in for comic relief.... This second strand is without interest, and those who value *The Searchers* filter it out, patiently waiting for a return to the main story line."[6]

No doubt people will continue to differ and argue when they talk about this film. But, regardless of one's opinion of *The Searchers*, it is almost impossible to write about Ford without acknowledging the uniquely influential place of this film both among Ford's works and in the ongoing conversation about cinema. When the subject is Ford, *The Searchers* is the 800-pound gorilla in the room — something we can't ignore.

This fact of life presents an intriguing challenge in an examination of notable women's roles and portrayals in Ford's films, because *The Searchers*—mainly the story of Ethan, his rage and racism, and his relentless quest—contains only minor female roles. In fact, none comes even remotely close to having as much screen time as the story's main supporting character, Martin Pawley (Jeffrey Hunter). And several of these roles consist of only a handful of screen moments and only a few spoken words.

Even though their roles appear marginal, however, the key female characters in *The Searchers* are tied much more closely to the film's essential action than we might initially assume. Ethan's quest, after all, is rooted in, and at least partially driven by, his deep feelings for his sister-in-law Martha and others. In addition, several female characters must deal with the repercussions of this search, repercussions that profoundly affect their lives in various ways.

So, for us to fully appreciate Ethan's quest—both in terms of the reasons driving it and its impact on the entire community of characters in the story—these female characters are roles of substantial importance. Likewise, for the film to achieve its very ambitious aims, each of these roles, while small, needs to be very credible, convey something deeply affecting, and contribute something of real value to the story.

In a way, Ford was asking each of the actresses he tapped for these roles in *The Searchers* to pull a "Mildred Natwick" (see Chapter 8), or to create a well-defined, compelling, and memorable character in seconds. Yet, while most of the actresses he worked with here did not have Natwick's gifts, he—and the actresses—usually succeeded in doing what they needed to do. Together—making up a close-knit but highly contrasting tapestry of frontier women—these roles and actresses are among the film's clear strengths.

The actresses themselves were a very diverse lot. The ranged in age during filming from the 59-year-old Olive Carey who played Mrs. Jorgensen to the nine-year-old Lana Wood who played the younger Debbie. They varied greatly in celebrity too. The most famous among them was Lana's older sister, Natalie Wood, then on the cusp of major stardom, who played the teen-age Debbie. The most obscure was Beulah Archuletta, a Native American actress and screen extra, who played Wild Goose Flying in the Night Sky, or "Look." Among them, perhaps the two most talented were Natalie Wood and Vera Miles, who played Mrs. Jorgensen's daughter, Laurie. Certainly the best connected were Carey, a long-time friend of Ford, and Dorothy Jordan, who played Martha and who, in real life, was married to Ford's good friend and business partner, Merian C. Cooper.

Yet, even though they might be best characterized by their diversity, these actresses all had one experience in common: as Ford often did with his minor characters, he gave them all moments to shine.

"Ethan?"

The very first word spoken in *The Searchers*—the main character's name with a question mark—tips us off to what lies ahead. While this story is about many things, the main character's identity is foremost among them. Who is Ethan Edwards? What dark things has he done in the past? What drives him now? And what drives the search he will soon embark on?

We are told we are in Texas in 1868. We first see Ethan as he rides up to the small ranch house of his brother Aaron (Walter Coy), Aaron's wife Martha, and their three children. The American Civil War has been over for three years, but where has Ethan been during this time? We get hints that he may have been fighting in Mexico, may have been in prison, or may now be wanted for a crime. He also has freshly minted gold pieces. Where and how did he get them? We don't know anything for sure. And, even though a word is never spoken that suggests it, Ethan is also deeply in love with Martha, his brother's wife, and she is with him. We see their feelings expressed in numerous glances and other tender gestures from his kiss on her forehead when he first arrives to the way she holds his coat near to her body before she brings it to him the next morning. Although Martha and Aaron have two daughters, Lucy (Pippa Scott) and Debbie, Ethan seems to have a special interest in the younger, eight-year-old Debbie. When we do the math, we realize that Debbie was born just before Ethan left to fight in the Civil War. All this has led to much speculation that Debbie might be Martha's daughter not by Aaron but by Ethan. Beyond Ethan and Martha's strong feelings for each other, however, we don't know very much for sure. Anything is possible here.

Soon, the local contingent of Texas Rangers led by the Captain Reverend Samuel Johnson Clayton (Ward Bond) arrives and recruits Ethan and Martin Pawley to help investigate some cattle rustling by Indians. Sensing danger, Ethan advises Aaron to stay close to home. Forty miles away, Ethan figures out that the Indians are Comanche and that their interest is not rustling but killing—specifically, they're about to attack either the neighboring Jorgensen ranch or his brother's. As he rests and wipes down his horse for the journey back, we see immense worry and sadness on his face. This is serious.

At the Edwards ranch, the family is preparing for dinner as deep red from the nearby rock monuments turns deeper red in the waning light (and also foreshadows bloody events). Aaron and Martha sense that an attack is imminent. They quietly work to prepare, not wanting to alarm their children. As the others hunker down in the house, they tell little Debbie to go to a hiding place and stay there no matter what she hears. It is next to her grandmother's grave in a nearby family plot. As she huddles next to the headstone, an ominous shadow covers it. We see a Comanche chief in war paint (Henry Brandon's Scar). He looks curiously at the child. Then, without a second thought, he blows a horn to initiate the attack.

When Ethan and Martin return, the worst has happened. Aaron, Martha, and their son have been killed. Before she died, Martha was also raped. Lucy and little Debbie have also been kidnapped.

The small community of settlers gathers for a funeral, but Ethan is anxious to go after the attackers and the girls. He is joined by Clayton's small band of Texas Rangers. As they leave, we meet two new characters, Mrs. Jorgenson and her daughter Laurie. Mrs. Jorgensen, an intelligent, sensible woman Ethan respects, asks him not to waste the lives of the young men, particularly Martin and her son Brad (who is smitten with Lucy), in vengeance. Laurie, we learn, is in love with Martin.

After a falling out with Clayton and the rangers, Ethan, Martin, and Brad continue the search by themselves. Soon, it takes them to a narrow rock-lined passage, where Ethan, we eventually learn, finds and buries the raped and murdered Lucy. The news of this drives Brad into hysterics. He rides alone into a party of Comanche and is swiftly killed. That leaves Ethan and Martin, who grows increasingly worried that — as time passes and Debbie becomes a young woman and ultimately a Comanche's wife — Ethan will consider her defiled and attempt to kill her.

The years drone on and Ethan and Martin continue their search for Debbie, who, they learn, is probably with a group of Comanche led by a war chief named Scar. At one point, they return to the Jorgensen ranch, where Laurie, young and brimming with sexual energy, emphatically tells Martin that she's not going to wait forever for him. Martin loves her too, but, if Ethan really does find Debbie and attempts to kill her, he must be there to stop him. So, much to Laurie's chagrin, Martin leaves to continue the search with Ethan.

Now another woman enters the picture. To learn information, Ethan and Martin begin trading with various native tribes. Through a misunderstanding, Martin finds that, instead of goods, he has unwittingly traded for a squaw. Her name is Wild Goose Flying in the Night Sky. Awkwardly, Martin keeps beginning statements about how this will not work out with the word "Look...." She indicates that she will be happy to answer to "Look." Later, when Look learns that the two men are pursuing Scar, she is frightened and leaves. Afterward, Ethan and Martin find her dead, killed ironically by the cavalry in an attack on a Comanche village.

Eventually, Ethan and Martin, again posing as traders, meet Scar and see Debbie, now one of Scar's wives. Alone, Debbie goes to their camp to warn them about Scar and plead with them to leave. Ethan draws a gun on her, horrifying Debbie, but a pursuing Comanche shoots an arrow into Ethan, wounding him. He and Martin must leave.

They return again to the Jorgensen ranch, this time to learn that Laurie is about to marry an oafish neighbor named Charlie McCorry (Ken Curtis). Tempers flare, punches are thrown, the wedding is called off, and news comes that Scar and probably Debbie are camped nearby.

With the assistance of the Texas Rangers and the cavalry, they storm the camp, Martin kills Scar, and Ethan chases Debbie down. But, instead of killing her, as Martin and others have feared, he raises her small, frightened body up in the air, and gently says, "Let's go home, Debbie."

The film ends, as it begins, at a doorway. Ethan and Martin have brought Debbie back to the Jorgensen ranch. The Jorgensens will take care of her now. And Martin and Laurie can finally be together. Everyone enters the ranch house except Ethan, who stands alone at the entrance and then walks away, forever the outsider, forever the loner. His work is done, and, in a changing world, he will be increasingly irrelevant. But, in his years of obsessive searching, he has found both Debbie and his own humanity.

* * *

While the main focus of *The Searchers* is Ethan and his quest, the film also tells the story of an entire community's search for a better, more civilized, more humane way of life. In fact, everyone in the film, the nomadic Native Americans as well as the settled white ranchers, is — either through violent or peaceful means — trying to find solutions. Change will come to this harsh, violent land, but it won't come quickly or easily. In the meantime, everyone — white settler or Native American, man or woman, adult or child — must cope with the present realities. Both as victims of the shared racial hatred and violence that triggers Ethan's search and as people who must face serious consequences because of it, the female characters within this world are all very much part of this equation.

The Women Who Trigger the Search

The first of the key female characters we meet is also the first person we see, Dorothy Jordan's Martha. Next to the towering John Wayne's Ethan, she is slight in stature. In fact, he has to bend mightily just to kiss her on the forehead. But, Martha's feeling toward Ethan is anything but slight. She is deeply in love with him, and, even though they have not seen each other in at least seven years, we feel that they haven't missed a beat. She is also married to Ethan's brother, however, and has borne his children. Was she unfaithful to her husband with Ethan? Is Debbie really Ethan's daughter? We never know for sure. We only know that she and Ethan share something profound and forbidden — certainly something strong enough to be the primary motivation for Ethan's quest.

Martha's role is brief, but it has several very moving moments. One is the scene when she picks up Ethan's coat, holds it against her body, strokes it tenderly, and then walks into another room to give it to him. While beautifully understated, the intensity of her deep feeling (and desire) is very clear. Another is when she sends Debbie to her grandmother's grave to hide from the Comanche attackers. She is trying to remain composed, but her fear, grief, and recognition of impending tragedy are striking when she lunges through the window as if trying to hug her daughter just one last time.

When she played Martha, Dorothy Jordan was in the midst of a brief comeback in films. Born in 1906, she began acting in early talkies in 1929, and — after playing roles in 24 films including 1930's *Min and Bill* with Wallace Beery and 1932's *The Cabin in the Cotton* with Bette Davis — she retired in 1933 to marry producer-director Merian C. Cooper, who was fresh from his resounding success with *King Kong*. In 1937, Jordan came out of retirement briefly to test for the part of Melanie Hamilton in *Gone with the Wind*, a role that eventually went to Olivia de Havilland. Then, in the 1950s, after Cooper and Ford had formed an independent production company together, she acted in three Ford films. In addition to *The Searchers*, these included 1953's *The Sun Shines Bright* and 1957's *The Wings of Eagles*. Jordan died in 1988 at age 82.

* * *

Another of the prime movers behind Ethan's quest is Debbie, who (here at age eight) is played by Lana Wood. Again, this is a small role with some very poignant moments. Soon after Ethan arrives, for example, Debbie asks him for a necklace just like the one he gave her older sister, Lucy. Ethan gives her a military medallion, and, not knowing the difference, little Debbie is thrilled. Then, in a completely different situation the next evening — again not quite understanding — she dutifully obeys her parents and hides by her grandmother's headstone. For security, she asks for her doll. And, knowing she must not be noticed, she calls her dog off. Then, at the headstone, she notices Scar standing over her.

In her first film role, young Lana Wood handles her small role well. Supported by Ford's direction, she never resorts to the sentimentality or overwrought fear that child actors are often prone to in the kinds of scenes she was asked to play here. She ably portrays the person she is supposed to portray, a nice young girl in a scary situation she doesn't quite understand.

Wood never reached the level of stardom that her older sister, Natalie, did. Born in 1946, Wood's role in *The Searchers* (and her connection with Natalie) led to numerous child roles in films and television shows. Then, in 1971, she played the role for which she is probably best known, the "Bond girl" Plenty O'Toole in *Diamonds Are Forever*, Sean Connery's last James Bond film (at least

In 1956's *The Searchers*, John Wayne's Ethan Edwards returns to his brother's Texas ranch after an absence of several years. Shown here (left to right) are his brother Aaron (Walter Coy with back to camera), Aaron's son Ben (Robert Lyden), Aaron's daughter Debbie (Lana Wood), Ethan, and Aaron's wife Martha (Dorothy Jordan). Neither Wood nor Jordan had many lines, but both made the most of their roles. Martha's unstated but powerful love for Ethan is beautifully rendered.

for a while). After a 23-year retirement, Wood returned to films in 2008, making several straight-to-DVD releases. In all, she has made appearances in more than 20 films and 300 television programs. She has also worked on two biographies about her sister.

* * *

A third woman whose experience must have shaped Ethan's attitudes and his desire for vengeance never actually appears in the story.

When little Debbie goes to hide by her grandmother's headstone, we see (for just a split-second) the grandmother's name, the circumstances of her death, her dates, and a few additional words. "HERE LIES MARY JANE EDWARDS," the top half of the stone reads, "KILLED BY COMANCHES."

After this moment, there is never another mention of the woman who was Ethan's mother or how she died, but the split-second shot tells us a great deal. Not only have the Comanches killed the woman he loved and kidnapped the

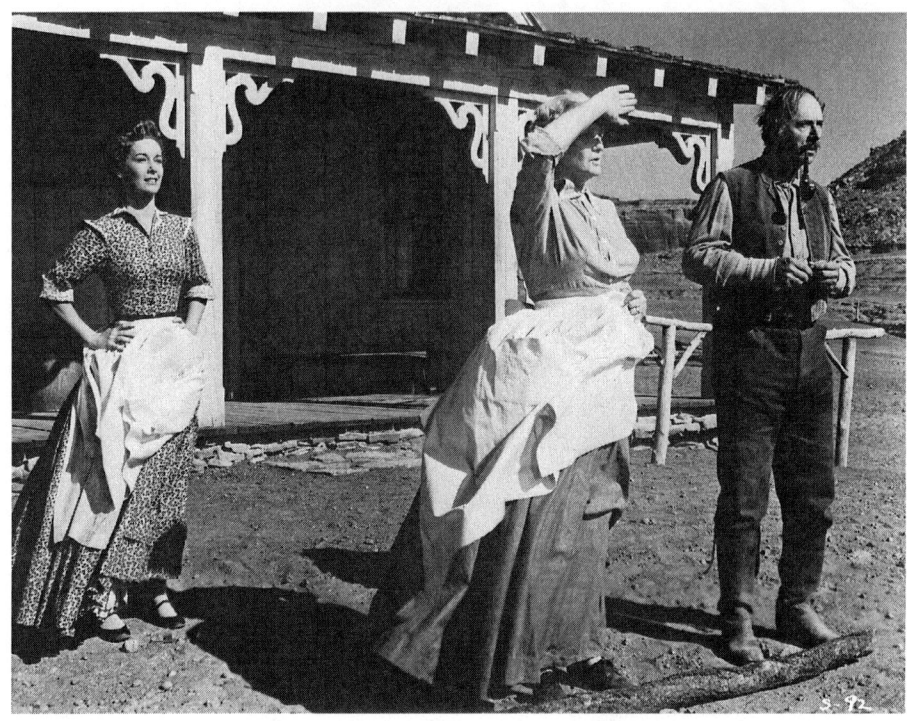

The Jorgensens, the other principal family in *The Searchers*, spot the returning Ethan (John Wayne) and Martin Pawley (Jeffrey Hunter). They are (left to right) Laurie (Vera Miles) Mrs. Jorgensen (Olive Carey) and Lars (John Qualen). Both Miles and Carey have standout moments in small but critical roles in this film.

girl who may be his daughter, but they have also killed his mother. Many seeds for his racist-fueled vengeance have been planted.

* * *

Initially, of course, the search is for both Debbie and her older sister, Lucy. Yet, while it's only suggested, we get the sense that Ethan has a much stronger connection to, and affection for, Debbie. For him, Lucy often seems to be an afterthought. If we accept this view, the suggestion that Debbie might indeed be Ethan's daughter becomes all the more credible.

The Women Who Bear the Consequences

In addition to the women who help set Ethan's search into motion, several other women are deeply affected by it. We meet two of them at the end of the funeral for Martha, Aaron, and their son, Ben.

The first is Mrs. Jorgensen, whose mature presence and gentle authority will be felt throughout the story. She is in the tradition of Ford's strong, stoic mothers dating back to his silent films, and we certainly see parts of her in Jane Darwell's Ma Joad in *The Grapes of Wrath* and Irene Rich's Mary O'Rourke in *Fort Apache*.

What's especially intriguing about Mrs. Jorgensen is her special understanding of her time and place: she seems to see many of the story's key issues more clearly than any of the other characters. After the funeral, as Ethan and others mount their horses to begin the search for Debbie and Lucy, for example, she approaches Ethan by herself and pleads, "Ethan, those girls mean as much to me as though they were my own.... Martha would want you to take care of her boys as well as her girls, and, if the girls are dead, don't let the boys waste their lives in vengeance." Then, with an added urgency because she fears she isn't getting through to him, she adds, "Promise me, Ethan."

Eventually, her worst fears are realized when Ethan's search leads to the death of her son, Brad.

On his first visit back, Ethan manages to express his remorse. "I got your boy killed," he says, feeling both responsibility and guilt.

Mrs. Jorgensen simply says: "Don't go blamin' yourself for that."

She has as much a right to feel vengeful as Ethan does, but that's not what she's about. In fact, when her husband, Lars, foolishly says that it's the land that killed their son, she responds with one of the more memorable short speeches (and Carey's moment to shine) in the film. "It just so happens we be Texicans," she says. "And a Texican is nothin' but a human man way out on a limb this year and next and maybe for a hundred more. But I don't think it'll be forever. Someday this country's going to be a fine, good place to be. Maybe it needs our bones in the ground before that time can come."

We've already seen that Mrs. Jorgensen is a good, caring, and practical woman. Here we see that she's also wise, far-sighted, and absolutely devoid of bitterness. As this society of settlers evolves, she will clearly be one of its unofficial leaders, a person with the vision and presence of mind to point people in the right direction.

Born in 1896, Olive Carey had been a friend of Ford's since he first came to Hollywood in the 1910s. The wife of silent film star and one of Ford's first leading men, Harry Carey, Sr., she was also the mother of another actor who regularly appeared in Ford films in later years, Harry Carey, Jr. After acting regularly in silent films for several years beginning in 1913, she appeared occasionally in sound films and on television shows (often westerns) up through the 1960s. Some other notable film appearances include Nicholas Ray's 1952 film noir *On Dangerous Ground*, John Sturges's 1957 *Gunfight at the OK Corral*, and Ford's 1961 *Two Rode Together*. Carey lived a long life, passing away at age 92 in 1988, and during her later years — because of her nearly 60-year association with Ford — she generously helped several Ford scholars on their biographies and other writings.

* * *

The other woman we first see in the funeral scene is Laurie, the Jorgensens' daughter. Several times here she is paired visually with Martin. We notice a mutual attraction, and we suspect that Laurie is not at all happy about Martin joining Ethan and the others on this search. Unlike her mother, her interest is less selfless — she wants Martin for herself.

As the story progresses, we see how the search affects — or perhaps more accurately, gnaws at — her. She's a young, vibrant, pretty, and passionate woman who's clearly — as she openly states — "not cut out to be an old maid." Every time she sees Martin, she's both brimming with sexual energy and frustrated by Martin's insistence on staying with Ethan to prevent him from killing Debbie. After years of waiting, she agrees to marry the oafish Charlie McCorry. But, when Ethan and Martin return immediately before the ceremony and news arrives that Scar (and probably Debbie) are camped nearby, the wedding is called off. Martin must again leave almost as soon as he arrives. Before he does, though, Laurie, young and virginal in her white wedding dress, makes one of the most startling admissions in the film, telling Martin that she wholeheartedly supports Ethan's desire to kill Debbie — to "put a bullet in her brain."

It's a shocking moment, and we feel the tremors on a couple of levels. First, Laurie's words reinforce how racism isn't just confined to Ethan but also how it infects everyone in this society of settlers, including this otherwise kind and caring young woman. Second, it's an expression of Laurie's own intense frustration with Martin, which includes, we presume, a good measure of sexual angst. She's had her eye on Martin since they were children. At this point she's waited years for Martin while he's searched for Debbie. She knows Martin loves her too. More than anything — even Debbie's well being — she wants the search to end and Martin to return to her. But she is repeatedly stifled, and her anger (and perhaps jealousy toward Debbie) manifests itself in this very disturbing way.

The moment also turns Laurie into *The Searchers'* most complex female character. For most of the film she appears to be little more than the ingénue, the long-suffering love interest, but when we see this side of her, our whole perception of her changes. Like Ethan, she hates the Comanche for taking away her true love. And, like Ethan, she is capable of dark, horrible thoughts. When Ethan and Martin finally return with Debbie at the end of the film, it's curious to wonder how Laurie will feel. Now that she finally can be with Martin, will she also move beyond her racism? Or will it always be a part of her?

Long-time Hollywood extra and bit player Beulah Archuletta, flanked here by John Wayne's Ethan (left) and Jeffrey Hunter's Martin, brought both humor and poignancy to her role of "Look" in *The Searchers*.

Miles, who's excellent here but even better six years later in Ford's last great western, *The Man Who Shot Liberty Valance*, makes this fairly small but important role truly memorable. This drama involving Debbie is deeply affecting Laurie's life, and she doesn't like it one bit. Something has to erupt, and it does.

(We'll discuss Miles' life and career in Chapter 13, which focuses on her portrayal of Hallie in *The Man Who Shot Liberty Valance*.)

* * *

Another woman deeply affected by the search is not one of the white settlers but a Comanche woman named Wild Goose Flying in the Night Sky and simply called "Look." Played by Native American actress Beulah Archuletta and inserted into the film largely for comic relief, Look is a "bartered bride," traded to an unwitting Martin to be his wife. But she also serves more than a purely comic function. There's a genuine sweetness and goodness to her; she wants to be a good dutiful wife and hopes that Martin will eventually accept her. It's also quite disturbing how she is treated: first, by Martin who at one point doesn't want her to sleep beside him and kicks her down a hill, and second, when soldiers kill her in an attack on a village. "She never done nobody any harm," Martin says with great sadness when he learns this. From the cavalry's point of view, she is just another savage Comanche. Yet, from Martin's point of view — and ours — she is another good, innocent person who becomes collateral damage, a victim in this ongoing, racially motivated conflict. He even theorizes that, good-hearted as she is, she may have gone to this village in an effort to find Debbie for him. While we can sympathize with Scar's personal losses (two of his sons have died in the ongoing hostilities) up to a point, Look is the film's only sympathetically portrayed Comanche. Her story, while brief and marred by some silliness, gives the film additional — and much needed — texture and dimension.

Little is known about Archuletta, who is probably best remembered for this role. She was born in Arkansas in 1912, grew up in New Mexico, and from the 1940s to the 1960s worked mostly as an un-credited extra in films, mostly westerns. Among her better known films are John Huston's 1948 *Key Largo*, Howard Hawks' 1952 *The Big Sky*, and 1963's *How the West Was Won*, co-directed by Ford, Henry Hathaway, and George Marshall. Archuletta died in Los Angeles in 1969 at age 57.

* * *

The final female to experience the consequences of Ethan's search is also one of the females who helped to set it in motion: Debbie.

When Ethan finally finds Debbie, it is years later and Lana Wood's older and more famous sister, Natalie, has stepped into the part. At this point, we learn for sure that Debbie is alive and one of Scar's wives. We also know that she still remembers Ethan and Martin, and, for their safety, wants them to leave. She is, however, also surprised and horrified to find out that, because she is now Scar's wife, her Uncle Ethan is ready, willing, and maybe even eager to kill her.

For many fans of *The Searchers*, the moment near the end of the story when Ethan chases after Debbie, catches her, and — instead of killing her — holds her trembling body in the air and says, "Let's go home, Debbie" is one of the most remarkable in the film. Here, the man obsessed with killing Debbie, embraces her, and, rather than ending her life, chooses to give Debbie a new life with the Jorgensens. In the process, he also brings back to life his own long-dead humanity.

Even though the role of the older Debbie is (once again) quite small, Ford sought a star of Wood's stature and charismatic screen presence for the part because of its great importance to the story. It's clear, too, that this casting decision paid off in a big way. When we first see Wood as Debbie in Scar's teepee, she pops off the screen. Along with Ethan and Martin, we receive a major jolt and find it hard to contain ourselves. It is a major moment.

Natalie Wood had been working in Hollywood for more than a decade before she appeared in *The Searchers*. A child star in the 1940s, she played, among many other roles, Maureen O'Hara's daughter in the perennial holiday favorite, 1947's *Miracle on 34th Street*. By 1955 — when she co-starred with James Dean in Nicholas Ray's landmark film of teen alienation and angst, *Rebel Without a Cause*— she was transitioning very easily into young adult roles. After *The Searchers*, she became one of the leading Hollywood stars of the 1960s, appearing in a string of highly successful films such as *Splendor in the Grass*, *West Side Story*, *Gypsy*, *Love with the Proper Stranger*, *Sex and the Single Girl*, *Inside Daisy Clover*, and *Bob & Carol & Ted & Alice*. In the 1970s, she took time off to raise her children while also starring in several television projects. For her work, she was nominated for three Academy Awards and received a Golden Globe Award. Married three times — first to actor Robert Wagner, then to British producer Richard Gregson, then to Wagner again — Wood drowned in 1981 while cruising with Wagner and two others on a weekend boating trip to Santa Catalina Island near Los Angeles. She was 43.

As the older Debbie in *The Searchers*, Natalie Wood — then 17 and on the verge of major stardom — gave her small role the kind of screen charisma it required.

Making *The Searchers* What It Is

As even many of its detractors will concede, *The Searchers* is filled with some of the most affecting and disquieting moments ever put onto film. And, for a story in which women play only brief roles, it's fascinating how many of these moments belong to the female characters — and the actresses who played them. What person who has ever looked at this film closely can ever forget the scenes when Martha walks through her doorway, stares at the distant lone rider approaching her home, holds her hand up to shade her eyes — all to the melody of the moody, lovely Civil War love song "Lorena"; when Martha lovingly holds Ethan's coat against her body and strokes it before giving it to him; when Martha and young Debbie walk into the frame and stand as they watch Ethan leave that morning; when Martha lunges toward Debbie in a last, desperate attempt to hug her; when Scar's dark shadow covers young Debbie's face at her grandmother's headstone and Debbie looks up helplessly; when Mrs. Jorgensen transcends the bitterness of her son's death and foresees a better world in "maybe" a hundred years; when a frustrated, angry Laurie tells Martin she hopes Ethan can find Debbie again and "put a bullet in her brain;" when Debbie, now Ethan's captive, fears for her life and then sees his startling change of heart; or when Mrs. Jorgensen brings her apron up to her face to cover her tears as she watches Ethan bring Debbie to her home?

For many people who love the cinema, these moments will live forever. While brief, they are by no means marginal. They are critical to giving the story its great complexity, depth, and resonance. They are instrumental to making *The Searchers* what it is. And they are all almost entirely dependent on credible, well-defined female characters as well as the actresses who skillfully portrayed them.

13

Reconnection and Regret
Vera Miles' Hallie in *The Man Who Shot Liberty Valance*

As one of John Ford's best known and most highly regarded films, *The Man Who Shot Liberty Valance* has received an enormous amount of critical attention since its initial release in 1962. Not only has it been the subject of countless essays, articles, and blogs, but many of the best-known Ford authorities have also written about it at great length. In his in-depth examination, 1986's *John Ford: The Man and His Films*, for example, film scholar Tag Gallagher devotes 30 pages to the film, 15 more than he gives to *The Searchers* and 24 more than he allots to *The Grapes of Wrath*.[1] And in his 2010 book, *Hollywood Westerns and the American Myth: The Importance of Howard Hawks and John Ford for Political Philosophy*, University of Chicago professor Robert Pippin spends nearly 50 pages discussing it.[2] Over the years, the film has certainly provided plenty of grist for the critical mill. Everyone, it seems, with anything to say about Ford or westerns, has something—and often quite a bit—to say about it.

Aside from passing references and a paragraph or two here or there, however, relatively little attention has been paid to one of the film's most essential and captivating components, the character of Hallie and Vera Miles' portrayal of her. This is quite perplexing. First, even though Hallie's character is a supporting role, she is far more complex than most leading roles in films. She is, for example, so capable, strong, vibrant, imaginative, and hopeful while also being, at different times, so haunted and tragic. Second, she is portrayed with such intelligence, sensitivity, and delicacy. Ford biographer Joseph McBride has called Miles' effort "one of the richest female performances in Ford's work."[3] When ranked against the hundreds of performances by dozens of accomplished actresses in Ford films spanning nearly half a century, that's quite a compliment.

And it's absolutely deserved.

* * *

Born Vera June Ralston in Boise City, Oklahoma, in 1930, Miles grew up in Pratt and Wichita, Kansas, where she worked nights as a Western Union operator and typist and, in 1947, graduated from Wichita High School. She then competed in numerous beauty contests including Miss Wichita, Miss Texas Grapefruit, and Miss New Maid Margarine. Soon, she made it to the big-time beauty pageant circuit, being crowned Miss Kansas in 1948 and then named the third runner up in that year's Miss America pageant.

In 1950, she moved to Los Angeles and landed several small roles in television and low-budget films, signing with various studios but never staying long term. As she reportedly remarked, "I was dropped by the best studios in town."[4]

By 1955, her most notable achievement to date was probably Tarzan's love interest in a film called *Tarzan's Hidden Jungle*. Yet, that year her fortunes changed dramatically when Ford cast her as Laurie Jorgensen, a key female role in *The Searchers*. Based on her work both in *The Searchers* and in another film she did that year, Henry Hathaway's mystery-thriller *23 Paces to Baker Street*, she caught the eye of Alfred Hitchcock, who signed her to a five-year contract.

Hitchcock was quite excited by his new find, seeing in her the potential to be the next Grace Kelly, who was retiring from acting to marry Prince Rainier III of Monaco. After working with her in an episode of his television anthology show, *Alfred Hitchcock Presents*, he cast her opposite Henry Fonda in his magnificent and greatly under-appreciated 1956 film, *The Wrong Man*. Her performance, as the loyal but emotionally fragile and increasingly depressed wife of the wrongly accused Henry Fonda, was widely praised, and Hitchcock immediately tapped her for the female lead in his upcoming psychological thriller, *Vertigo*. Then, much to Hitchcock's dismay, Miles announced that she was pregnant and wouldn't be available for the film, and the role eventually went to Kim Novak. Although Hitchcock later cast Miles in the important role of Marion Crane's (Janet Leigh) sister, Lila, in 1960's *Psycho*, he never quite forgave her for bowing out on *Vertigo*.

Ford, however, returned to Miles without hesitation six years after they had worked on *The Searchers* together to play the critical role of Hallie in *The Man Who Shot Liberty Valance*.

Remembrance of Things — and Choices — Past

As *The Man Who Shot Liberty Valance* opens, it is about 1910.

A living American legend, Senator Ransom Stoddard (James Stewart), and his wife Hallie arrive in the Western town of Shinbone. They are returning to pay their respects to Tom Doniphon (John Wayne), an old friend who has just died. Soon, Maxwell Scott (Carleton Young), an ambitious newspaper editor, pressures Stoddard into telling his story. Who was this Tom Doniphon? Why is his death important enough to warrant a visit from a national leader of such stature?

Stoddard, as if releasing himself from a great burden, begins to talk, and the film fades to flashback.

Decades before, when Stoddard first arrives in Shinbone as a young lawyer fresh from the East, the notorious Liberty Valance (Lee Marvin) robs the stage he is riding on, brutally beats him, and leaves him for dead. Tom finds him and takes him to his girlfriend, Hallie, to be nursed.

Soon, young Ranse becomes active in Shinbone, working first in a restaurant and then for a crusading newspaper editor, Dutton Peabody (Edmond O'Brien), starting a law practice, and even teaching school. Yet, the menacing, chaotic presence of Valance looms. The local law officer, Link Appleyard (Andy Devine), is — according to Ranse's account — a cowardly, doddering fool who is of no help. The only person who is not afraid of Valance is Tom, but he has plans of his own to work his ranch and to marry Hallie. He's content to stay out of the way — that is, unless Valance threatens him personally.

In 1962's *The Man Who Shot Liberty Valance*, Vera Miles gave a striking performance as Hallie, the young woman torn between two men and the destinies that go with them, and as Hallie, the older woman who must live with her sadness and regret. Shown here with co-star James Stewart as Ransom Stoddard, Miles is memorable in numerous scenes. As the older Hallie especially, she is excellent at conveying her character's strong and complicated emotions.

Then destiny intervenes. Angered by Valance, a totally outmatched Ranse faces the outlaw in a showdown in the street at night. The shots are fired, and, amazingly, Valance is the one who falls. Ranse is immediately christened "the man who shot Liberty Valance," is hailed as a hero, leads the successful campaign for statehood, and becomes a successful politician and eventually a major figure in American politics. Hallie, as we know from the first moments of the story, has gone with him and long been Mrs. Stoddard. Unknown at first to Ranse and

Hallie, however, he had help. Along with his hired hand, Pompey (Woody Strode), Tom was waiting in an alley with a Winchester. It was his bullet, fired simultaneously, that killed Valance, and, because his act wasn't self-defense, no one must know. So, Ranse and Hallie go off together, both living with the unsettling reality that the act that built Ranse' reputation, his shooting of Valance, is a lie. Saddened by the loss of Hallie, Tom withdraws to lead what apparently is a lonely, empty life.

We return to 1910. Now that Tom is dead, Ranse — even though it may cost him dearly — finally reveals the truth. When he does, however, it's not what his listeners want to hear. In one of Ford's most famous moments, newspaperman Scott refuses to print the truth because it would be too devastating to the people who've believed in Stoddard all these years. "This is the West, sir," he says. "When the legend becomes fact, print the legend."

The Man Who Shot Liberty Valance has many themes. On one hand, it is about the trade-offs that must take place as a more primitive society transitions to a more developed, more "civilized" one. What is gained, and what is lost? Yes, these people have statehood, a railroad, better schools, and paved streets. But, to get these things, have they given up something basic and true and good about themselves: something Tom so roughly and eloquently represented? On another hand, the film is about the bad things we sometimes do in the name of good. Was it right to suppress the lie for all those years when this decision probably led to a greater good than would have otherwise occurred? Was it right to "print the legend" after the lie was finally revealed? How essential to any society are its founding myths and heroes? The issues the film brings up, and the questions they provoke, are numerous.

Of special note too is the film's ambiguity: it's drenched in it. The big questions the film asks are never neatly answered. If anything, these questions simply lead to more curiosity and more questions: Is the press an extension of our right of free speech or a mechanism to manipulate public perception? Is public education a way to nourish and enrich people's minds or to control and direct those minds? Is the sedate and utterly bland Shinbone we encounter in 1910 really a major improvement over the raucous, vibrant place we see decades earlier? So much is open-ended, up in the air, unresolved. All these ambiguities inspire more speculation and are a major reason why the film continues to captivate.

The Two Hallies

At the heart of *The Man Who Shot Liberty Valance* — and at the center of this swirling vortex of questions — is a love story. And at the heart of this is

Hallie: a woman who must ultimately choose between two very different kinds of men and the destinies that go with them.

Throughout the film, Hallie resonates deeply with us. One reason why is the story's flashback structure. After the film's first 20 minutes, we are acutely aware of two Hallies, the spirited young woman in the extended flashback and the haunted white-haired woman she is decades later. For much of the film, we also can't help but wonder exactly how one becomes the other.

The young Hallie is of course the bright, pretty, ambitious, and illiterate waitress torn between two men and what they offer. It is clear that she loves and desires Tom. We see this in the scene when she stands in long shot at the back door of Peter's Place, watches Tom walk away, and clutches her apron in a gesture of longing for him. At the same time, she is also increasingly attracted to Stoddard and what he represents: civilization, education, progress, and all the presumed benefits that come with such things. Yet, in contrast to her relationship with Tom, sex doesn't seem to be a big part of the attraction here. Her instincts toward Ranse are far more maternal. He is less wild and less threatening to her, and almost immediately she finds great personal satisfaction in being Ranse's comforter and in many ways his protector. (She's the one who actually saves Ranse's life when he goes after Valance by telling Pompey to find Tom.) Throughout the film we know which man Hallie eventually chooses. But do we really know why? Does she simply outgrow Tom, seeing Ranse as a man more compatible with her own ambitions? Does she fear Tom's sexuality? Does she prefer to play the comforter/protector role, a part she can only play with Ranse? Or, by bowing out, does Tom simply make the decision for her?

The older Hallie is even more intriguing. In many respects, she has had the best life a once-illiterate waitress from nowhere could hope for. Her husband is now an American political icon, and she is his utterly dignified, almost regal wife. But she's also a very sad person. She's not merely grieving for Tom. She's also weighted down with guilt and regrets. How responsible does she feel for Tom's wasted life? How much does she regret choosing Ranse over Tom (a prominent life over a passionate one)? And how difficult is it for her both to live with her husband's lie and to know that her high station in the world is also a direct result of this lie? What are her distant eyes — eyes that seem so fixed on the past and lost possibilities — telling us?

Two scenes involving the older Hallie, one near the beginning and one at the end of the film, stand out for their poignant elegiac poetry.

The first is when Hallie and Link Appleyard ride out to Tom's ranch and Link cuts a cactus rose for Hallie. The music is Alfred Newman's "Ann Rutledge" theme reprised from Ford's 1939 film, *Young Mr. Lincoln*, a piece about lost, never-to-be-recovered love. The bittersweet feelings flow freely. Striking too is how Link (clearly a key "link" between the present and the past in the story) is so thoughtful, sensitive, and insightful — quite different from the buffoon Ranse characterizes him as in the flashback. Link knows it all too: how much Hallie and Tom loved each other, how empty Tom's life was afterward, perhaps even how they all lived with the lie about who really shot Valance.

The second of these two scenes is at the very end of the film. Ranse and Hallie are on the train heading out of Shinbone and back to their very prominent lives. She still seems sad and far away, but her eyes brighten and tears of joy begin to form when Ranse suggests retiring in Shinbone. "My heart is here," she says. Then, after Ranse asks her, she acknowledges that she is the one who put the cactus rose on Tom's coffin. The twin admissions stun Ranse. Was Tom the *only* man Hallie ever really loved? In addition to the public lie they've both lived with for years, has their marriage also been a lie?

Now, it appears that Ranse shares more fully in the tragedy too. He seems to finally understand that no matter what he ever says or does, Tom — emotionally dead for years and now physically dead as well — will always have a special hold over Hallie, a place in her heart he can never share. Part of Tom's parting shot to Ranse at the end of the flashback is the line "Hallie's your girl now." The irony is that, even though she marries Ranse and is with him for decades, she will never be his girl the way she is, and will always be, Tom's.

So, the older Hallie reconnects with Shinbone, Link, Pompey, and, in a way, Tom. In her gestures and manner, we see that she is clearly more engaged in the reunion (and overall a much more empathetic and less patronizing person) than Ranse. There is, however, no emotional cleansing for her, no catharsis. All Hallie can do now is offer the dead Tom a cactus rose he'll never see. It's a powerful statement. But, ultimately, it isn't — and never will be — enough. She will remain another one of those genuinely good people in Ford films who unwittingly causes heartbreak or other harm. She will continue to live with her guilt and her regrets. And she will continue to die a little bit inside each time she hears a person call her husband "the man who shot Liberty Valance."

While Hallie's character is beautifully conceived and written, it is Miles' performance that ultimately makes her so appealing. Whether she's the young or the older Hallie, Miles inhabits every inch of the character every moment she is on screen. Although there is lots of talk in this film, she has the ability to say so much more with just a glance, smile, disgruntled glare, or far-away look.

Miles is a greatly under-appreciated actress, and Hallie is one of her most effectively rendered roles — a fascinating, very moving study of a person haunted by the choices she has made. What would her life have been like if she had picked Tom instead of Ranse? Near the end of her life, she can only imagine. And, as the train that carries her and Ranse away from Shinbone chugs into the distance, that's all we can do too.

* * *

After making *The Man Who Shot Liberty Valance*, Miles continued to work steadily both in films and television until her retirement in 1995. She worked with John Wayne again in two late 1960s efforts, *Hellfighters* and *The Green Berets*, although her small role in the latter film was cut from the final release. Between 1964 and 1974, she also played the female lead in six films for Disney opposite such leading men as Fred MacMurray and James Garner. Then, in 1983, she re-created her role of Lila Crane in the first sequel to *Psycho*, *Psycho II*, also with Anthony Perkins. In addition to films, Miles acted in numerous television shows, including guest roles on such classic series as *The Twilight Zone*, *The Fugitive*, *The Outer Limits*, *Colombo*, and the long-running *Murder, She Wrote*.

She has been married and divorced three times and has four children and several grandchildren. Since her retirement, she has lived in relative seclusion in Southern California, never granting interviews or making public appearances.

14

No Other Way Out
Anne Bancroft's Dr. Cartwright in *7 Women*

"So long, you bastard," are the parting words of Dr. Cartwright (Anne Bancroft) to Mongolian warlord Tunga Khan (Mike Mazuki) at the end of John Ford's 1966 film, *7 Women*.

They are also the last words any character ever utters in a John Ford feature film.

Roundly panned by critics and preview audiences, *7 Women* received no real marketing support from its studio, MGM, and failed miserably at the box office. In the process, an upcoming MGM/Ford project called *The Miracle of Merriford* was abruptly scrapped just a week before shooting was to start. And, while there would be talk of other projects, the writing was on the wall: the 50-year career of the 71-year-old Ford, America's most celebrated filmmaker, had come to a sudden, embarrassing end. Lifetime honors and tributes would follow of course, but it's as if "So long, you bastard" could have also been the film industry's parting words to the crotchety, often tyrannical old taskmaster many now considered long past his prime, irrelevant, out of touch, and maybe even a little senile.

Thankfully, there's another side to this story. It began at a movie theater on 42nd Street in New York the day the film opened there in January 1966. One of the people who saw *7 Women*, which was playing that day on the bottom half of a double bill with a forgettable B-movie called *The Money Trap*, was respected *Village Voice* film critic Andrew Sarris. Writing about his experience, Sarris called *7 Women* "a genuinely great film" and one that "is at once too profound for the art-film circuit and too personal for the big, brassy Broadway houses."[1] At the end of 1966, Sarris also ranked it the third best film of the year. Soon, other voices chimed in. *Cahiers du Cinéma*, the influential French film magazine, named *7 Women* the sixth best film of 1966.[2] And Ford himself told Peter Bogdanovich he thought it was "a hell of a good picture."[3]

14. No Other Way Out

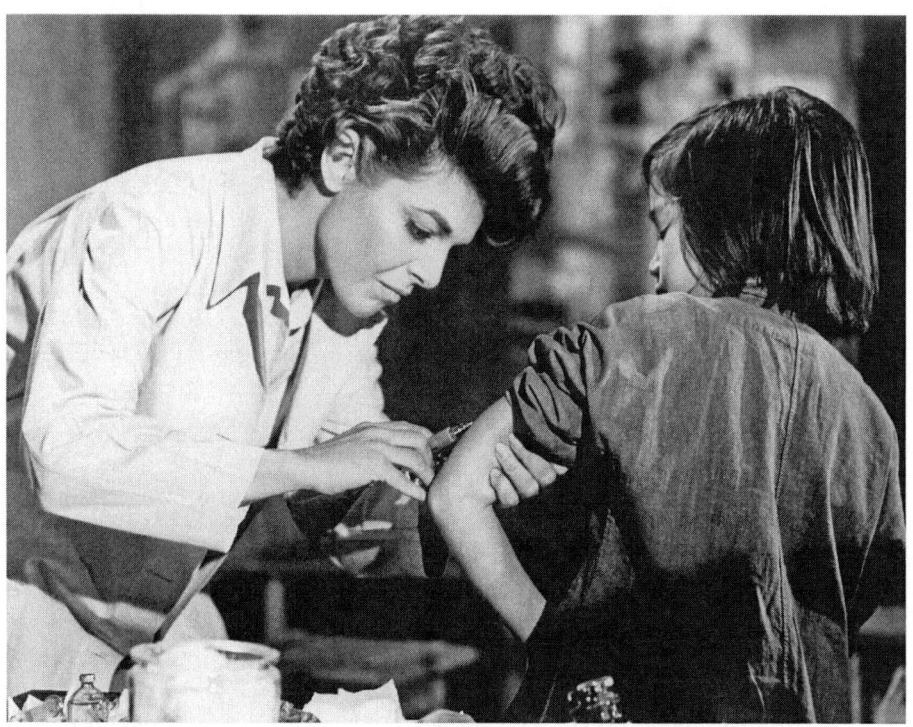

As the embittered but highly competent and caring Dr. Cartwright in 1966's *7 Women,* Anne Bancroft (here administering a shot to a young Chinese girl) is excellent as the physician who saves a group of hapless Christian missionaries in China in 1935. A last-minute replacement for actress Patricia Neal, who had a serious stroke just as production was getting underway, Bancroft very ably captures the many facets of her intriguing character.

Usually, time has a way of resolving such extreme differences of opinion, with most people eventually gravitating toward one critical camp or another. With *7 Women*, however, the arguments (and sometimes very heated ones) have continued unabated. Writing in 1999, for example, Ford biographer Scott Eyman described the film as a disaster, saying, "Ford directs without evincing any interest or creativity."[4] But, writing in 2001, Ford biographer Joseph McBride called it "one of Ford's masterpieces."[5]

So, who are we to believe? Is *7 Women* a misbegotten mess or a much-maligned masterpiece? Decades after it opened in New York and found one of its most ardent champions, it remains one of Ford's most persistently polarizing films.

Amid the arguing, however, it's often easy to lose sight of *7 Women's* main character and one of its main assets, Anne Bancroft's Dr. Cartwright. Cartwright is, in a word, fascinating. On one hand, she is an unrepentant pagan in a flock of pious missionaries, a person who swears, smokes, drinks, flaunts authority, tells of a sexual indiscretion, and smugly smiles at their revulsion toward her and her ways. Yet, she is also a passionately dedicated doctor who has taken an oath to preserve human life — an oath she has committed to with all her heart. While embittered by her personal experiences, she is nevertheless hopeful for other human beings and capable of great courage. Simultaneously, she is a savior, a healer, a catalyst who triggers changes in other characters, and someone who herself experiences a fundamental change. And Bancroft plays — or, more precisely, underplays — the role with just the right amount of toughness, tenderness, and vulnerability. Cartwright is not one to be overtly emotional, but, if we look closely at Bancroft's facial expressions, gestures, and other movements, a wide array of feelings are subtly and very effectively conveyed. This is a very skillful and sensitive performance.

* * *

Born Anna Maria Louisa Italiano in the Bronx in 1931, Anne Bancroft was the daughter of a dress pattern maker (her father Michael) and a telephone operator (her mother Mildred), both the children of Italian immigrants. After studying at both the American Academy of Dramatic Arts and the Actors Studio, she began her professional career in Hollywood as a contract player in the 1950s just as the old studio system was breaking down. While she had roles in such distinguished films as Jacques Tourneur's 1957 noir classic *Nightfall*, she was generally frustrated by constantly working low-budget, low-quality films such as 1954's *Gorilla at Large*. Returning to New York in the late 1950s, she soon became the toast of Broadway, winning back-to-back Tony Awards for her roles in the stage productions of William Gibson's *Two on a Seesaw* in 1958 and *The Miracle Worker* in 1959. After her success with *The Miracle Worker* on stage, she returned to Hollywood to reprise her role as Annie Sullivan in the film version in 1962. For their work in the film, Bancroft and her co-star, the 16-year-old Patty Duke, both won Oscars. Two years later, Bancroft received a second Academy Award nomination for her work in the British drama *The Pumpkin Eater*, directed by Jack Clayton and co-starring Peter Finch and James Mason. Soon after that, she was widely praised for her work in 1965's *The Slender Thread*, the first directorial effort of Sidney Pollack.

Bancroft wasn't the first choice to play Dr. Cartwright in *7 Women*. In fact, she wasn't even the second. Reportedly, Ford considered both Katharine Hepburn and Jennifer Jones before settling on another recent Academy Award winner, Patricia Neal. But, just three days into production, Neal suffered a debilitating stroke and Ford and producer Bernard Smith contacted Bancroft. She was available and immediately flew to Hollywood from New York to take over the role.[6]

"The last place on Earth"

7 Women opens on plain, nondescript hills. It is, we are told, 1935. We are in China near the Mongolian border, and feuding warlords and marauding bandits are all about. Then, in one dramatic shot after another, we see tough, scary men on galloping horses approaching one other, uniting behind one man on a majestic white stallion, and riding off together: menacing, unstoppable, invincible. The dust from all these thundering hoofs overwhelms us, and the scene fades to black.

Now, a new scene appears: we are at an isolated outpost run by the Unified Christian Missions Educational Society, a spot one character will soon call "the last place on Earth." This is a sedate but dreary compound managed by the painfully rigid and repressed Agatha Andrews (Margaret Leighton). She and the others there soon learn that the doctor they have long waited for, a Dr. D.R. Cartwright, will soon arrive. One of her teachers, Charles Pether (Eddie Albert), and his wife, Florrie (Betty Field), are delighted. Florrie is 42, pregnant for the first time, and anxious to have a doctor on hand when she delivers.

The doctor, however, doesn't arrive as expected. Pether, who has been sent to pick the doctor up, comes back empty-handed. Then several days later, as if from nowhere, the doctor arrives on of all things a mule. And — something else that's unexpected — the doctor is a woman.

Immediately, tensions begin to develop. Dr. Cartwright uses coarse language, smokes, and has a curt, tough manner — all quite off-putting to the prim and proper missionaries. She comes into her first dinner at the mission smoking a cigarette, puts it out when Andrews says grace, but, defying Andrews' wishes, lights it again afterward. In turn, Cartwright finds the missionaries to be a pathetic lot. After she examines Florrie and warns her and Charles of the dangers of giving birth at her age in the primitive hospital, Charles tells her that they will simply trust in the Lord. When he leaves, she can't help but roll her eyes in exasperation at his passivity and lack of common sense.

Soon, however, Cartwright and the missionaries must put aside their differences to handle refugees from a nearby British mission who, we learn, are fleeing the brutal Mongolian marauder and warlord, Tunga Khan. Cartwright also finds out that they have brought cholera with them, and she works day and night to bring the outbreak under control. Then, one evening Charles and Cartwright see a huge fire in the night sky — Tunga Khan is near. Charles goes into town to investigate and is killed. Then, just as the dust from their horses overwhelmed the screen in the film's opening shots, Tunga Khan (atop his white stallion) and his band overwhelm the hapless mission. The women are held prisoner. Chinese people, including women and children, are killed indiscriminately as the bandits laugh. For the mission women, whose lives have thus far been spared such horrors, this is an indescribable nightmare. Amid these horrors, however, Dr. Cartwright manages to deliver Florrie's baby, a boy.

Cartwright also does something else that is quite remarkable. At Tunga Khan's suggestion, she agrees to have sex, her only bargaining chip, with him in exchange first for her medical bag to help the baby and then for food and better shelter for the other women as well as the baby. The missionaries all find this quite disturbing but respond in different ways. True to her rigid principles, Andrews denounces Cartwright as the "whore of Babylon." But Miss Binns (Flora Robson), one of the British missionaries, and Miss Argent (Mildred Dunnock), Andrews' assistant, while uncomfortable with it all, are deeply moved. They understand that this is a sacrifice being made for the baby and for them.

Then, an amazing succession of scenes occurs. Cartwright, now dressed as a rich Asian man's mistress might be, tells the rest of the women that she has arranged passage for them out. When all but Argent leave the room, Cartwright takes a bottle of poison from her medical bag, hides it in her clothing, and gives the bag to Argent, effectively anointing her as the group's new leader. In very moving moment, she hugs Argent tightly and kisses her desperately on the cheek. Argent understands: this brief embrace will be the last honest connection Cartwright will ever have with an empathetic human being. Argent warns Cartwright that suicide is a sin, and Cartwright respectfully responds, "Then pray for me." Moments later, Cartwright sees the group off, and we see her from the point of view of the ox cart carrying the women away. She stands alone at the mission gate holding a lantern. As they move forward, she becomes a smaller and lonelier figure. Sadly, she turns and re-enters the compound, puts down the lantern, walks down the dark hall of the residence, and enters Tunga Khan's room. He is delighted to see her and orders her to fix drinks for them. Secretly, she puts poison in both, gives one to him, and toasts him with a big smile, saying: "So long, you bastard." Not knowing what she's said, he smiles, drinks, and quickly falls over dead. She looks soberly at her drink and takes it. Then the scene fades to black.

While *7 Women* is probably not one of Ford's great masterpieces, it is by no means the disaster Eyman and some others believe it to be. Ably addressing such Ford pre-occupations as intolerance, the perils of Puritanical thinking, and the need for sacrifice so a new society can emerge from the old, it is a very thoughtful and thought-provoking story. It also moves with great speed and energy, communicating very effectively and economically through its terse script, telling visual compositions and juxtapositions, and intriguing staging. One virtuoso moment, for example, is when Cartwright returns to Tunga Khan to fulfill her part of their "deal." First, she ups her asking price, emphatically insisting on milk for the baby and food for the missionaries. Tunga Khan quickly agrees. Then she silently walks across the room, looks away from the others in the scene (and in a direction where only the audience can see her face), and waits grimly for him to order the others out of the room. As they leave, one Chinese woman touches her arm gently, attempting to provide some comfort. Then Cartwright walks to a bench by the room's window, sits, lights a cigarette, smokes, and stares squarely at Tunga Khan with a fearless, uncompromising air. He can have her body, she seems to be saying, but this is by no means a surrender. The film's score by Elmer Bernstein is also quite good, consistently providing just the right musical complement, from rousing orchestra to a single, lonely horn, to heighten a scene's desired mood. The film's acting, while uneven, also includes Bancroft's fine performance and strong supporting turns by Flora Robson and Mildred Dunnock.

Certainly some of the criticism that's been leveled at the film is valid. A few of the acting performances, especially Sue Lyon's naïve Emma Clark and Betty Fields' hysterical, childish Florrie, are just poorly rendered. Also, Margaret Leighton's Agatha Andrews is uneven. In some scenes, for example, she is very moving. She has an excellent moment when she shares with Dr. Cartwright that, by itself, a life of devotion and service to God hasn't given her the kind of happiness she has always wanted — that, as she puts it, "God isn't enough." This is an extremely painful thing for her character to admit, and Leighton pulls the scene off very effectively. Then, in other scenes, as when Andrews calls Cartwright the "whore of Babylon" or later a "scarlet woman," she seems more like a caricature of a crazed religious zealot.

Other frequent criticisms, however, miss the point. Often ridiculed, for example, is the film's studio-bound look, which, to mid–1960s audiences accustomed to lots of location shooting and much more "realism" in films, must have seemed hopelessly out of date. Yet Ford, who had been a pioneer in location shooting and never hesitated to go on location when he thought it appropriate, wasn't attempting realism here. In fact, his whole visual treatment suggests full-on expressionism. The religious mission is isolated, suffocating, drab, and dreary in much the same way Hannah Jessop's farm is in the first part of *Pilgrimage*. We see this very artfully conveyed in the dull, dark skies and occasional fog that hangs over the proceedings as well as in the dark, muted colors — often dull browns and other earth tones, grays, and black — that fill frame after frame. Yet, while this approach reminds us of *Pilgrimage* and other black-and-white expressionistic Ford films, the director never made another color film that looks anything like *7 Women*. It's highly effective. Another criticism is the way Tunga Khan's band is characterized: everyone in it is so barbaric. They even kill women and children and laugh about it. Again, realism isn't Ford's aim. He wants to create a women's nightmare: a merry band of rapists, looters, and murderers who are horrific almost beyond imagination. This is Liberty Valance and his henchmen on steroids.

Without a doubt, *7 Women* has its flaws. On balance, however, the film succeeds in more ways than it doesn't. It is definitely one of those efforts that, to be fully appreciated, needs to be understood and then accepted on its own terms. And, for many viewers, it may take some work to get to that point. This is not an easy film, but it can be a very rewarding one.

"Then pray for me"

Who is Dr. Cartwright, the woman at the center of this story?

This is an intriguing question because there are so many ways to answer it.

Our first glimpse of Cartwright is a curious one. As children at the mission sing "Yes, Jesus Loves Me," she rides in on a mule, an act reminiscent of Jesus riding a donkey into Jerusalem on Palm Sunday. The suggestion here is very clear — she is the story's Christ figure, and she will eventually sacrifice herself to save several of the people there. But, she's also a very unlikely Christ figure: a chain smoking, tough talking woman in pants and a cowboy hat. Yes, saviors can come in most unexpected forms.

Cartwright's name is curious too. We never know her first name. All we ever get are her initials, D.R., which are, of course, also the abbreviation for a doctor, a healer. Her last name also points to the story's end, when the other women and the baby are all leaving in an ox cart — a cart going in the right direction, away from the nightmare; a cart carrying a community of people that has been upended, but now, through the doctor's efforts, has been righted.

In essence, Cartwright personifies *both* saviors and healers. Without her medical expertise, the cholera would have overwhelmed the mission, killing everyone. And, without her medical skills, her willingness to play concubine for Tunga Khan, and her consistent resourcefulness, the missionaries and the baby would likely never have been spared.

Her role as savior and healer goes deeper too. As well as curing people of their physical ills, she also acts as a catalyst, getting at least some of the missionaries to see through their delusions. Perhaps the greatest of these delusions is that Andrews is an able and truly Christian leader. As the pressures mount and people need real solutions, they turn increasingly to Cartwright. In the process, Andrews becomes increasingly irrelevant and eventually suffers a mental breakdown. We see this shift in perspective occur with several of the missionaries, including Miss Binns and Emma, but it is with Miss Argent that the change is most dramatic. Early in the film, Argent is as trusting and compliant as can be, taking in every word from Andrews as if it were gospel. But, the more she interacts with Cartwright, the more clearly she sees Andrews for the intolerant deluded wreck that she is. The brief embrace and kiss she shares with Cartwright is transformational. For Argent, the non-believer Cartwright has become the most Christ-like among them in her devotion to her fellow human beings. Accepting the symbol of leadership, the medical bag, she joins the others on the cart. Then, as Andrews continues her intolerant prattling, it is the gentle, soft-spoken Argent who fiercely rises up, telling Andrews: "Oh, be quiet! I never want to hear your voice as long as I live."

In addition to being a catalyst of change in others, Cartwright is a dynamic character, a person who undergoes a major internal transformation.

When she first arrives at the mission, she seems to be a complete mismatch for the place. We know that her life hasn't been easy. As a female doctor in the 1930s, she tells how she endured discrimination and made do working in "hell holes" of hospitals. She's also had an ill-fated love affair. Her life experience has made her bitter, skeptical, and guarded, teaching her that she must compensate for being a woman by acting tough and adopting predominantly male habits such as smoking and swearing.

But this mission soon becomes Cartwright's home too, and she finds herself a valued and respected member of the community. This bonding begins to occur during the cholera crisis, when people discover her talent and resourcefulness, and when this crisis is over, she — with the help of some alcohol — feels comfortable enough to confide her personal story to the others. Slowly but surely, these missionaries are becoming her family. From this point forward, she is gentler and more open with the others, stops making her sarcastic quips, and even curtails her swearing. No longer is there a need to posture.

Her relationship with the community reaches a more committed level after Tunga Khan's arrival and her decision to trade her body for what she needs to help the others in her newly adopted family. She does all this partly because of her doctor's oath to preserve human life. But she also does it out of the deep feeling — perhaps love — she has developed for the others. She sees Emma as "a good kid" who deserves a decent chance at life. She hopes that Florrie's baby boy will someday become "an All-American fullback." And she truly wants the others, even Andrews, to live and get help.

Then her relationship reaches its most profound level when she decides to sacrifice herself in return for the freedom and safety of the others. She sees no other way out, and her "family's" welfare is paramount. One touching example of the enormous change that's taken place within Cartwright is her response to Miss Argent's warning that suicide is a sin. If she had heard that early in the story, Cartwright would probably have just rolled her eyes in exasperation as she did earlier at Pether's remark about trusting in the Lord. Now, however, she doesn't. With the greatest respect, she simply tells Argent: "Then pray for me." Rather than mocking Argent's beliefs, Cartwright, a doctor to the end, is giving her a prescription for finding some personal peace in this terrible situation. It's clear too that Cartwright has now found a level of personal peace she probably has never had before.

Some critics have found the film's ending pessimistic, even nihilistic. Yet, it's actually quite the opposite. In one respect, Cartwright's act is redemptive and very much in the tradition of Sidney Carton's going to the guillotine at the end of *A Tale of Two Cities*. (It's also interesting that these two characters have similar last names.) She is sacrificing her life to save the lives of people dear to her. What greater way can a person express love for others? In another respect, Cartwright's act is the result of hard-boiled logic. It is extreme and tragic, yes. But her existence as Tunga Khan's concubine would most likely be miserable and short-lived. And being who she is, Cartwright has already worked this out in her mind. So, if she wishes to save the others, she must stay with Tunga Khan. And, if she's going to die, she would rather die on her terms, not his. It's a terrible choice, but, for her, it's also the best choice.

In portraying the many facets of Cartwright, Anne Bancroft gives a very subtle and accomplished performance. Cartwright is a very deliberate, guarded, and complex woman, and Bancroft is excellent at showing us both the strong emotions and the vulnerability beneath the tough, usually shielded exterior. The great personal change Cartwright experiences occurs naturally, with seeming effortlessness, and throughout, every word Cartwright speaks and every gesture she makes is entirely credible. In fact, many of her visual moments are especially striking and eloquent — the way she defiantly smokes her cigarette as Andrews glares at her from across the dinner table, the way she looks at Tunga Khan right before she lives up to her end of their unholy bargain, the way she sits alone and stares ahead in horror after Argent leaves with the medical bag for the last time. This is the work of a very accomplished actress.

* * *

While the critical and commercial failure of *7 Women* spelled the end of Ford's feature film career, it didn't harm Bancroft's in the least. Her next part, Mrs. Robinson in Mike Nichols' *The Graduate*, is one of the iconic roles in all of American film. For her portrayal, she received a third Academy Award nomination as well as a Golden Globe Award. Afterward, she kept working regularly in films, on the stage, and in television productions for the next 35 years, adding two Emmys to her list of recognitions and becoming one of a handful of actors to win at least one Oscar, Tony, Emmy, and Golden Globe Award. After *The Graduate*, some of her other well-known films include 1972's *Young Winston*, 1975's *The Prisoner of Second Avenue*, 1977's *The Turning Point*, 1980's *The Elephant Man*, 1983's *To Be or Not to Be*, 1985's *Agnes of God*, 1987's *84 Charing*

Cross Road, and 1995's *How to Make an American Quilt*. In all, she made more than 50 film appearances.

After a brief and unhappy marriage in the mid–1950s, Bancroft met comedian Mel Brooks when both were guests on Perry Como's television show in the early 1960s and immediately recognized each other as kindred souls. In a 1984 interview, she admitted that she told her psychiatrist the next day, "'Let's speed this process up. I've met the right man.'" Then, she added: "See, I'd never had so much pleasure being with another human being. I wanted him to enjoy me too. It was that simple." The two were married in 1964. And, in 1972, they had a son, Max.[7]

In 2005, after a battle with uterine cancer, Bancroft died at age 73. The night of her death, the lights of Broadway were dimmed in her honor.[8]

Among the many people who paid tribute to her at the time was Mike Nichols, who had directed her in *The Graduate*. "Her combination of brains, humor, frankness, and sense were unlike any other artist," Nichols said. "Her beauty was constantly shifting with her roles, and because she was a consummate actress she changed radically for every part."[9]

"At least for a later time..."

In his 1966 review of *7 Women*, Andrew Sarris proclaimed that the film's "beauties" were "for the ages, or at least for a later time when the personal poetry of film directors is better understood...."[10] To some extent at least, both he and Ford have achieved vindication. Bad movies are quickly forgotten, but *7 Women* has remained a subject of ongoing interest and discussion among people who care about Ford's films and films in general for a long time now. Love it or hate it, there *is* something about this challenging and unusual film that provokes strong feelings and calls out for ongoing attention.

It would be wonderful as well that at some "later time" more people will appreciate the richness of the Dr. Cartwright character and Anne Bancroft's superb portrayal of her. The bitter, irreverent woman who first arrives at the mission embarks on an extraordinary personal journey, and Bancroft takes us every step of the way with the clarity and conviction of a master. Cartwright is the last of the Fordian heroes, those often-misunderstood loners (played by people from Harry Carey, Sr., to John Wayne) who make sacrifices so that new social orders can be born, and she deserves to be counted among the best of them.

15

Snapshots
Other Fine Female Roles and Performances in Ford Films

When the subject is John Ford, there is always more to say, and this sentiment clearly remains true when the subject is women's roles in Ford films.

In addition to the roles and actresses spotlighted in the preceding chapters, here is a series of short portraits — snapshots, if you will — of some more very intriguing roles and the actresses who played them. Again, these choices are unabashedly subjective, and undoubtedly some Ford aficionados will feel that some fine roles and actresses have been overlooked. If so, apologies are in order, because they are probably right.

Ford's First "Profound" Character: Karen Morley's Laura Nash in *Flesh*

Ford scholar Tag Gallagher has called Laura Nash, the heroine in Ford's virtually forgotten 1932 film, *Flesh*, the director's "most profound character" up to that time and notes that, with Laura, "such an explored study of alienation is new to Ford." Gallagher also suggests that this major step forward in Ford's development as an artist might be at least partially due to the influence German expressionistic director F.W. Murnau had on him. Murnau, Gallagher contends, taught Ford "that people live and breathe and feel within décor, and that consciousness is a continuously renewing dialectic between inner self and outer world."[1] The point is well taken. Before *Flesh*, Ford's characters, especially his females, lacked the depth, complexity, neuroses, and contradictions of Laura. They weren't as credible or well rounded, as fully human. Afterward — in fact, as soon as Ford's very next film, *Pilgrimage*— we would see such complex female characters often in his work.

Another critical element in play here is the actress who portrays Laura, MGM contract actress Karen Morley. While not caring much for the film overall, director and Ford scholar Lindsay Anderson rates Morley's work in *Flesh* as "a first-rate, unsentimental performance."[2] His point is also well taken. Morley ably portrays a complicated, deeply divided, and emotionally lost woman, making her credible and sympathetic even as she does despicable things. In *Flesh*, she rises well above marginal material.

In many respects, the story of *Flesh* is reminiscent of many sordid Pre-Code Hollywood melodramas. Laura, an American released from a German women's prison because she's pregnant, repeatedly takes advantage of a slow-witted but kind-hearted German wrestler named Polakai

In 1932's *Flesh*, Wallace Beery's smitten Polakai tries to befriend Karen Morley's troubled Laura Nash. Morley's memorable performance is the film's saving grace.

(Wallace Beery), trying to steal his money, talking him into getting her "brother" (actually her lying, abusive lover) Nicky out of jail, and even marrying Polakai without telling him she is carrying Nicky's child. Later, after Laura, Polakai, and the baby move to America, she tries to get Polakai to wrestle in fixed matches, something he finds repugnant. To top it off, she begs the no-good Nicky, who has also come to America, to take her back. Eventually, though, Laura grows to appreciate Polakai's goodness, and, as the film ends, they agree to stay together.

Granted, this is the stuff of soap opera. And granted, the film is uneven. Wallace Beery also plays Polakai as so blockheaded at times that he's often painful to watch. Through it all, however, *Flesh* has a genuine appeal, and a major reason why is Morley's performance as Laura.

Although Laura does bad things throughout the film, we empathize with her from the beginning. When she is released from prison, she asks pitifully about Nicky, hoping he is being released too. Once out, she finds herself alone and pregnant with no money or place to live. She is truly desperate. She is also in love with Nicky and keeps pursuing him because she believes that she's not good enough for anyone better. As she says after one of Nicky's slights, "I must be rotten inside to take that from any man."

Yet, Laura isn't simply a down-and-out masochist. She is also bright, witty, likeable, and sensitive to moral issues — especially when Nicky isn't around. When she describes the nature of the relationship between her and the German Polakai early in the film, she says, "This is a Teutonic friendship," her pun on "Platonic." None of the other characters gets it of course. This is her little joke — and ours. Her wit suggests a kind of strength, a way of asserting her personality, and it helps to make her transformation at the end of the film far more credible than it otherwise would have been. As the story progresses, she also develops a greater sense of moral awareness and responsibility, feeling worse and worse when she does things she considers bad. This capability helps to enable her change as well.

Another key contribution to the character's success is Morley's excellent portrayal. Film historian Danny Peary has also called her one of "the great unsung actresses" of the early and mid–1930s,[3] and she really is. In addition to her role in *Flesh*, she's terrific in *Scarface, Dinner at Eight, Arsene Lupin, Our Daily Bread*, and several other films during the period. When her MGM contract ended and she went freelance in the mid 1930s, however, she didn't have the studio support and received fewer roles. Then, in 1947, her film career ended abruptly when the studio bosses blacklisted her for not naming names of suspected Communists before the House Un-American Activities Committee. She was 37. Just before she died at 93 in 2003, however, she was interviewed for the Turner Classic Movies documentary, *Complicated Women*, about actresses and the provocative roles they played in the Pre-Code era. The documentary, which premiered just after Morley's death, was dedicated to her.

* * *

Hillbilly at the Hair Stylist: Lucille La Verne in *Pilgrimage*

Lucille La Verne may be one of the most obscure actresses featured in this book, but most of us have seen, or at least heard, her work. Probably her most famous role is the voice of the Wicked Witch in Disney's *Snow White and the Seven Dwarves* in 1937.

Like the star of Ford's 1933 film, *Pilgrimage*, Henrietta Crosman, La Verne spent the vast majority of her career on the stage, and very little of her work remains for us to enjoy today. Luckily, though, we can see her in a handful of

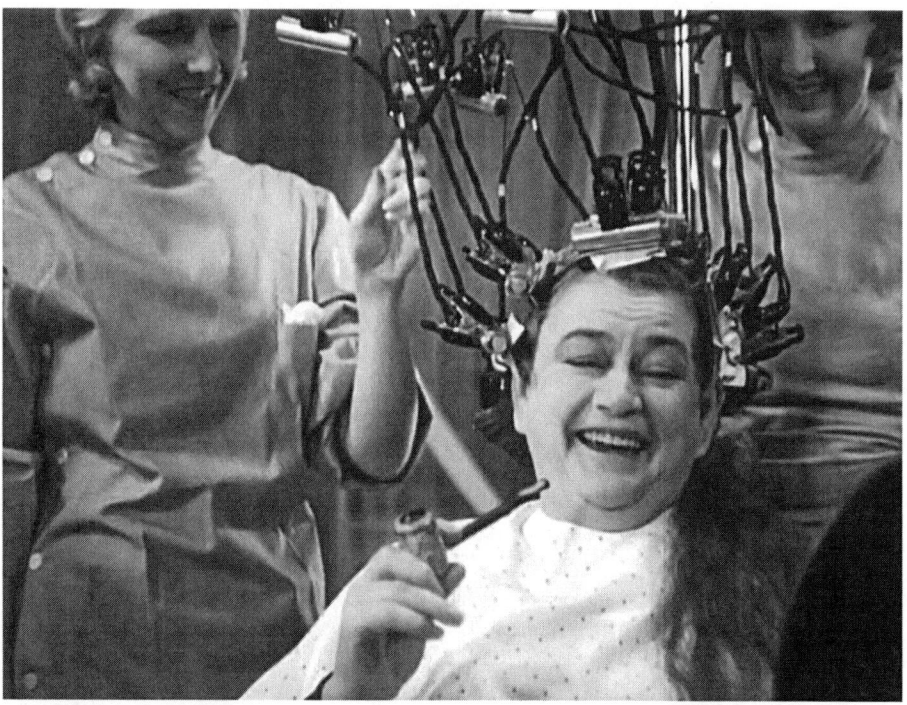

As the rustic Tilly Hatfield who befriends Hannah Jessop on the boat to France in 1933's *Pilgrimage*, Lucille La Verne infuses her important supporting role with both comic vitality and wise authority.

films, including *Pilgrimage*, where she gives a remarkable supporting performance as Tilly Hatfield, a hillbilly woman who is among the Gold Star Mothers who accompany Hannah Jessop (Crosman) to France to visit the graves of the sons they lost in World War I.

As soon as we meet her, La Verne's Tilly is a delight: warm, friendly, spirited, open to new experiences, and endlessly curious. Her role in the story is essentially a catalyst, helping the very repressed Hannah to open up, see life's experiences differently, and enjoy herself more. Along the way, Tilly has several wonderful scenes. One is getting the kick of her life in a Parisian beauty parlor while smoking her corncob pipe. Another, which also involves her pipe, takes place in a fine Parisian restaurant. Tilly has just finished dinner and notices all the very smart, sophisticated Parisians chicly smoking their cigarettes. Figuring that it's all right for her to smoke too, she pulls out her pipe, loads it, and lights it. The chic smokers are aghast, but Tilly just stares right back at them. After we grow to see Tilly as a basically comic character, Ford pulls one of his fast ones on us. When the subject finally comes up in conversation, we learn that Tilly lost, not one, but three of her sons in the war. It's another one of the film's very poignant moments.

Born in Nashville, Tennessee, in 1872, La Verne quickly showed an ability to play a wide range of characters and to master the roles with great speed. At age 14, for example, she played both Shakespeare's Juliet and Lady Macbeth back to back in a touring troupe. The following year, at 15, she made her Broadway debut and for most of her career worked in theater in numerous capacities: running a theatrical company, directing, and playwriting as well as acting. Her best-known stage triumph came in the hit 1923 play *Sun Up* by Lula Vollmer, in which she acted in more than 3000 performances on Broadway and in the play's U.S. and European tours. In the late 1920s, a Broadway theater was also named for her.

After *Pilgrimage,* La Verne continued to act in films for a few more years. In addition to her work in *Snow White and the Seven Dwarfs,* she also received praise for her portrayal of a bloodthirsty old hag (with a great cackle) in MGM's 1935 version of *A Tale of Two Cities* starring Ronald Colman. La Verne died in Culver City, California, at age 72 in 1945.

* * *

A Certain Sad Dignity: Marian Nixon's Mary Saunders in *Pilgrimage*

Marian Nixon had a special quality about her, and, between her film debut in 1923 and her decision to retire from acting at age 32 in 1936, she was much in demand, making more than 70 films. She only worked with Ford twice, and both times it was in 1933. She had a small role in *Dr. Bull* as May Tupping, a telephone operator who tenderly cares for her bedridden husband. She probably was cast as May based on her work in the film Ford made immediately before *Dr. Bull, Pilgrimage.*

In *Pilgrimage,* Nixon plays Mary Saunders, a sensitive young woman whose life is far from easy. She lives on an Arkansas farm with her alcoholic father (Charlie Grapewin), and, while she is in love with her earnest young neighbor, Jim Jessop (Norman Foster), Jim's overbearing mother, Hannah (Henrietta Crosman) is determined to break them up. When Mary and Jim declare their independence, Hannah, to ensure that the two are separated, has Jim drafted into the Army during World War I. Soon, Mary finds out that she's pregnant. She tells Jim, but he is on the way to the front, and there is no chance to get married. Then he is killed; Hannah will have nothing to do with her or little Jimmy (Jay Ward), the child Mary bears; and Mary must raise the boy by herself.

This is heart-wrenching stuff, and this is also material that can easily go awry. With a lesser actress in Mary's role, this very painful story could have quickly descended into farce. But Nixon brings a quiet strength, maturity, and sincerity to her role that makes it quite moving. She accepts her life's choices without self-pity, lives with the pain and loss she has experienced, makes the best life she can for her son, and keeps moving forward. She has several very good scenes, but two — both at the local train station — particularly stand out. The first is when she tells Jim she is pregnant and then must watch as his fellow soldiers drag him against his will back into the train and on to the front. Here she is quite moving, conveying a range of feelings from her happiness at seeing him to her regret for not

As Mary Saunders, an unwed mother who must struggle alone in 1933's *Pilgrimage*, Marian Nixon holds young Jay Ward, who plays her son Jimmy.

having told him about their baby sooner, to her shock and distress at how Jim is dragged away. The second scene is years later when she and young Jimmy offer Hannah a small bouquet of flowers to put on Jim's grave when Hannah visits France. Mary has great difficulty facing the fierce, extremely intimidating Hannah. But she loved Jim too, and she wants her feelings, and her expressions of those feelings, to be respected. There is great strength to this slim, almost fragile-looking young woman.

Born in 1904, Nixon began working in show business as a chorus dancer on the vaudeville circuit and, by age 19, was appearing in major supporting roles in silent films. She successfully made the transition to sound films and, while she often played supporting roles, was cast as the lead in the 1932 film adaptation of *Rebecca of Sunnybrook Farm*. That year she also co-starred with James Cagney in the boxing film, *Winner Take All*. She died in 1983 at age 78. Her grandsons, the screenwriting team of Ted and Nicholas Griffin, are active in Hollywood today. Among Ted's credits are the 2001 version of *Ocean's 11* with George Clooney, Brad Pitt, and Matt Damon.

* * *

Presence Personified: Hattie McDaniel's Aunt Dilsey in *Judge Priest*

Best known for her Oscar-winning role as Scarlet O'Hara's wise, nononsense mammy in 1939's *Gone with the Wind*, Hattie McDaniel had prominent parts in numerous Hollywood films in the 1930s and 1940s.

Her role as Judge Priest's housekeeper and confidant, Aunt Dilsey, in Ford's 1934 *Judge Priest* is her first major film part, and she adds a great deal to the story with her exuberance, rich singing voice, and great sense of comedy. Several of her scenes are gems. In one, she's cooking in the kitchen, unconsciously becomes caught up in another character's harmonica playing, and begins dancing, her large body moving with amazing ease and grace. In another, she does a charming duet with Judge Priest as she also does the dusting, communicating to him in extemporaneous lyrics that she empathizes with him and supports him as he tries to find a just solution in a difficult case. McDaniel really had presence, and, whenever she's onscreen, viewers' eyes automatically turn to her no matter who's talking.

Sharing a smile with co-star Will Rogers who played the title role in 1934's *Judge Priest*, Hattie McDaniel, as Aunt Dilsey, brought her special charisma to a small but an important role.

In addition to *Judge Priest* and *Gone with the Wind*, McDaniel was featured in such films as the 1936 version of *Showboat* with Irene Dunne and Paul Robeson and 1935's *Alice Adams* with Katharine Hepburn. During the run of *Alice Adams*, several Southern film reviewers betrayed their own racial prejudices by criticizing McDaniel for being so good that she stole several scenes from the film's "rightful" star, Hepburn.

As well as films, McDaniel worked frequently in radio and later on television. In the late 1940s, she became the first African American performer to star in her own radio show, a comedy series called *Beulah*. She died in 1952.

* * *

Crushed Spirit: Maureen O'Hara's Angharad in *How Green Was My Valley*

Often, when people share their favorite examples of Ford's visual poetry, they cite the aftermath of the second wedding that takes place in his 1941 masterpiece, *How Green Was My Valley*. In stark contrast to the film's earlier and much happier wedding, this is a tense, stiff affair. As the characters leave the church, we see the bride and groom, Maureen O'Hara's Angharad Morgan and Marten Lamont's Iestyn Evans. He seems very smug and self-satisfied. She appears to be in an almost zombie-like trance. As they board their carriage, a gust of wind causes her wedding veil to soar high into the air. After a moment, the veil is captured and contained and the bride and groom ride off. Then, we are left with a long shot of a man standing alone in silhouette underneath a tree next to the church. This, we know, is the man Angharad really loves, the man who also wants to marry her but feels he can't, the man who in fact has just performed the marriage ceremony. And why does the veil soar? Perhaps it is to represent Angharad's own once-soaring spirit, a spirit that has now been frustrated, contained, and essentially crushed. Or perhaps Ford had something else in mind. In any case, the mingling of visual beauty and emotional heartbreak in these moments is extraordinary. This is Ford at his poetic, ironic, bittersweet best. This is also one of many fine moments from Maureen O'Hara in this, the first of five films she made with Ford.

While Angharad is loving and loyal to her family, the Morgans (the people the film is mainly about), her story arc focuses more her ill-fated love for Walter Pidgeon's Mr. Gruffydd, the local minister. As is her way, Angharad falls for him deeply and completely. He has feelings for her too but doesn't

In the first of her five roles for Ford, Maureen O'Hara played Angharad, who marries the wrong man in 1941's *How Green Was My Valley*. Here she poses with young Roddy McDowell who plays her young brother Huw.

want her to live as an impoverished minister's wife. She begs him and even comes to offer herself to him (something quite scandalous for 19th century Wales). He seems startled by both the intensity and immensity of her feeling, but he is also adamant about not marrying. Soon, she receives an offer from the wealthy but cold Evans, and the fates of these three characters are forever sealed.

Only 21 and a relative novice to films when she played Angharad, O'Hara portrays this very passionate woman with great discipline and restraint, giving her an uncommon dignity. This helps to intensify our feelings for Angharad as she runs the gamut of emotions from flushed exuberance to bitter frustration and ultimately to blank despair. We care deeply about her throughout, and no doubt many who have later questioned their own romantic choices in life relate closely to her as well. As written, Angharad is a complex, believable, and utterly sympathetic character. O'Hara starts there and gives Angharad fire and a soul. "I felt that I captured the sincerity of Angharad's tragedy," the actress noted years later.[4] We readily agree. This is a fine performance.

More information about Maureen O'Hara and her career is included along with a discussion of her roles in Ford's *Rio Grande* and *The Quiet Man* in Chapter 11.

* * *

The Young Widow: Anna Lee's Bronwyn in *How Green Was My Valley*

Anna Lee was a favorite of John Ford's, and Ford was a favorite of Lee's. Despite what anyone else had to say about the director and his legendary feistiness, she constantly referred to him as a "lovely man."

Already an established actress in the UK (as well as the goddaughter of Sir Arthur Conan Doyle, creator of the Sherlock Holmes mysteries), Lee first came to Ford's attention when he cast her as Bronwyn in 1941's *How Green Was My Valley*. After that, she worked in supporting roles in seven more Ford films over the next quarter century. Some of her roles are quite small. In 1962's The *Man Who Shot Liberty Valance*, for example, she has only one line, and in 1958's *The Last Hurrah* and 1959's *The Horse Soldiers* her roles aren't much larger. While they aren't long, however, they are certainly memorable. In fact, her short turn in *The Horse Soldiers* as the Civil War widow who pleads to have her son (who appears to be no older than 12 or 13) relieved of military duty is one of the most memorable moments in that film. Another memorable role is her Emily Collingwood, the wife of George O'Brien's Sam Collingwood in 1948's *Fort Apache*.

Holding her baby and confiding to her mother-in-law Beth (Sara Allgood), Anna Lee's Bronwyn ponders widowhood and loneliness in 1941's *How Green Was My Valley*.

Her most important scene in this film comes near the end. The soldiers are all leaving on what nearly everyone sees as a doomed mission. Emily finds out that Sam has new orders, and others urge her to have Sam recalled. But Emily, like Sam, has her pride. She decides — against her more practical instincts — to let him go, saying that he can assume his new post when he returns, which of course never happens. As she watches — and the men become smaller and smaller in the distance — she finally says wistfully: "All I can see is the flags." This is one of those deeply moving and highly ironic moments we often see in Ford, and Lee pulls it off with great aplomb.

As these examples suggest, one curious similarity many of Lee's roles for Ford share is widowhood. Lee plays either a young or middle-aged woman who has already lost her husband when we first meet her or one who loses her husband in the course of the story.

Of Lee's many roles for Ford, the one she is probably best remembered for is Bronwyn, a kind, caring young woman from a neighboring village who marries the oldest Morgan son, Ivor (Patric Knowles); develops a special closeness with young Huw, the story's main character; and then — on the same day — gives birth to her and Ivor's first child and loses Ivor in a mining accident. After this, Bronwyn, lonely and now with a child to care for, carries on as best she can in her house next door to the Morgans, and, to help support her and to keep her company, Huw eventually comes to live with her. It's a sad story that mirrors the changes other members of the Morgan family experience throughout the film. While we don't have a great deal of backstory about Bronwyn, Lee brings such intense feeling to her role that her joys and tragedies have an especially strong impact on us as we watch her story unfold. We care about her deeply, and her character stays with us long after the film ends.

Lee was especially fond and proud of her Bronwyn. The intensity she brought to her performance also had an impact on her fellow actress in the film, Maureen O'Hara, who, in 1944, named her own newly born daughter Bronwyn, in Lee's honor.

Lee also had quite a career apart from Ford. She appeared in a number of noteworthy films such as 1947's *The Ghost and Mrs. Muir* and 1965's *The Sound of Music* as well as scores of television shows. Later in life, she played the role of Lila Quartermaine on the television soap *General Hospital* for decades. After two unsuccessful marriages, she married novelist Robert Nathan (whose books *The Bishop's Wife* and *Portrait of Jennie* were both made into hit films in 1947) and remained married to him until his death in 1985. She died in Beverly Hills in 1994 at age 91.

* * *

A Gentle Toughness: Cathy Downs' "Clem" in *My Darling Clementine*

Often included on critics' shortlists of Ford's greatest Westerns, his 1946 *My Darling Clementine* — one of several Hollywood films that dramatizes the legendary 1881 gunfight at Tombstone, Arizona's OK Corral — is not widely noted for its female characters. In his 1946 review of the film for the *New York Times*, for example, Bosley Crowther — after heaping high praise on the film's star, Henry Fonda (as Wyatt Earp), and other male performers — writes: "Mr. Ford is less knowing with the females. Linda Darnell (as the good-bad girl Chihauhua) makes a pin-up of a trull, and Cathy Downs (as Clementine) is simply ornamental as a good little girl from back east."[5]

As was often the case, Crowther was half-right. Darnell, then a major star and usually a very competent actress, is not especially effective in her role. But Downs, a newcomer in her first credited role, does a fine job giving real flesh and blood to a character that can too easily be dismissed as "a good little girl."

First, Downs's character is anything but simple or one note. Clementine, who scours the country — going from "cow town to cow town" — in search of her lost love, Doc Holliday (Victor Mature) before finding him in Tombstone, is a much more determined, self-assured, intelligent, and resilient young woman than her prim and proper demeanor suggests. When Holliday rejects her, for example, she fiercely pleads with him to give up his suicidal lifestyle and return to the East with her. She eventually accepts the fact that he won't, but she isn't going to go meekly either. She will have her say and tell him exactly what's on her mind. Then, she'll figure out what she wants to do, which, in this case is starting a school in a town that desperately needs one. As Tag Gallagher noted: "In contrast to (Howard) Hawks's western women, who are treated essentially as erotic fantasies..., Ford's Clementine has her feet firmly planted on the earth. She pursues Holliday not simply from desire but to help him; rejected, she is independent enough to stake out her own future in Tombstone."[6]

Downs's performance merits praise as well. She brings real credibility and authority to a role that requires these qualities as desperately as Tombstone needs a school. Not only does she hold her own with Mature's Holliday, but she also earns the right to be a worthy prospective partner for Fonda's Earp. After all, it isn't just Fonda but Fonda and Downs, who — when their characters walk arm-in-arm to church services to the strains of "Shall We Gather at the River?"— are so critical to making this and several other of the film's most memorable and magnificent scenes work as well as they do.

"It is remarkable how Cathy Downs's Clementine overshadows (Darnell's Chihauhau)," film historian Jim Kitses has written. "Darnell is given huge close-ups that reflect her stature (as a star) and the character's sensuality, but the film insists on a respectful distance with Clementine. The dramatic action, Ford's careful staging, and Downs's quiet performance all work to elevate the character to a supreme iconic significance."[7]

Born in Port Jefferson, New York, in 1926, Downs worked briefly as a model for *Vogue* magazine before being signed by a 20th Century–Fox talent scout in 1944 and brought to Hollywood. After a pair of uncredited bit parts, she was cast in *My Darling Clementine*, and with the success of the film, the studio began to groom her for stardom. Her next films, however, were not nearly as successful, and by the 1950s she was routinely assigned to low-budget westerns and science fiction films. She made a few television appearances in the early 1960s but increasingly could not find work. Married and divorced twice by the time she was 39, she died of cancer alone and penniless in Los Angeles in 1976. She was 52.

* * *

Flanked by Henry Fonda's Wyatt Earp and several impressive spires of cactus, newcomer Cathy Downs has many fine moments as Clementine in 1946's *My Darling Clementine*.

Society's Child: Arleen Whelan's Lucy Lee in *The Sun Shines Bright*

"Maybe there's one [film] that I love to look at again and again," Ford said in a 1968 interview with director Burt Kennedy. "That's *The Sun Shines Bright*. That's really my favorite picture."[8]

Although Ford (depending on his mood, the person asking the questions, and various other factors) often changed his opinions and versions of stories with interviewers, he was uncharacteristically consistent about *The Sun Shines Bright*. He loved this film.

What's especially curious is that it also remains one of his more obscure efforts during the last 15 years of his career. Made in late 1952 and then released in May 1953 between blockbusters *The Quiet Man* and *Mogambo*, this affectionate glimpse of small town Kentucky life circa 1900 received mostly mixed to negative reviews, drew meager audiences, was quickly forgotten, and has rarely been shown on television. It only became available on DVD in March 2013.

Over the years, however, the film has also become a favorite of such Fordophiles as Lindsay Anderson, Tag Gallagher, and Jonathan Rosenbaum, who all rank it among the director's best.

Their high regard is certainly understandable. Like good coffee or caviar, *The Sun Shines Bright* is an acquired taste. It can be difficult to connect with at first. But, once a connection is made, it's almost impossible to break. It's a film that gets into your bloodstream.

Loosely based on three stories by humorist Irwin S. Cobb (whose stories also inspired Ford's 1934 film *Judge Priest* with Will Rogers), *The Sun Shines Bright* focuses on several challenges facing an older Judge Billy Priest (here played by character actor Charles Winninger). The most interesting among them is his agreeing to officiate at a funeral for a sick, aging prostitute who has come home to die. It's also election time, and Judge Priest understands that this action might very well lead to his defeat in a closely contested race for his job. Still, he believes it is the right thing to do, and he follows through with the task.

Involved in all of this is Lucy Lee (Arleen Whelan), a young schoolteacher who has been raised by the good-hearted Dr. Lake (Russell Simpson). No one has ever told Lucy Lee who her mother is, and, as events unfold, she finds out that her mother is the prostitute, who is also the disgraced daughter of the town's leading citizen, General Fairfield. That's a lot to deal with of course, especially in the few short days that the story takes place, but Lucy Lee has many commendable qualities, including integrity, courage, and the ability to face difficult truths with grace. And she conveys them in an exquisitely orchestrated sequence when she visits the judge's house and demands to know the secret the townspeople have kept from her.

Previously, the judge has brought an oil painting of a young General Fairfield and his wife, Lucy Lee's grandmother (who happens to be the spitting image of Lucy Lee), into his home and covered it. Once this mysterious woman has come to town, Lucy Lee knows that something is up, and, as she stands in the judge's house, they share this exchange:

> **Lucy Lee:** Uncle Billy! Uncle Billy...! I had to see you, Judge. I must know what's going on. Who am I? I know Dr. Lake loved me like a daughter, but tell me, Judge, who am I?
>
> **Priest:** Why you're his adopted daughter, honey.
>
> **Lucy Lee:** That's not enough anymore, Uncle Billy.

A moment later, we see Lucy Lee from the point of view of the portrait. She stares at it with great seriousness, her face coming out of a shadow and into the light. Then, we see that the portrait is only partially draped, that the exposed part shows her grandmother and physical double. Slowly, as the truth sinks in,

As Lucy Lee in 1953's *The Sun Shines Bright*, Arleen Whelan brings dignity and restraint to her role as a young woman who finally learns the truth about her past.

a cello begins the song "Genevieve," the music associated throughout the film with motherhood. At last, Lucy Lee has learned the story of her past. She leaves, both shocked and comforted at the same time, carrying this new discovery with every dignified step.

These moments are an example of Ford's visual poetry in top form, and Whelan beautifully conveys both the bizarre and profoundly moving nature of this experience for Lucy Lee. She is stunned, but even in the midst of that moment, she also has the presence of mind to know that she needs this information to move on with her life.

Like many other actresses who gave fine performances in Ford films, Whelan was never close to being a major star. Known for her beauty and auburn hair, she was born in Salt Lake City in 1914, moved to Los Angeles with her family, and was working in a salon on Hollywood Boulevard when film director H. Bruce Humberstone dropped in for a shave, saw her, and recommended her to Darryl F. Zanuck. At 22, she signed a long-term contract with 20th Century–Fox and within two years she had a supporting role in Ford's 1939 film, *Young Mr. Lincoln*. After that, however, she was cast in mostly forgettable roles during the 1940s, had her second stint with Ford in *The Sun Shines Bright*, and — after working in some forgettable Republic westerns in the mid-1950s — retired at age 43 to become an avid golfer. She had three brief marriages and died at age 78 in 1993.

* * *

A Stranger in Her Own Land: Constance Towers' Mary Beecher in *Sergeant Rutledge*

The 1960 film, *Sergeant Rutledge*, is Ford's tribute to the African American "Buffalo Soldiers," who comprised two regiments of the U.S. Cavalry after the Civil

War. While the story centers on the court martial of one of these soldiers, Sergeant Braxton Rutledge (Woody Strode), for the rape and murder of a young white woman and then the murder of her father, it is really more of an exploration of racial attitudes between blacks and whites at the time. It also includes some of the best and worst of Ford during his later period. The film's artful look and frequent use of expressionism to give certain scenes an otherworldly, and often thought-provoking, atmosphere are very effective, but a contrived plot and heavy-handed and sometimes just plain hapless acting present some serious problems. In many cases, such as the courtroom confession at the end of the film, the actors involved just can't credibly convey what's required.

In an excellent performance in 1960's *Sergeant Rutledge*, Constance Towers plays Mary Beecher, a woman at odds with the white community's treatment of the film's African American title character.

A bright spot in *Sergeant Rutledge* that hasn't received the attention it should is the film's female lead, Mary Beecher, and Constance Towers' portrayal of her. Like other Ford ingénues such as Anne Shirley's Fleety Belle in *Steamboat Round the Bend* or Shirley Temple's Philadelphia in *Fort Apache*, Mary is much more than merely the young female love interest. In her case, she is a curious mix of many parts.

One fascinating characteristic is her relative isolation from all the white characters in the story except (at times) Lieutenant Cantrell (Jeffrey Hunter). When we first meet her we see a refined, intelligent, and insightful person returning to her native Arizona and her father after a 12-year absence. She admits she can barely remember either and soon finds the roughness and violence of the land quite a shock. In the courtroom scenes too, her distance from the other whites is emphasized. Unlike the white men, she is not ready for a lynching. And, unlike the white women, she is not in attendance just to hear the lurid details of the rape and double murder. In fact, her separation is shown visually both in where she sits (in a row by herself and across from most of the other women) and in the color of her dress (a serious dark blue as opposed to the lighter, paler colors the other women wear).

Of the white characters, she's also the most empathetic toward Rutledge. (Cantrell, who is torn between his devotion to duty and his concern for Rutledge, is more sympathetic than empathetic, more detached than involved emotionally.) Mary clearly prefers justice for Rutledge even if that means evading the law. At one point, she even urges Cantrell to simply let Rutledge ride off to Mexico. She doesn't have much faith in the court or in the military or civilian societies that support it to do the right thing.

What's particularly intriguing about Mary is that her own isolation and her empathy toward Rutledge are so closely intertwined, and that, more than any of the white characters, she identifies with him. Like him, she is an outsider in this violent, white dominated society. Like him, she (Her father is killed by Apaches.) is an innocent victim of local violence. Like him, she has little to no confidence in the white man's court. Finally, they share still another bond: at the train station, they each saved the other's life.

We know all along that Mary and Cantrell will get together at the end of the film. But the only way for that to happen is for Cantrell to prove Rutledge innocent and get him released. That is Mary's condition for romance; she will accept nothing less.

Amid *Sergeant Rutledge's* less than lofty acting performances, Towers truly towers. She plays a deceptively complex character in a very understated and convincing way and makes her special connection with Rutledge very real.

A student at both the Julliard School of Music and the American Academy of Dramatic Arts in New York, Towers began her careers as both an actress and singer in the early 1950s. After just a couple of films, she caught Ford's eye and was cast as Hannah Hunter, the female lead in 1959's *The Horse Soldiers*. After her work in *Sergeant Rutledge*, she made several notable films in the 1960s, including 1963's *Shock Corridor* and 1964's *The Naked Kiss* for cult film director Sam Fuller. She has also appeared in more than a dozen other films, in several noted musical theater productions, and on numerous television shows. On the stage, she appeared in a 1966 production of *Show Boat* at Lincoln Center in New York and in a 1977-78 revival of *The King and I* on Broadway. As of 2013, she was still playing the recurring role of the villainous Helene Cassadine on the daytime soap opera *General Hospital*.

Since 1974, Towers has been married to actor and former U.S. ambassador to Mexico, John Gavin. Before that, she was married to businessman Eugene C. McGrath, and in 1960 she and McGrath named their newborn son "Michael Ford" partly to salute the director who brought her to prominence in his film, *The Horse Soldiers*, the year before.

* * *

"Degraded Woman": Linda Cristal's Elena in *Two Rode Together*

Among Ford's later films, one of the most roundly reviled is his 1961 western, *Two Rode Together*, and one of its fiercest critics was Ford himself, who once called it as "the worst piece of crap I've done in 20 years."[9] Ford, who disliked the script, reportedly did it only to fulfill a commitment to Columbia, wanted to get through shooting as quickly as possible, and made no bones about letting his growing cynicism toward Hollywood and human beings in general show through.

Seeing the film, it's often hard to disagree. The story, which recycles many of the plot points of *The Searchers*, is about two ill-suited partners (this time James Stewart and Richard Widmark in place of John Wayne and Jeffrey Hunter) named McCabe and Gary who head out to retrieve a group of white settlers who have been kidnapped by the Comanche. For the most part, the film's quality ranges from middling to poor: the script and the staging are often clunky, the acting often forced and wooden, much of the humor tired and just not funny, and the visual presentation slap-dash. If you could take only 10 Ford films with you to that desert island, this would not be one of them.

That said, the film also has several fine elements.

One that film critics and scholars often point to is a stationary two-shot that runs uninterrupted for nearly four minutes of screen time showing McCabe and Gary sitting and chatting beside a river. The scene does absolutely nothing to advance the plot, but that's not the point. The point is to give texture to the characters and, indirectly, to showcase the two fine actors, Stewart and Widmark. The result is reminiscent of Louis Malle's quirky 1981 film, *My Dinner With Andre*— a delightful celebration of engaged conversation, mutual discovery, and deepening friendship.

Yet, while praise for *Two Rode Together* usually stops with this scene, there is still more to say in the film's behalf. For example, Stewart's performance throughout is quite good. McCabe's hardened cynicism and basic sense of morality constantly seem to be warring inside his head, and Stewart shows this conflict in biting, wry line deliveries that few actors of his time could have pulled off as well. Add to this, Ford regular Mae Marsh has a haunting cameo as Mrs. Clegg, a woman long held by the Comanche, who considers herself already dead and chooses not to return to her husband and sons.

Of the film's oft-neglected assets, however, one of the most impressive is Linda Cristal's performance as Elena, a well-born Mexican woman who has spent five years as a captive squaw and decides to escape with McCabe and Gary. Elena is introduced relatively late into the story, but, once she is, she quickly becomes one of the film's most alluring characters: excited by the prospect of

As a Comanche captive who struggles to find acceptance among "civilized" people after her escape, Linda Cristal's Elena, shown here with James Stewart's McCabe, is a highlight in 1961's *Two Rode Together*.

leaving the Comanche, but still immersed in their ways; filled both with hope for a new life and with despair over the cold, bigoted reception she receives when she returns to "civilization;" guilt-ridden over having lived as the squaw of a Comanche warrior, but sincere in her belief that she has done nothing she should be ashamed of. She also has a sweetness and vulnerability about her that serve as perfect counterpoints to McCabe's sourness and cynicism.

Of the scenes that Cristal and Stewart have together, three especially stand out. In the first, she tells him of her life before she was taken, of the father and the fiancé she loved, of them all traveling to what apparently was going to be the site of her wedding, and of the Comanche meeting them. Then she abruptly stops, caught up in the grief that comes with this memory and hiding her face in her clenched hands. We don't need any further explanation. In the second, which Tag Gallagher has called "lovely,"[10] she tells McCabe how acutely she feels the prejudice of the white people toward her, how they see her as a "degraded woman," and why it might be better for her just to go back to the Comanche. "These people — they smile at me and show their teeth," she says of the whites. "But it's the eyes that bite." After some prodding from McCabe, though, Elena agrees to accompany him to a dance that evening and feels a renewed sense of hope. There's an invigorating freshness about this scene that sharply contrasts with much of the rest of the film. Like the more famous "river scene," much of it was probably improvised, and here, Cristal proves herself as worthy a match for Stewart as Widmark was by the river. In the third of Elena's three key scenes, she confronts her detractors directly at the dance and tells them what her life was like with the Comanche. When she is too pained to continue, McCabe — once so detached — steps in to make an even more impassioned plea for tolerance. Now we can see that, through her openness and basic decency, she is winning over this once-hardened man.

These three scenes nicely encapsulate the changes Elena and McCabe both go through, and Cristal plays all three with great conviction and is very affecting. Because she has a larger role and the opportunity, she also gives us a much better sense of what her character has been through with the Comanche (and what she must now endure from bigoted whites) than we ever get from another Ford character in a similar situation, Natalie Wood's Debbie in *The Searchers*.

Born in Argentina in 1934, Cristal made her English-language film debut in a 1956 Dana Andrews western, titled (ironically, considering her character's story in *Two Rode Together*) *Comanche*. Then, in 1960, she was cast as Flaca in John Wayne's *The Alamo*, a role that brought her great notoriety and likely led to her being cast in *Two Rode Together*. After a "semi-retirement" of a few years to raise her two children, Cristal was persuaded to return to acting full time to play the role for which she is best remembered — Victoria, the young wife of Leif Erickson's "Big John" Cannon on TV's *The High Chaparral*. The series ran on NBC from 1967 to 1971, and in 1969 Cristal won a Golden Globe for her role. After the series ended, Cristal worked occasionally in both film and TV until the 1980s, taking only roles that particularly appealed to her. She has been married and divorced twice.

16

Dare We Call Ford a Feminist?
The Director's Achievement in Context

John Ford would have been the last person to think of himself as a feminist. In fact, if anyone had ever called him one, it's intriguing to imagine his response. Maybe he would have fired back a string of expletives and kicked the person out of the room. Or maybe he would have simply smiled at the irony of it all — the rough, tough "man's director" as feminist — and replied: "I've been called worse things."

Labels are always tricky, and, with someone as complex and often contradictory as Ford was, they are especially tricky. Another issue to consider is the time in which Ford worked. Still another is that so many of his films are period pieces. In *Drums Along the Mohawk*, for example, we have a Hollywood director making a film in 1939 that tells a story involving two frontier women in the 1770s and 1780s. How do we consider feminism in *either* of those contexts?

Yet, if we begin with the general agreement that a feminist is someone who believes that women should be acknowledged as the natural equals of men; offer perspectives that are of significant interest and value to men; and be accorded the same respect, rights, privileges, and opportunities as men, then we can probably call Ford a feminist.

For his time especially, this point of view was quite progressive. Between 1917 and 1965, the years when he directed feature films, men totally dominated the U.S. film industry, and women were almost entirely shut out. With rare exceptions (the actress Mary Pickford, who co-founded United Artists, was one), women had no role whatsoever in producing or distributing films. During this time, too, only three women managed to have directorial careers of even minor significance. Lois Weber[1] (1879–1939) was a pioneering director, screenwriter, and actress whose career faded in the mid–1920s. Dorothy Arzner[2] (1897–1979) made nearly 20 films featuring such actresses as Clara Bow, Katharine Hepburn, Joan Crawford, Lucille Ball, and Ford favorite Maureen O'Hara from the mid–1920s to the early 1940s. And the fine actress Ida Lupino[3] (1918–1995) directed seven feature films in the late 1940s and early 1950s before turning to directing television shows. That's a sum total of three females out of what very likely were thousands of film directors working in Hollywood for nearly half a century.

As it still is in many ways, Hollywood when Ford worked there was a man's world. Many women distinguished themselves as actresses, film editors, costume designers, (occasionally) screenwriters, and in other artistic and production jobs, but the men, in every meaningful sense, called the shots. As we would expect, the stories chosen and the films produced overwhelmingly reflect their particular preoccupations and obsessions — their views of the world.

The key word here is "views" in its plural, not singular, form. While we generally accept that films during the classic period in Hollywood were male dominated and steeped in sexism, the male directors were by no means monolithic in their thinking. The ways they viewed human experience in general and female experience in particular varied widely.

On one hand among the major auteurist directors were people such as Alfred Hitchcock and Howard Hawks. While brilliant as craftsmen and at conveying certain kinds of human experience, women's characters were simply not their strengths.

From time to time, such as in his fine 1943 film, *Shadow of a Doubt*, Hitchcock would present credible and compelling females. The story's main character, Charlotte "Charlie" Newton (Teresa Wright), and her mother, Emma (Patricia Collinge), are two of the most interesting and authentic female characters in all his work: both of them good but sheltered people trying to come to terms with the evil that resides within someone they both love. A big part of their success, however, may also be due to playwright Thornton Wilder, who worked on the script for the film and likely had a hand in giving *Shadow of a Doubt* a level of emotional depth missing in most Hitchcock vehicles. Much more often, Hitchcock's prominent females are his stock-character icy blondes played by Madeline Carroll, Grace Kelly, Kim Novak, Eva Marie Saint, Tippi Hedren, and other actresses. Rather than true-to-life characters, they were projections of his imagination — objects of his obsessions. To his great credit, Hitchcock also showed amazing self-awareness and courage by taking on such subjects as sexual obsession head on. His 1958 film *Vertigo* is certainly proof of this. Still, his films are still almost entirely about his male heroes. We know relatively little about the women. As the actor Joseph Cotton, who worked with Hitchcock on *Shadow of a Doubt* and then 1949's *Under Capricorn*, once wryly observed, "Hitch had very strong feelings about women in his films. To him, the most feminine and most vulnerable women were usually blondes.... He loved blondes and couldn't understand women not bleaching their hair for the privilege of working with him."[4]

Then there's Hawks. Some critics like to talk about the "Hawksian woman," a term first coined by writer Naomi Wise in the 1970s to describe a kind of female character we see over and over and over again in Hawks' films.[5] This woman is forthright about speaking her mind, up to matching her male counterparts in witty (often sexually suggestive) comebacks, and assertive about getting what she wants. Yet, while this character is fun to watch in a few films, it is still a "type" and gets old and predictable very quickly. We also have to wonder just how much this kind of character is, more than anything else, merely a reflection of Hawks' own fantasies about women. In real life, the director made no bones about liking his women young, slim, sassy, and sexually assertive — women who could give as well as they got, and that's what he gives us on screen in role after role played by numerous actresses over the decades. Often, he even coaches these actresses to speak in similar suggestive cadences. Just compare Lauren Bacall in 1944's *To Have and Have Not* with Angie Dickinson in 1959's *Rio Bravo*. The two characters are virtually interchangeable. In fact, in *Rio Bravo*, it looks as if Dickinson is trying her best to do a slinking Bacall impersonation. The director in charge here is clearly not someone very interested in exploring real female experience or conveying real female perspectives.

These two directors had their distinct styles and views of the world of course, but one characteristic they shared with each other as well as many other male directors of the day is what some feminist film critics have referred to as ability to accommodate the "male gaze," both their own and the gazes of the males in the movie-going audience. Cult western director Budd Boetticher has explained this viewpoint this way: "What counts is what the heroine provokes, or rather what she represents," he once noted. "She is the one, or rather the love or fear she inspires in the hero, or else the concern he feels for her, who makes him act the way he does. In herself the woman has not the slightest importance."[6]

On the other side of the spectrum from directors such as Hitchcock and Hawks, however, were directors who seemed far more interested in conveying legitimate female experience and perspectives and in taking considerably more care in creating more honest and recognizable female characters. One was George Cukor, whose work developing female leads portrayed by such actresses as Katharine Hepburn, Judy Holliday and Judy Garland is often cited. Another was Clarence Brown, who worked with actresses from Garbo to Joan Crawford, to Elizabeth Taylor to develop an array of vivid female characters. Still another was Frank Capra who collaborated very successfully with actresses such as Barbara Stanwyck and Jean Arthur. Yet another was the very under-appreciated William Wellman, who directed numerous (and very good) late-silent and Pre-Code films featuring complex and very real female characters that were excellently portrayed by such actresses as Louise Brooks, Ruth Chatterton, Barbara

Stanwyck, and Loretta Young. We can easily add other directors to this list, too.[7]

Among all these directors, Ford is today most often associated with Hawks. (In fact, many people assume that Hawk's 1948 film, *Red River*, is a Ford western.) There are several likely reasons why. Both worked in a variety of genres, excelled in westerns, directed John Wayne in both westerns and non-westerns, had reputations as crusty characters, and were long-time friends.

In portraying women, however, Ford comes much closer to the Cukor/Brown end of the spectrum than to Hawks. And, if any major director of the period might be a true kindred spirit of Ford's with respect to female characters, it might be Wellman, another so-called man's director best known today for his aviation films such as 1927's *Wings* and 1954's *The High and the Mighty* and dark westerns such as 1943's *The Ox-Bow Incident* and 1954's *Track of the Cat*. Wellman, who, in addition to his work with women in many fine Pre-Code films, also co-wrote and directed the 1937 version of *A Star is Born* with Janet Gaynor, is generally not recognized for the variety of vivid female characters in his early films. A major difference, however, is that Wellman delivered his most interesting, complex female characters during a fairly limited period while Ford delivered interesting, complex female characters for more than three decades.

One of Ford's great strengths as a conveyor of women's experiences and perspectives is the great variety of female characters featured in his films. There is no one type of "Fordian female" the way there is a "Hawksian woman." Hannah Jessop in *Pilgrimage* is cruel and selfish but also capable of acknowledging her sins and changing. Beth Morgan in *How Green Was My Valley* is patient and loving with her family but incapable of letting go of the past and adapting to change. Mary Kate in *The Quiet Man* is passionately in love with, but increasingly frustrated by, a basically good man who doesn't appreciate her need to be her own person with her own possessions and financial resources. Dr. Cartwright in *7 Women* must work through her bitterness about being belittled in her male-dominated profession and draw upon all her resources to save the lives of others. These are four completely different individuals in four completely different situations, all confronting completely different issues. They are also only four of dozens of distinctly different female characters we see in these films.

To achieve this kind of diversity and originality with his female characters Ford clearly had to have a sincere, ongoing interest in women's stories and perspectives. In some cases, such as *Four Sons*, *Pilgrimage*, and *7 Women*, he based his films on literature written by women (I.A.R. Wylie and Norah Lofts). In addition, like other great storytellers, he constantly observed human behavior both with a keen eye and great understanding and empathy.

From these starting points, he based his female characters both on stories about distinctive women and his own experiences as an observer. In developing these characters, he might start with a stereotype such as a saintly mother or a prostitute with a heart of gold. Then, he and his scriptwriters would "cultivate" the characters, making them more and more distinctive — and real. For example, the mother figures in *The Grapes of Wrath, How Green Was My Valley,* and *The Searchers* are all in some respects similar. Mostly, however, they are different from each other because they are all so distinctively drawn. Each is truly her own person. The French critic Jean Mitry once described the process this way. After starting with the easily recognizable stereotype, Mitry noted, Ford then gives these characters "life and realism by stuffing them with a thousand details, a thousand original or singular nuances, nuances which burst the seams of the ready-made clothing the characters wore at first, when it was necessary to define them and situate them dramatically."[8]

Ford was influenced by many prevailing film industry trends during his career ranging from the use of expressionism to socially conscious westerns. Yet, when portrayals of women became more negative and demeaning in the 1940s, 1950s, and 1960s with the numerous portrayals of stereotypes from *femme fatales* to "Bond girls," he never followed the pack. Not all of the women he portrays are exemplary of course. Many, such as Grace Kelly's Linda Nordley in *Mogambo* and Margaret Leighton's Agatha Andrews in *7 Women* are deeply flawed. Yet, we see no stereotypical *femme fatales* in his work, and women are never objectified. Maybe Sean Thornton in *The Quiet Man* might find the mere sight of Mary Kate sexually arousing, but, along with him, we soon learn a great deal about who Mary Kate is, how she views the world, and what she's concerned about. When it came to female characters, Ford rarely (if ever) condescended.

In many Ford films, too, the wisest and/or strongest characters are the women. Sometimes these characters are major players in the story such as Jean Arthur's Wilhelmina in *The Whole Town's Talking*, Jane Darwell's Ma Joad in *The Grapes of Wrath*, or Anne Bancroft's Dr. Cartwright in *7 Women*. Other times, while women's roles are relatively small, their wisdom and strength loom large in the story. Numerous examples range from Lucille Laverne's Tilly Hatfield in *Pilgrimage* to Mildred Natwick's Sarah Tillane in *The Quiet Man*, to Olive Carey's Mrs. Jorgensen in *The Searchers*. Still other times, the key female characters experience major personal changes as the stories proceed, becoming much wiser and stronger by story's end. Examples here include Henrietta Crosman's Hannah in *Pilgrimage*, Claudette Colbert's Lana in *Drums Along the Mohawk*, and Ava Gardner's Honey Bear in *Mogambo*.

While the lives of many of Ford's female characters center on their families, the director never depicts them as the natural subordinates to men. They are always full partners in the family enterprise (whether it be a farm or a steamboat) who pitch in and do what needs to be done to keep family and community going. Sometimes they are also the de facto leaders of the community. In *Drums Along the Mohawk*, we see examples of both — Claudette Colbert's Lana, who works in the fields and even takes up arms when she needs to, and Edna May Oliver's Mrs. McKlennar, who ably runs what seems to be the most prosperous land holding in the area.

In many of Ford's films, women also have careers outside the home (and not necessarily just in a brothel). In *The Whole Town's Talking*, Jean Arthur's Wilhelmina works in an accounting firm. In *My Darling Clementine* and *The Sun Shines Bright* Cathy Downs' Clem and Arleen Whelan's Lucy Lee both choose to be teachers. In *They Were Expendable* Donna Reed's Sandy is a career Army nurse. And in *7 Women* Anne Bancroft's Dr. Cartwright is of course a physician.

Even when women must work as prostitutes, Ford shows great sensitivity toward them, consistently giving us the women's points of view in very sympathetic and often very moving ways. Claire Trevor's Dallas in *Stagecoach* has great difficulty doing this kind of work, and it isn't easy for us to watch her in such emotional pain. Joanne Dru's Denver in *Wagon Master* is tougher and maybe a little harder; the work isn't ideal, but she has more or less come to terms with it. In *The Sun Shines Bright*, Ford's surrogate, Judge Priest (Charles Winninger), treats a community of prostitutes — as they pay their final respects to one of their own — with the utmost respect. Showing these women in these ways neither condemns nor glorifies them; it merely illustrates, and often, as in *The Sun Shines Bright*, quite eloquently, that these women are human beings and, as such, deserve respect. If Ford is making any value judgments in these and other cases, he is commenting on the societies he often depicts in his films — hypocritical societies that make snap moral judgments about "fallen women" but that actually offer women scant few other professional options or opportunities for economic independence.

* * *

When put together, the two words "feminism" and "Ford" seem a bit odd, and doubtless people will disagree with the assessment that Ford was at heart (or perhaps intuitively) a feminist. Yet, even though he could be crotchety and cruel, Ford loved people. Joseph McBride and numerous others have written about the lengths that Ford went to in order to conceal his enormous sensitivity and concern for those around him.[9] As actress and life-long friend Olive Carey also described him, he was "a pussycat in a lion's costume."[10] Yet, while he concealed this part of his nature in real life, this "pussycat" freely showed this deep feeling in his films — a feeling for all human beings, women as well as men, ethnic and racial minorities as well as white people who traced their roots to Western Europe. As we see repeatedly in his films, one way he expressed this feeling was

Ford (far right) chats on the set with his principal female cast members in his final feature film, 1966's *7 Women*. From the far left, they include Anne Bancroft, Sue Lyon, Mildred Dunnock, Betty Field (lying down), Jane Chang, Margaret Leighton (standing), Flora Robson and Anna Lee.

by constantly learning about different kinds of people, enriching his understanding of them and their stories, and then conveying their stories as fully, honestly, and forcefully as he could. He was, as his work over the decades clearly tells us, endlessly interested.

From Ford's early work we see exuberant support for a collectivist vision of people from different ethnic backgrounds and with different points of view and beliefs joining forces to achieve a greater good. While his 1923 western epic, *The Iron Horse,* has its Native American stock character bad guys, for example, it is also brimming over with people from different ethnic backgrounds who unite to build the Transcontinental Railroad. Every major ethnic group in America, it seems, is represented in the adventure. While complications abound among the various characters, the camaraderie is exhilarating. For us truly to become one human race, Ford seems to be saying even way back then, we need to acknowledge each other's humanity, treat one another with respect, pull together, and achieve together.

While full acknowledgment of women as partners in this process would come a few years later, it nevertheless came — and it stayed. By the early 1930s, we see the emergence of genuinely original, complex, engaging female characters in Ford films to stand along side his males. And for the next three decades, his films included scores of these characters — Hannah Jessop, Wilhelmina Clark, Dallas, Ma Joad, Beth Morgan, Sandy Davyss, Denver, Kathleen York, Mary Kate Danaher, Honey Bear Kelly, Hallie, Dr. Cartwright, and others as fully realized and memorable as many of the best female characters in many of the best Hollywood films made from the 1930s to the 1960s.

Ford wasn't always successful of course. As noted earlier, his ambitious collaborations with high-profile actresses such as Katharine Hepburn in 1936's *Mary of Scotland* and Barbara Stanwyck in 1937's *The Plow and the Stars* produced dismal results. As a studio director for much of his career, he also received his share of lackluster, "assembly-line" assignments without the freedom to improve upon uninteresting female characters or other script shortcomings.

Yet, even when the female characters in a Ford film weren't very interesting, they were never objectified or treated with condescension. And, when a Ford film shined, his female characters usually did too.

Dare we call Ford a feminist? Why not? He was certainly called worse things.

Conclusion
Electric Moments

The work of few filmmakers sticks with us the way certain electric moments in Ford can stick. They are the cinematic equivalents of great lines from Shakespeare or Keats. They are Ford's poetry at its best.

The longer we think about it, the longer our list of these moments can also grow. In one of Ford's great films, there can be dozens of such moments. In his body of work, there are certainly hundreds, maybe even thousands. Coming from the so-called "man's director," it is also intriguing how many of them center on his female characters — the moments when Ma Joad looks into the mirror and poses with her earrings; when Angharad's bridal veil flies wildly into the air outside the church immediately after she has married the wrong man; when Mary Kate Danaher pleads for her "fortune;" when Hallie asks Link Appleyard to cut a cactus rose for her; when Hannah Jessop, learning that her son has died, tries to piece together the photograph of him she once tore up in anger. This list can go on and on.

As we see time and again in Ford's work, women and their experiences were extremely important to him. He took great pride in conveying these experiences artfully and with great understanding and empathy. In many films, he was quite successful, and once we scratch the surface of his work, we see the evidence all about.

Most of the characters in most Ford films are, of course, men. Male themes and male-dominated stories often appealed to him, and he was, after all, living and working in very much of a man's world. Yet, as his work tells us, Ford's artistic intent was always to explore a wide spectrum of human experience, not just male experience. In fact, part of what distinguishes him from most (if not nearly all) of the auteurist directors of his time was his ability to effectively portray an incredibly wide array of human beings. This amazing breadth has prompted film director Walter Hill to compare Ford to Dickens[1] and Joseph

McBride to liken Ford to Tolstoy.[2] In both cases, this is high praise indeed, and it is richly deserved. As with the complete works of Dickens or Tolstoy, literally thousands of characters populate the films of Ford. They come from every walk of life. They can be comic or tragic. They represent the best among us, the worst among us, and all that's in between. Hundreds and hundreds of these characters are women, and together, these female characters add immense depth and dimension to the author's work.

To overlook the women in Ford films is — purely and simply — to overlook a major part of Ford's artistic achievement. Just imagine watching his films without ever seeing Ma Joad pose with her earrings, Mary Kate plead for her "fortune," Hallie ask for the cactus rose, or scores of other electric Ford moments that are all about the women. It would be an entirely different experience, wouldn't it?

Recommended Resources for Further Reference

"We love him like we love the Lord. We're students of the great John Ford."
— author unknown (from 1948 lyric found in Ford's papers)

An immense amount of information about John Ford and his films is available — so much that it's often difficult for people who want to learn more about Ford to know where to start. Among the many available resources, here are several well worth investigating.

1. Joseph McBride, *Searching for John Ford* (New York: St. Martin's Griffin, 2001). Among the Ford biographies, this is probably the best. Not only does it correct many inaccuracies found in earlier works, but it's a very thorough and impressive piece of scholarship. McBride spent more than 30 years working on this book and, in the process, interviewed Ford and scores of people who worked with him. While McBride is unabashed in his great love for Ford's films, however, he never lets his partisanship get in the way of probing, well-balanced scholarship. For a newcomer to Ford who is interested in getting as much of the "whole story" as possible and who is willing to invest some time in the pursuit of this goal, *Searching for John Ford* is a great place to start.

2. Tag Gallagher, *John Ford: The Man and His Films* (Berkeley: University of California Press, 1986). The main focus here is Ford's films, and time and time again Gallagher has brilliant — and often very radical — insights into them. He is especially effective at showing the subversive undercurrents in many of Ford's great films such as *How Green Was My Valley*, *Fort Apache*, and *The Man Who Shot Liberty Valance*. While I sometimes disagree with Gallagher's assessments (for example, he sees much more in 1963's *Donovan's Reef* than I do), this is an exhilarating read from start to finish.

3. Peter Bogdanovich, *John Ford* (Berkeley: University of California

Press, 1978). As well as being a highly respected film director in his own right, Peter Bogdanovich is one of the foremost authorities on Ford and his work. This book, one of the first ever written about Ford, remains an excellent resource. In addition to several very perceptive essays, it includes an in-depth interview with Ford himself and perhaps the first comprehensive, detailed Ford filmography.

4. Lindsay Anderson, *About John Ford* (London: Plexus, 1981). Like Bogdanovich, Lindsay Anderson was a film critic turned film director who knew Ford well for many years, championed him when he was out of fashion, and wrote a major book about him. Anderson has his own controversial opinions. He calls 1953's *The Sun Shines Bright* Ford's last great film, for example, and feels that *The Searchers* is highly overrated. He also is sharply critical of many younger Ford scholars, who, he believes, often overestimate the quality of Ford's later work. But, agree with him or not, Anderson is always compelling.

5. Andrew Sarris, *The John Ford Murder Mystery* (Bloomington: University of Indiana Press, 1975). Andrew Sarris, the legendary film critic who promoted the French "auteur" theory (that the best films are directed by people with distinctive artistic visions who serve, in effect, as the films' authors) in the U.S. and singled out Ford as one of cinema's great auteurs, offers a thoughtful, affectionate, and sometimes poetic appraisal of Ford's work.

6. Scott Eyman, *Print the Legend: The Life and Times of John Ford* (Baltimore: Johns Hopkins University Press, 1999). This biography includes parts of interviews with many people who knew Ford and who aren't included in McBride's biography or other books on Ford. It's also an interesting counterpoint to the takes McBride, Gallagher, and others have on many of Ford's films.

7. Robert Pippin, *Hollywood Westerns and the American Myth: The Importance of Howard Hawks and John Ford for Political Philosophy* (New Haven: Yale University Press, 2010). This book consists of three very perceptive extended essays on Howard Hawks' *Red River* as well as Ford's *The Searchers* and *The Man Who Shot Liberty Valance*. The essay on *Valance* is especially good at explaining the issues the film explores and how they relate to both traditional and contemporary American political attitudes.

8. Jim Kitses, *Horizons West: Directing the Western from John Ford to Clint Eastwood* (London: BFI, 2004). This is a very thoughtful look at six directors who shaped the western genre from Ford to Eastwood. By far the longest and most detailed entry is on Ford and includes in-depth discussions not only of his westerns but also of other important Ford "Americana" films such as *Pilgrimage* and *Drums Along the Mohawk*.

9. Peter Bogdanovich, *Directed by John Ford* (television documentary), Turner Classic Movies, 2006. This is an exceptionally good two-hour retrospective of Ford and his work. As well as many wonderful clips from Ford films, it includes interviews both with people who worked with Ford (John Wayne, James Stewart, Henry Fonda, Harry Carey, Jr., etc.) and with contemporary directors (Steven Spielberg, Martin Scorsese, Clint Eastwood, etc.) who discuss Ford's contribution to film and his enduring influence.

10. **Directed by John Ford** (www.directedbyjohnford.com). This excellent website was created and is managed by April Lane, who writes often about Ford's films and other classic film subjects. Lane has made this site an online "Ford Central" filled with galleries of photographs of Ford and of scenes from Ford films, information about actors and others who worked for Ford, links to articles and YouTube videos about Ford, information about upcoming events in which Ford films are featured, news about upcoming Ford DVD releases, and much more.

Chapter Notes

Abbreviations of Frequently Cited Sources

Anderson: Lindsay Anderson, *About John Ford* (London: Plexus, 1981).
Bogdanovich: Peter Bogdanovich, *John Ford* (Berkeley: University of California Press, 1978).
Eyman: Scott Eyman, *Print the Legend: The Life and Times of John Ford* (Baltimore: Johns Hopkins University Press, 1999).
Gallagher: Tag Gallagher, *John Ford: The Man and His Films* (Berkeley: University of California Press, 1986).
Kitses: Jim Kitses, *Horizons West: Directing the American Western from John Ford to Clint Eastwood* (London: BFI, 2004).
McBride: Joseph McBride, *Searching for John Ford* (New York: St. Martin's Griffin, 2001).
Sarris: Andrew Sarris, *The John Ford Murder Mystery* (Bloomington: University of Indiana Press, 1975).

Introduction

1. Sarris, p. 30.
2. The five actresses nominated for Academy Awards in Ford films include one for Best Actress, Ava Gardner for *Mogambo* in 1953, and four for Best Supporting Actress: Edna May Oliver for *Drums Along the Mohawk*, 1939; Jane Darwell for *The Grapes of Wrath*, 1940; Sara Allgood for *How Green Was My Valley*, 1941; and Grace Kelly for *Mogambo*, 1953. Darwell was the only Oscar winner.
3. Joseph McBride, David Shepard, and Jonathan Rosenbaum have praised Crosman's performance. McBride, Andrew Sarris, Tag Gallagher, Danny Peary, and others have praised Bancroft's performance.
4. Bogdanovich, p. 110.

Chapter 1

1. Joseph McBride, *Audio Commentary of Pilgrimage on DVD* (Beverly Hills: Twentieth Century–Fox Home Entertainment, 2007).
2. McBride, pp. 194–5.
3. Bogdanovich, p. 24.
4. Andre Sennwald, "Henrietta Crosman Scores in *Pilgrimage*, Which Has Premiere at the Gaiety," *The New York Times*, July 13, 1933.

Chapter 2

1. Much has been written about the pre-code era, a period in Hollywood that has become endlessly fascinating to today's classic film enthusiasts. Two books worth looking at for more information are Thomas Doherty's *Pre-Code Hollywood: Sex, Immorality, and Insurrection in American Cinema* (1999) and Mick LaSalle's *Complicated Women: Sex and Power in Pre-Code Hollywood* (2003).
2. Stephen Harvey, "Jean Arthur: Passionate Primrose," in *Close Ups: Intimate Profiles*

of Movie Stars by Their Co-Stars, Directors, Screenwriters, and Friends, Danny Peary, ed. (New York: Workman, 1978), p. 432.
  3. Andre Sennwald, "A Whirl of Laughter at the Music Hall in 'The Whole Town's Talking,'" review, *The New York Times*, March 1, 1935.
  4. Michael Costello, "The Whole Town's Talking," Allmovie review by rovi.
  5. Edward G. Robinson and Leonard Spigelgass, *All My Yesterdays: An Autobiography* (New York: Hawthorn, 1974).
  6. John Oller, *Jean Arthur: The Actress Nobody Knew* (New York: Lamplight Editions, 1997).
  7. Charles Champlin, "An Appreciation — Jean Arthur's Legacy of Indelible Performances," *The Los Angeles Times*, June 20, 1991.

Chapter 3

  1. Gallagher, p. 125.
  2. Sarris, p. 58.
  3. Stepin Fetchit, whose real name was Lincoln Perry, specialized in roles that depicted subservient black stereotypes in — depending on the viewer's interpretation — either a mocking or straightforward manner. Eventually, Hollywood saw him as an embarrassment, and, after the mid–1940s, he rarely worked. His presence in older films usually gives today's race-conscious viewers a very uncomfortable feeling. But in Ford's films his characters are generally treated affectionately and respectfully.
  4. Gary Brumburgh, "Anne Shirley (1918–1993)," IMDb.

Chapter 4

  1. McBride, p. 258.
  2. Rudy Behlmer, ed., *Memo from Darryl F. Zanuck: The Golden Years at Twentieth Century–Fox* (New York: Grove, 1993), pp. 6–7.
  3. Shirley Temple Black, *Child Star: An Autobiography* (New York: Warner Books, 1988), p. 182.
  4. Ibid., p. 185.
  5. Sarris, p. 76.
  6. Quoted in Leslie Halliwell, *Halliwell's Filmgoer's Companion* (New York: Scribner, 1984).

Chapter 5

  1. Bertrand Tavernier, "Notes of a Press Attaché: John Ford in Paris," *Film Comment* 30 (July–Aug. 1994).
  2. Joanne Dru interview with Hedda Hopper, 1957.

Chapter 6

  1. Kitses, pp. 51–3.
  2. Frank Nugent, "John Ford's Film of 'Drums Along the Mohawk' Opens at the Roxy — 'One Hour to Live' at the Rialto," *The New York Times*, November 4, 1939.
  3. Zanuck, p. 22.
  4. Kitses, p. 53.
  5. Ibid., p. 54.
  6. Nugent.
  7. "Obituary: Claudette Colbert," Tributes.com.
  8. Thomas McWilliams, "Edna May Oliver," IMDb.
  9. "A Biography of Edna May Oliver," http://www.angelfire.com/tx2/rainbow11/EDNABIO.html.

Chapter 7

  1. Rudy Behlmer, *Memo from Darryl F. Zanuck: The Golden Years of Twentieth Century–Fox* (New York: Grove Press, 1993), p. 36.
  2. Bosley Crowther, "How Green Was My Valley," *The New York Times*, October 29, 1941.
  3. Gallagher, pp. 185–6.
  4. "Biography for Jane Darwell," IMDb.

Chapter 8

  1. Eyman, p. 228.
  2. Ibid.
  3. Ibid., pp. 228–9.
  4. Ibid., p. 347.
  5. Peter Flint, "Mildred Natwick, 89, Actress Who Excelled at Eccentricity," *The New York Times*, October 26, 1994.

Chapter 9

  1. Sarris, p. 114.

2. Larry Rohter, "Dear Donna: A Pinup So Swell She Kept G.I. Mail," *The New York Times*, May 25, 2009.
3. Anderson, p. 108.
4. Ibid., p. 107.
5. Sarris, p. 114.
6. Susan King, "Classic Hollywood: The Donna Reed Show," *The Los Angeles Times*, December 26, 2011.

Chapter 10

1. Maureen O'Hara and Johnny Nicoletti, *'Tis Herself* (New York: Simon & Schuster, 2004), p. 166.
2. Rudy Behlmer, *Memo from Darryl F. Zanuck: The Golden Years at Twentieth Century–Fox* (New York: Grove Press, 1993), p. 43.
3. O'Hara and Nicoletti, p. 165.
4. Sarris, p. 135, quoting Molly Haskell, *From Reverence to Rape: The Treatment of Women in the Movies*.
5. O'Hara and Nicoletti, p. 170.
6. Ibid., p. 303.
7. Sé Merry Doyle, dir., *John Ford: Dreaming The Quiet Man* (Dublin: Irish Film and Television Network, 2012).

Chapter 11

1. Gallagher, p. 312.
2. Dorris Rollins Cannon, *Grabtown Girl: Ava Gardner's North Carolina Childhood and Her Enduring Ties to Home* (Asheboro, NC: Down Home Press, 2001).
3. "Biography for Ava Gardner," IMDb.
4. Laura Jacobs, "Grace Kelly's Forever Look," *Vanity Fair*, May 2010.
5. Ibid.
6. James Spada, *Grace: The Secret Lives of a Princess* (New York: Dell, 1987) p. 65.
7. Dore Schary, *Heyday* (New York: Berkeley Books, 1979), p. 256.
8. Gallagher, p. 311.
9. Joseph Cotton, *Vanity Will Get You Somewhere* (Lincoln, NE: toExcel Press, 1987), p. 114.
10. Spada, p. 73.
11. Ibid.

Chapter 12

1. Steven Spielberg, *Steven Spielberg on Watching John Ford Films*, American Film Institute Archive video, retrieved from You Tube, March 15, 2013.
2. J. Hoberman, "American Obsession," *The New York Times*, February 22, 2013.
3. Bosley Crowther, "The Searchers," *The New York Times*, May 31, 1956.
4. "The Searchers," *Variety*, May 13, 1956.
5. Anderson, p. 160.
6. Roger Ebert, "The Searchers, 1956," *Chicago Sun-Times*, November 25, 2001.

Chapter 13

1. Gallagher, pp. 384–413.
2. Robert Pippin, *Hollywood Westerns and the American Myth: The Importance of Howard Hawks and John Ford for Political Philosophy* (New Haven: Yale University Press, 2010).
3. McBride, p. 628.
4. Quoted on Wikipedia, no source given.

Chapter 14

1. Sarris, p. 185.
2. *Cahiers du Cinema* Top Ten List, 1966, http://alumnus.caltech.edu/~ejohnson/critics/cahiers.html#y1966.
3. Bogdanovich, p. 107.
4. Eyman, p. 523.
5. McBride, p. 663.
6. Ronald L. Davis, *John Ford: Hollywood's Old Master* (Norman: University of Oklahoma Press, 1997), p. 332.
7. "Anne Bancroft Dies at 73," NBC News, updated June 10, 2005.
8. "*Graduate* Star Anne Bancroft Dies," BBC News, June 8, 2005.
9. Ibid.
10. Sarris, p. 185.

Chapter 15

1. Gallagher, pp. 84–6.
2. Anderson, p. 57.
3. Danny Peary, *Alternate Oscars* (New York: Dell, 1993), p. 20.
4. Maureen O'Hara and John Nicoletti. *'Tis Herself* (New York: Simon & Schuster, 2004), p. 71.

5. Bosley Crowther, "'Darling Clementine,' With Henry Fonda as Marshal of Tombstone, a Stirring Film of West," *The New York Times*, December 4, 1946.
6. Gallagher, p. 232.
7. Kitses, pp. 58–9.
8. Burt Kennedy, "Burt Kennedy Interviews John Ford," *Action*, August 1968.
9. McBride, p. 618.
10. Gallagher, p. 377.

Chapter 16

1. Lois Weber was a major Hollywood player in the 1910s and early 1920s, and her films often tackled female poverty, spousal abuse, birth control, and other feminist issues at a time when these subjects were considered extremely provocative. Although she made many films, only a handful of them have survived. One excellent drama restored in the 1990s now available on DVD is 1921's *The Blot*.
2. In addition to being the only woman director in Hollywood from the late 1920s to the early 1940s, Dorothy Arzner made films that often dealt with the struggle of women to protect their female integrity in a male-dominated world. An interesting example of her work now on DVD is 1940's *Dance, Girl, Dance*, which teams Maureen O'Hara and Lucille Ball.
3. While on suspension from Warner Bros. for turning down an acting role in the mid–1940s, Ida Lupino became interested in directing. And, by the late 1940s, she had become the first woman to direct film noir. Of Lupino's seven films, two — 1953's *The Hitch-Hiker* and *The Bigamist* — are probably her most intriguing. After the mid-1950s, she went on to direct in television, including episodes of such classic series as *The Twilight Zone* and *Have Gun, Will Travel*.
4. Joseph Cotton, *Vanity Will Get You Somewhere* (Lincoln, NE: toExcel Press, 1987), p. 66.
5. Naomi Wise, "The Hawksian Woman," Reprinted in Jim Hillier and Peter Wollen, eds., *Howard Hawks, American Artist* (London: BFI, 1996).
6. Patricia Erens, "Introduction," *Issues in Feminist Film Criticism*, Patricia Erens, ed. (Bloomington: Indiana University Press, 1990), pp. xvi.
7. There is an enormous amount more that can be said about these directors and the female characters presented in their films. Here are just a few more comments. Among Cukor's films, a favorite for its female lead is 1952's *The Marrying Kind* with Judy Holliday. Among Brown's, one standout is 1944's *National Velvet* with Elizabeth Taylor, Anne Revere, and Angela Lansbury. Among Capra's, two excellent examples are 1939's *Mr. Smith Goes to Washington* with Jean Arthur and 1941's much darker *Meet John Doe* with Barbara Stanwyck. Among Wellman's, 1928's *Beggars of Life* with Louise Brooks and 1931's *Safe in Hell* with Dorothy Mackaill, are well worth seeing. Also, other noted directors occasionally collaborated very successfully with actresses. One example is Michael Curtiz and Joan Crawford in 1945's *Mildred Pierce*. Another is Fritz Lang and Gloria Grahame in 1953's *The Big Heat* and 1954's *Human Desire*.
8. Gallagher, p. 466 (Mitry quote translated by Gallagher).
9. McBride, pp. 2–3.
10. Ibid., p. 3.

Conclusion

1. Peter Bogdanovich, *Directed by John Ford* (New York: Turner Classic Movies, 2006).
2. Joseph McBride, *Audio Commentary of Pilgrimage on DVD* (Beverly Hills: Twentieth Century–Fox Home Entertainment, 2007).

Selected Bibliography

Anderson, Lindsay. *About John Ford.* London: Plexus, 1981.
Behlmer, Rudy, ed. *Memo from Darryl F. Zanuck: The Golden Years at Twentieth Century-Fox.* New York: Grove Press, 1993.
Black, Shirley Temple. *Child Star: An Autobiography.* New York: Warner Books, 1988.
Bogdanovich, Peter. *Directed by John Ford.* New York: Turner Classic Movies, 2006.
_____. *John Ford.* Berkeley: University of California Press, 1978.
Cannon, Dorris Rollins. *Grabtown Girl: Ava Gardner's North Carolina Childhood and Her Enduring Ties to Home.* Asheboro, NC: Down Home Press, 2001.
Champlin, Charles. "An Appreciation—Jean Arthur's Legacy of Indelible Performances." *The Los Angeles Times,* June 20, 1991.
Colman, Juliet Benita. *Ronald Colman: A Very Private Person.* New York: William Morrow, 1975.
Cotton, Joseph. *Vanity Will Get You Somewhere.* Lincoln, NE: toExcel Press, 1987.
Cowie, Peter. *John Ford and the American West.* New York: Harry N. Abrams, 2004.
Crowther, Bosley. "'Darling Clementine,' With Henry Fonda as Marshal of Tombstone, a Stirring Film of West." *The New York Times,* December 4, 1946.
_____. "How Green Was My Valley." *New York Times,* October 29, 1941.
_____. "The Searchers." *The New York Times,* May 31, 1956.
Davis, Ronald L. *John Ford: Hollywood's Old Master.* Norman: University of Oklahoma Press, 1997.
Doyle, Sé Merry, dir. *John Ford: Dreaming The Quiet Man.* Dublin: Irish Film and Television Network, 2012.
Ebert, Roger. "The Searchers, 1956." *Chicago Sun-Times,* November 25, 2001.
Epstein, Dwayne. *Lee Marvin: Point Blank.* Tucson: Schaffner Press, 2013.
Erens, Patricia. "Introduction." *Issues in Feminist Film Criticism.* Ed. Patricia Erens. Bloomington: Indiana University Press, 1990.
Eyman, Scott. *Print the Legend: The Life and Times of John Ford.* Baltimore: Johns Hopkins University Press, 1999.
Flint, Peter. "Mildred Natwick, 89, Actress Who Excelled at Eccentricity." *The New York Times,* October 26, 1994.
Gallagher, Tag. *John Ford: The Man and His Films.* Berkeley: University of California Press, 1986.
Harvey, Stephen. "Jean Arthur: Passionate Primrose." *Close Ups: Intimate Profiles of Movie Stars by Their Co-Stars, Directors, Screenwriters, and Friends.* Ed. Danny Peary. New York: Workman, 1978.
Hoberman, J. "American Obsession." *The New York Times,* February 22, 2013.

Jacobs, Laura. "Grace Kelly's Forever Look." *Vanity Fair*, May 2010.
Kennedy, Burt. "Burt Kennedy Interviews John Ford." *Action*, August 1968.
King, Susan. "Classic Hollywood: *The Donna Reed Show*." *The Los Angeles Times*, December 26, 2011.
Kitses, Jim. *Horizons West: Directing the Western from John Ford to Clint Eastwood*. London: BFI, 2004.
Lane, April. *Directed by John Ford*. www.directedbyjohnford.com.
McBride, Joseph. *Audio Commentary of Pilgrimage on DVD*. Beverly Hills: Twentieth Century–Fox Home Entertainment, 2007.
_____. *Searching for John Ford*. New York: St. Martin's Griffin, 2001.
Mast, Gerald, and Bruce Kawin. *A Short History of the Movies*. New York: Pearson Longman, 2006.
Nugent, Frank. "John Ford's Film of 'Drums Along the Mohawk' Opens at the Roxy—'One Hour to Live' at the Rialto." *The New York Times*, November 4, 1939.
O'Hara, Maureen, and John Nicoletti. *'Tis Herself*. New York: Simon & Schuster Paperbacks, 2004.
Oller, John. *Jean Arthur: The Actress Nobody Knew*. New York: Lamplight Editions, 1997.
Peary, Danny. *Alternate Oscars*. New York: Dell, 1993.
Pippin, Robert. *Hollywood Westerns and the American Myth: The Importance of Howard Hawks and John Ford for Political Philosophy*. New Haven: Yale University Press, 2010.
Robinson, Edward G., and Leonard Spigelgass. *All My Yesterdays: An Autobiography*. New York: Hawthorn, 1974.
Rohter, Larry. "Dear Donna: A Pinup So Swell She Kept G.I. Mail." *The New York Times*, May 25, 2009.
Sarris, Andrew. *The John Ford Murder Mystery*. Bloomington: University of Indiana Press, 1975.
Schary, Dore. *Heyday*. New York: Berkeley Books, 1979.
Sennwald, Andre. "Henrietta Crosman Scores in *Pilgrimage*, Which Has Premiere at the Gaiety." *The New York Times*, July 13, 1933.
_____. "A Whirl of Laughter at the Music Hall in 'The Whole Town's Talking.'" *The New York Times*, March 1, 1935.
Spada, James. *Grace: The Secret Lives of a Princess*. New York: Dell, 1987.
Spielberg, Steven. *Steven Spielberg on Watching John Ford Films*. American Film Institute Archive video.
Wise, Naomi. "The Hawksian Woman." Reprinted in *Howard Hawks, American Artist*, Jim Hillier and Peter Wollen, eds. London: British Film Institute, 1996.

Index

Academy Awards 2, 6, 12, 41, 62, 63, 64, 72, 73, 74, 78–79, 89, 97, 110, 118
All About Eve 71
All My Yesterdays 32
All the King's Men 53
Allgood, Sara 7, 9, 72–82, 161
Altman, Al 110
American Film Institute 120
Anderson, Lindsay 1, 93, 121, 153
Anne of Green Gables (novel and 1934 film version) 35
Archuletta, Beulah 122, 131–132
Arthur, Jean 25–33
Arzner, Dorothy 172
Astaire and Rogers 99
Aster, Mary 7
August, Joe 26, 30, 92

Bacall, Lauren 174
The Bachelor and the Bobby-Soxer 44
Bancroft, Anne 2, 142–151, 178; meeting Mel Brooks 151
Bancroft, George 55
The Barefoot Contessa 118
Barefoot in the Park (1967 film) 89
Beery, Wallace 153
Bergman, Ingmar 6
Bernstein, Elmer 147
Blackmail 74
Blair, Charles 108
Bluebeard's Eighth Wife 65
Boetticher, Budd 174
Bogdanovich, Peter 15, 16, 19, 142
Bond, Ward 88, 92
Born to Kill 60
Bright Eyes 43
British Film Institute (*Sight & Sound*) 120
Brown, Clarence 7, 174

Brumburgh, Gary 42
Bucking Broadway 8
Burke, Billie 7

Cameo Kirby 28
Candida (stage play) 84
Candy, John 108
Capra, Frank 6, 32, 64, 174
Carey, Harry, Jr. 56, 88
Carey, Harry, Sr. 8
Carey, Olive 122, 128, 129–130, 177
Carroll, Madeline 7
Champlin, Charles 32–33
Chang, Jane 178
Charlie Chan's Secret 24
Cheaper by the Dozen (1950 film) 82, 89
Cheyenne Autumn 26
Child Star 47
Citizen Kane 54, 78–79
Cleopatra (1934 film) 64
Cobb, Irwin S. 165
Colbert, Claudette 6, 62–71
Collinge, Patricia 173
Complicated Women 154
Cooper, Gary 53, 112
Cooper, Merian C. 122, 126
Coppola, Francis Ford 6
Costello, Michael 32
Cotten, Joseph 118, 173
The Country Girl 119
Coy, Walter 127
Crisp, Donald 77
Cristal, Linda 7, 169–171
Crosman, Henrietta 7, 15–24
The Crowd 29–30
Crowther, Bosley 121, 162
Cukor, George 7, 17, 174
Curly Top 43

193

Index

Dallas (TV series) 97
Dance, Girl, Dance 101
Darwell, Jane 7, 9, 12, 72–82, 88
David Copperfield (1935 film) 65
DeMille, Cecil B. 64
Devine, Andy 55
Dial M for Murder 119
Diamonds Are Forever 127
Dickenson, Angie 174
Dieterle, William 30
Dietrich, Marlene 7, 53
Disney, Walt 82
Dr. Bull 34
Donna Reed Foundation for the Performing Arts (and Donna Reed Festival) 98
The Donna Reed Show 97
Downs, Cathy 97, 162–164
Dru, Joanne 7, 52–61
Drums Along the Mohawk 62–71, 172
Dunnock, Mildred 7, 147, 178

Eastwood, Clint 6
Ebert, Roger 121
The Egg and I 71
Emmy Award 71, 97
Eyman, Scott 85, 143

Fabares, Shelley 97
The Far Horizons 97
Field, Betty 21, 147, 178
Flesh 152–154
Fonda, Henry 5, 10, 73, 75, 82, 107, 164
Ford, John: with female characters 6–14, 172–179; in film history 5–6; portrayal of mothers 9, 21–22; silent era work 6–9; treatment of family 70
Fort Apache 8, 43–51, 62
Four Sons 9, 21
Fourteen Hours 112
From Here to Eternity 97
From Reverence to Rape 106–107

Gable, Clark 109–110, 116
Gallagher, Tag 15, 16, 34, 41, 109–110, 135, 152, 163, 170
Garbo, Greta 7
Gardner, Ava 2, 6, 12, 109–119
Gaynor, Janet 7
Gilbert, John 28
Godard, Jean-Luc 6
Golden Globe Award 71, 97
The Grapes of Wrath 6, 22, 62, 72–82
Guestward Ho! 60
Gunfight at the O.K. Corral 129

Hammond, Virginia 71
Hangman's House 8
Haskell, Molly 106
Hawks, Howard 6, 11, 173–174, 175
Hayes, Helen 7
Hepburn, Katharine 7, 12
High Noon 112
Hill, Walter 180
Hitchcock, Alfred 11, 26, 71, 136, 173
Hoberman, J. 120
How Green Was My Valley 6, 22, 72–82, 100, 101, 159–162
The Hucksters 111
Humberstone, H. Bruce 166
The Hunchback of Notre Dame (1939 film) 100
Hunter, Jeffrey 128, 131

The Informer 85
The Iron Horse 8, 52, 178
It Happened One Night 64
It's a Wonderful Life 91, 97

Jacobs, Laura 112
Jamaica Inn 100
John Ford: Dreaming The Quiet Man 108
John Ford Stock Company 88–89, 117
Johnson, Ben 56, 88
Johnson, Nunnally 75
Jolson, Al 53
Jones, Shirley 7
Jordon, Dorothy 122, 126
Judge Priest 34, 158
Juno and the Peacock 74

Kelly, Grace 2, 7, 12, 109–119, 136
Key Largo 60
The Keys of the Kingdom (1944 film)
The Killers (1946 film) 111
King Kong (1933 film version) 126
Kipling, Rudyard 45
Kitses, Jim 63, 67, 69, 163
Kurosawa, Akira 6

Lancaster, Burt 111
Lang, Fritz 26
Laughton, Charles 100, 108
La Verne, Lucille 7, 154–156
Lean, David 6
Lee, Anna 7, 49, 160–162, 178
Leighton, Margaret 7, 147, 178
The Little Colonel 43
The Littlest Rebel 43
Llewellyn, Richard 77

Index

Lofts, Nora 175
Logan, Joshua 84
The Long Voyage Home 84–86
The Los Angeles Times 32
The Lost Patrol 7, 96
Loy, Myrna 7, 99
Lukas, George 6
Lupino, Ida 173
Lydia 192
Lyon, Sue 147, 178

The Man Who Shot Liberty Valance 11, 62, 79, 100, 131, 135–141
Mann, Margaret 10
Marsh, Mae 169
Mary of Scotland 12–13
Mary Poppins (1964 film) 82
Mayer, Louis B. 110
Mayerling 118
McBride, Joseph 14, 15, 135, 143, 180–181
McDaniel, Hattie 7, 70, 158
McDowell, Roddy 159
McLaglen, Victor 46–47
Men Without Women 8, 96
Midnight (film) 65
Miles, Vera 7, 14, 122, 128, 131, 135–141
The Miracle of Merriford 142
Miracle on 34th Street 101
Mr. Hobbs Takes a Vacation 108
Mitchell, Thomas 12–13, 55
Mitry, Jean 176
Mogambo 11, 100, 109–119, 164
Monroe, Marilyn 11
Montgomery, Robert 91, 92, 96
Morley, Karen 7, 152–154
Motion Picture Producers and Distributors of America (MPPDA) 25
Motion Picture Production Code 25–26
Mourning Becomes Electra (1947 film) 82
Murder, My Sweet 41
Murnau, F.W. 10, 21, 152
My Darling Clementine 82, 97, 162–164

Natwick, Mildred 7, 83–89, 122
Neal, Patricia 143, 144
New York Film Critics Awards 72
The New York Times 24, 29, 67, 78, 120, 121
Nichols, Dudley 10, 16
Nichols, Mike 151
The Night of the Iguana (1964 film) 118
Nixon, Marian 7, 156–157
Nugent, Frank 67, 70

O'Brien, George 84

O'Connor, Una 84
O'Hara, Maureen 2, 7, 21, 99–108, 159–160
Oliver, Edna May 7, 62–71
On Dangerous Ground 129
On the Beach 118
Only the Lonely 108
Otis, Elizabeth 75
Our Man in Havana (1959 film) 108
The Ox-Bow Incident (1943 film) 82
The Palm Beach Story 71
The Parent Trap 108

Peary, Danny 154
Pickford, Mary 172
Pilgrimage 7, 13, 15–24, 147, 154–156
Pippin, Robert 135
The Playboy of the Western World 74
The Plow and the Stars 12
Pommer, Erich 100
Portrait of Jennie 30
Powell, William 99
Pre-Code period 25
Pride and Prejudice 71
The Pride of St. Louis 60

Qualen, John 128
The Quiet Man 11, 84, 87–88, 99–108, 164

Raw Deal 60
The Real McCoys 82
Rear Window 119
Red Dust 109, 113
Red River 53, 175
Reed, Donna 7, 90–98
Renoir, Jean 6
Rich, Irene 49
Rio Bravo 174
Rio Grande 11, 21, 99–108
Robinson, Edward G. 26, 32
Robson, Flora 7, 147, 178
Rogers, Will 6, 34–35, 36
Romeo and Juliet (1936 film version) 65
The Royal Family of Broadway 17

Sabotage 74
Sarris, Andrew 9, 34–35, 51, 90, 94, 142, 151
Schary, Dore 112
Scorsese, Martin 6
Screen Actors Guild Lifetime Achievement Award 51
The Searchers 22–23, 26, 120–134, 136; influence on other films 121

Sennwald, Andre 24
Sergeant Rutledge 11, 26, 166–168
Seven Days in May 118
7 Women 11, 13, 21, 142–151
Shadow of a Doubt 173
She Wore a Yellow Ribbon 8, 53, 84, 87
Shepard, David 15
Shirléy, Anne 7, 34–42
Show Boat (1951 film version) 111
The Sign of the Cross 64
Simpson, Russell 92
Since You Went Away 44
Snow White and the Seven Dwarves 83
Spada, James 119
Spielberg, Steven 6, 120
The Spiral Staircase 82
Stagecoach 52–61, 62
Stand Up and Cheer! 43
Stanwyck, Barbara 7, 12, 41
Steamboat Round the Bend 30, 34–42, 52
Steinbeck, John 74, 75
Stella Dallas 41
Stevens, George 32
Stewart, James 14, 137, 169
Stone, Oliver 6
Straight Shooting 8
The Sun Shines Bright 82, 126, 164–166, 177

A Tale of Two Cities (1935 film) 65
Taxi (1950 film) 112
Technicolor 62–63
Temple, Shirley 2, 7, 43–51; political career 51
They Were Expendable 11, 30, 90–98
3 Bad Men 8
3 Godfathers 82, 84, 86
Thunder Bay 60
Tierney, Gene 7
Time Magazine 71
To Catch a Thief 119
To Have and Have Not 174
Toland, Gregg 75
Tom Sawyer (1930 film) 74
Towers, Constance 7, 166–168

Tracy and Hepburn 99
Trevor, Claire 7, 52–61
Trotti, Lamar 10
The Trouble with Harry 89
The Two Mrs. Glenvilles 71
Two Rode Together 129, 169–171

Up the River 30

Variety 121
Vertigo 173
Vidor, King 29
Von Sternberg, Josef 7

Wagon Master 11, 52–61
Ward, Jay 157
Wayne, John 5, 8, 14, 53, 55, 60, 91, 99–108, 128, 131, 175
Wead, Spig 92
Weber, Lois 172
Wee Willie Winkie 43–51
Welles, Orson 6, 14, 54
Wellman, William 82, 174–175
Whelan, Arleen 7, 164–166
The Whole Town's Talking 25–33
Widmark, Richard 169
Wilder, Billy 26
Wilder, Thornton 173
Wiley, I.A.R. 9, 175
The Wings of Eagles 21, 100, 126
Wise, Naomi 174
Wood, Lana 122, 126–127
Wood, Natalie 7, 122, 132–133
Wright, Teresa 173
The Wrong Man 136
Wuthering Heights (1939 film) 80

Young, Loretta 7
Young Mr. Lincoln 62, 139

Zanuck, Darryl F. 10, 43–44, 67, 72, 75, 166
Zinnemann, Fred 112
Zukor, Adolph 17